1972

THE SERIES THAT CHANGED HOCKEY FOREVER

SCOTT MORRISON

Published by SIMON & SCHUSTER
New York London Toronto Sydney New Delhi

SIMON &
SCHUSTER
CANADA

Simon & Schuster Canada
A Division of Simon & Schuster, Inc.
166 King Street East, Suite 300
Toronto, Ontario M5A 1J3

This Simon & Schuster Canada edition May 2022

SIMON & SCHUSTER CANADA and colophon
are trademarks of Simon & Schuster, Inc.

For information about special discounts for bulk purchases,
please contact Simon & Schuster Special Sales at 1-800-268-3216
or CustomerService@simonandschuster.ca.

Manufactured in the United States of America

1   3   5   7   9   10   8   6   4   2

Library and Archives Canada Cataloguing in Publication
Title: 1972 : the series that changed hockey forever / Scott Morrison.
Names: Morrison, Scott, 1958– editor.
Description: Simon & Schuster Canada edition.
Identifiers: Canadiana (print) 20210189258 | Canadiana (ebook) 20210189266 |
ISBN 9781982154141 (hardcover) | ISBN 9781982154318 (ebook)
Subjects: CSH: Canada-U.S.S.R. Hockey Series, 1972.
Classification: LCC GV847.7 .M65 2021 | DDC 796.962/66—dc23

ISBN 978-1-9821-5414-1
ISBN 978-1-9821-5431-8 (ebook)

Contents

Foreword

A columnist I know once wrote: "Phil Esposito fell nineteen years before the Soviet Union did. Only Esposito stood back up and blew a kiss at stone-faced Soviet leader Leonid Brezhnev. Esposito and Canada then toppled the Soviet hockey empire in the famed 1972 Summit Series."

The fall he referred to was me landing on my ass during the introductions prior to the first game in Moscow, the fifth game in the series. The Soviets were leading 2-1-1, which was a shocker to say the least and had everyone in Canada hyperventilating, except for the ones who were booing us. Brezhnev was proudly watching from a private box, figuring his boys were going to put us away in the four games on home ice and score a big win for the motherland. And, yes, I blew him a kiss and everyone around him laughed.

We went on to fall again that night, blowing a lead, losing the game, and putting ourselves in a position where we needed to win the final three games to salvage our pride and our reputation as the best hockey nation on the planet. As improbable as it once seemed that the Russians would take a stranglehold on the series, it seemed just as improbable that we would come back.

And, as if the stakes weren't big enough already, we were fighting for our country.

There is a reason why, fifty years later, people are still talking about 1972. It's quite simple, actually. It's not because I got up off my ass, but because we as a team did and we won. Everybody loves a winner; nobody cares about a loser.

So, there you have it.

It was a great series, but it was also, in my opinion, something that should never have happened, at least not the way it was played. I believed it then and I believe it now. In fact, when I first got called and asked to play, I said no. Three times, in fact, I said no before Bobby Orr called and urged me to play, and I said yes. I was an NHL player—who the hell wanted to play in an exhibition series like that? And we were told it wasn't going to be anything more than that, an exhibition series with all the intensity of an all-star game. That's the truth. I didn't care.

I cared about my NHL team, the Boston Bruins, the Stanley Cup champions. My brother, Tony, the reigning Vezina Trophy winner, cared about his NHL team, the Chicago Blackhawks. We had training camp coming up, and it was the first time I was making a half-decent salary. I didn't want to get hurt in an exhibition series. Remember, there were no guaranteed contracts back then.

I also totally disagreed with us being called Team Canada and I made that perfectly clear the very first day of training camp. If we don't have the likes of Bobby Hull and Gerry Cheevers and other stars who were going to play in the rival World Hockey Association—they're all Canadians—how are we called Team Canada? But that was the start of the politics in a series that became very political on so many levels.

One thing I will say: if we'd had our best players (meaning the WHA guys, too) and trained for a month knowing how intense the series was going to be, the Soviets wouldn't have been able to win a game. Okay, maybe one game—and that's not taking anything away from them, because they were good. But I think having Bobby Hull, the rest of those WHA guys, and Bobby Orr would have made a huge difference. Anyway, there's lots more about that in the pages ahead.

I also didn't like that we had to play by international rules with international officials. We were the NHL, the best league in the world. So if you're going to play the best league in the world, then you should play by their rules, not by international rules. And who sets the international rules? At the time it was a guy named Bunny Ahearne, who was the head of international hockey, and you know who he wanted to win.

That's why I said we should never have played under those circumstances. I had no interest. None.

Having said all that, fifty years later, the competitor and Canadian in me is glad I ultimately agreed to be a part of it, even though that series took a huge toll on a lot of us and we still feel it to this day. It was supposed to be nothing more than a lopsided exhibition series (and an unwelcome interruption to summer) between the so-called amateurs from the Soviet Union (trust me, they were not amateurs in any sense of the word) and what was supposed to be the best Canadian team (like I said, it wasn't) in the first ever best-on-best series.

Well, it turned out to become the greatest hockey series ever, one in which we had everything to lose and nothing to gain. And we did become Team Canada in the sense that, before it was over, we truly were representing our country, not just the NHL.

If we had lost—and it damned near happened, of course—would we still be talking about it today? I don't think so. It would have been long forgotten, at least by us. But we're still talking about 1972 because everybody loves a winner. In the end, everyone *was* a winner—Team

Canada for sure; the Soviets feel like they were winners (and still celebrate the anniversaries) because of how well they played; and hockey fans won because the entertainment and drama was so damn good.

But only one team truly won the series on the ice!

Part of what made it the greatest series ever was that the world was a much different place in 1972. It was a hockey series with pride and bragging rights on the line, but it was also a battle of political ideals. It became country versus country, society against society. It was our way of life versus their way of life. That's how it felt. The Russians were saying communism was better, we were saying capitalism was better. I hated communism and still do. And this battle of "political" and "social" issues was being fought on the ice. The Russians were the enemy, a big, powerful country feared on the political stage. Like I said, it wasn't just hockey pride that was on the line, it was real-life pride.

I didn't like them at all. I didn't like their society. At one point in the series, I was quoted as saying I would kill to win. I did say that: "I would kill to win." And that scared me a lot. I hated them in the beginning, and I got more emotional as the series went on. Everyone was emotional. That's another reason why this series was like no other. That emotion, those stakes, will never be re-created.

Some exhibition series, eh!

I played my entire National Hockey League career in the United States—four seasons in Chicago; eight with Boston, which included two Stanley Cup wins; and six seasons with the New York Rangers, later becoming their general manager and coach. I was also a founder of the expansion Tampa Bay Lightning, which have gone on to win the Stanley Cup three times, the last two back-to-back. I still do colour commentary on radio for Lightning games. Yes, America has been very good to me.

But I still consider myself a proud Canadian—Sault Ste. Marie is my hometown—and my pride and the pride of all my teammates and everyone associated with that Canadian team shone through in 1972, from the shocking opening-night loss in Montreal to the struggles in the remaining games in Canada, including the fourth game in Vancouver, when we were booed by our home fans. It still hurts me to this day. I felt bad for all the guys.

What makes me really proud, looking back, is we showed the spirit that separates Canadian hockey players from the rest—our refusal to quit, no matter how dire the circumstances. Never count out a Canadian hockey player. Years later, the Russians admitted to me that until they could match our emotions, they couldn't beat us. They were right.

Since that great series, of course, so much has changed in the world and on the ice. People over there have confirmed to me that things started to change in Russia after we won. Did it have something to do with the Soviet Union going like us and communism falling? I don't know. But I do know it was a completely different feeling when I went over there years later. It was like being in Toronto, or New York. It wasn't anything like what we saw in '72, which was dreadful, not even close. Back then, they couldn't say a word about their lifestyle; now they're more capitalistic than us.

That series opened the door to other great international competitions, a sharing of hockey ideas that eventually led to the Soviets and Europeans coming to play in North America. I've often said: Russians, Canadians, Americans, Swedes. Who cares? It's a big world. Everyone is the same. They all want to win the Stanley Cup.

As for the series—was it my finest hour? Others have said it was. I say no. For me, it was about winning the Stanley Cup, but it was a great series and it will always have a special place in my memory.

People still ask me, why did we win? It's like I said, we never quit. That's the trademark of the Canadian hockey player. Fast-forward to the 1987 Canada Cup, which was the 1972 for the next generation. The Canadians were behind in that three-game final against the Soviets. They lost the first game, needed double overtime to win the second, and in the final game they trailed 3–0 eight minutes in and 4–2 after the first period. But they battled back, scoring with just 1:26 left to win 6–5. Does any of that sound familiar?

But that series and so many others that have followed wouldn't have happened without 1972. And without us winning. That's why we're still talking about it.

—Phil Esposito
Tampa Bay, Florida
January 2022

Introduction

1972.

For those of a certain vintage, and even for so many who don't have black-and-white memories, 1972 is all you have to say and they will know exactly what you are referring to—the greatest hockey series ever played, a defining event in a country's history, a tipping point for the game itself.

No matter that it was never really supposed to be quite all that. Historic, yes. Special, certainly. But it was never expected to be the greatest hockey series ever, at least not quite in the way that it ultimately turned out to be.

It was supposed to be more of a coronation, or a confirmation—or so most of Canada either thought or was led to believe. It was the first time Canada's best professionals (or at least most of them), its National Hockey League stars, would play the so-called amateurs of the Soviet Union, who had dominated the international game for years, winning World Championships and Olympic gold aplenty. But never against the best that Canada could put on ice.

It was originally billed simply as Canada vs. USSR, but it was later renamed the 1972 Summit Series, a showdown that was long

1

overdue, a series that was going to be a measuring stick for two hockey superpowers. And so it was.

"It was time to play," said Team Canada goaltender Ken Dryden, who had played with the Canadian National Team and had been humbled by the Soviets a few years earlier. As such, he was maybe just a little more cautious than most with his series expectations. "The Europeans, in particular the Soviets, had run out of opponents. It was time."

While some politicians tried to suggest it was something more culturally and politically noble, and the Soviets insisted it was about learning and growing, make no mistake: deep down it was always about declaring global hockey supremacy, plain and simple.

Most Canadians thought they knew not only how the series would end, but also how it would get there. It was going to be a romp, a walk in the park. Most of the media said it. The scouts said it. The players and fans believed it. Canada, with its professionals, was finally going to flex its muscle, stick out its chest, and teach the mysterious and brazen "amateurs" a lesson once and for all. There would no longer be any confusion as to whose game it really was.

"It was supposed to just confirm what people had been told for umpteen years," said Team Canada defenceman Rod Seiling. "We couldn't win the Olympics, we couldn't win the World Championships, because we weren't sending our best. But once we sent our best, the world would go on the way it was supposed to."

Had the Canadians followed that imagined script, had they won all eight games handily, the series might not have become the greatest ever played, but in some ways it still would have been great.

"I think it was supposed to be [great]," said Dryden. "And it would be that in a very different way. It would be that as this incredible demonstration of us and of the strength of us and the power of us, and that's what was going to make it this incredible event. After not having had a chance to play our best against theirs, having that chance and then going out and just demonstrating how much superior we really are—that's what I think the greatest was supposed to be."

"No one expected it to be the greatest," said Team Canada defenceman Brad Park. "Not until we got our asses handed to us in the first game. It only took seven goals . . ."

Indeed, that shocking first game on September 2 at the steamy Montreal Forum sent nervous tremors across the country, not to mention through the Team Canada dressing room. That game turned out to be a romp, after all, but it was the Soviets applying a 7–3 beating on Team Canada, who had scored just thirty seconds into the game and again six minutes later, just the way all Canadians had expected.

But, looking at the bigger hockey picture, in many ways that series opener was far more important and impactful than any other game in the series because that night the Soviets and hockey were both winners. The Soviets proved they could play with Canada's best, and the hockey world was about to change forever as a result, especially with how the rest of the series unfolded. All of a sudden, it was much more than just an exhibition series. It was a great series. It had to be a great series.

"That's right," said Team Canada coach Harry Sinden, "there was a real series when a lot of people weren't expecting one."

Which is why victory became more than a matter of bragging rights on the ice. It was a battle between two terrific teams, but also two different cultures. It became personal. It became political, a conflict of systems—communism versus democracy, our way of life versus theirs. But it also became a brilliant clash of two different hockey worlds and styles, a Cold War on ice.

"As the series went on, it felt like we were playing for our way of life," said Team Canada winger Ron Ellis. "We were playing for democracy. Whoever won that series was going to have the bragging rights, and the Soviets sure wanted to win, I truly believe, to show that their way of life was better, and that they could also produce the best players in the world."

For Team Canada, it quickly became complicated. Several of them had been reluctant to play in the first place because if it was going to be a romp, why bother? And it was cutting into their precious off-season. Most spent three weeks in August alternately having fun at night and trying to get into shape by day, but not with the conviction (at least by day) that was required, because they had been led to underestimate the enemy sight unseen. They were an oversized roster of thirty-five players assembled from ten different NHL teams, many of whom really didn't like each other, but were now trying to put egos and personal history aside and pull together as one.

But there was no real urgency until they realized the hard way— with those seven goals on opening night—that the opponent was more than just formidable and their pride and reputations were at stake.

And there were roughly 15 million Canadians, about two-thirds of the population at the time, watching on television and suddenly agonizing and asking the question: What just happened here? In their minds, it wasn't that the Soviets were better than advertised, it was that the Canadians weren't as good as promised. More pressure.

"Going over there, that's when it became a war, not a friendly international match like it was billed," said Ellis. "Now the stakes were very, very high, representing your country, representing the NHL, representing Canadian fans, the pressures and the stress really started to build."

With all of that, the series became even greater because of the special oneness, because of the unexpected, from the opening-night shocker, to the roller-coaster ride of emotions and all the drama, to finally a storybook ending. And because it still became an "incredible demonstration of us." Only in a different way. A collection of moments—and one really big moment—that hockey fans of the day will never forget. Because it was different.

"A lot different," said Dryden.

"It became a war, our society versus theirs, whether we wanted it or not," said Team Canada star Phil Esposito, who never wanted to play in the series but soon became arguably the best in it. "I remember saying, I would have killed to win that series. Looking back, I wasn't very proud of that, but that's how I felt. It was war and it was hell."

The world really was a different place back then, on and off the ice. The World Wide Web had yet to be invented, and what we knew about the Soviets, the Communists, was only what we saw on the nightly news. And we mostly didn't like it. They frightened us. The two superpowers in world politics and the arms race were the United States and the Soviet Union. It was a divided world back then—the West and its freedom and democracy and the East growling behind the Iron Curtain. It was a Cold War. To us, the Soviets were the evil empire, the enemy, that we feared. The Soviet Union was a foreign place for many reasons, not the least of which was that back in 1972 not many Canadians, or Americans, had been outside of North America, never mind there.

"For me, I don't like to refer to it as a war on ice, but it was a battle between two ideologies," said Canadian forward Peter Mahovlich, whose brother, Frank, was also on the team. Their parents had left Yugoslavia before they were born and relocated in Timmins, Ontario, to get away from the Communist regime and find a better way of life. "It was communism or socialism or whatever it is. You think democracy is the best form of government. A lot of politics is based on how you perform through sports, or how well you develop technology. That's a reason why the 1972 series was so important."

At the time, Canada had its own issues. The country had celebrated its centennial in 1967—with the famous Expo 67 held in Montreal—and was feeling pretty good about itself. The economy was strong, and across much of the country there was a feeling of hopefulness. But it was author Pierre Berton who later referred to 1967 as Canada's "last good year." World events chipped away at that hopefulness, and relations between the French and English in Canada became strained. In October 1970, a terrorist organization known as the Front de libération de Québec (FLQ), which was looking to gain independence for Quebec from the rest of Canada, clashed with the federal government. There were the kidnappings of Quebec government minister Pierre Laporte and British trade commissioner James Cross that led to Prime Minister Pierre Elliott Trudeau invoking the War Measures Act. In the fall of 1972, Canada was in the midst of a federal election that would take place a month after the series ended and would be one of the closest decisions ever.

It was a nationalistic time, a time of protests and anger, and a hockey series was supposed to give us all relief from that. A distraction the country desperately needed. And ultimately it did, and what happened on the ice created a legacy that is still felt today and will be felt forever more.

"I look back now, and there was a division in Canada with the FLQ," said Peter Mahovlich. "This series galvanized Canada and brought the country together. You're too busy playing at the time to know. Even a deep thinker like Kenny Dryden didn't realize it at the time. But now, fifty years later, the importance continues to grow."

As the series progressed, after the shock and anger of the Canadian fans in the beginning turned to a rallying cry behind the Iron

Curtain, it felt like Canada was a country that desperately needed to feel good and affirm a belief that its way of life was better, and its hockey was better, a country that came together for twenty-seven days in September.

"There was no such thing as a Francophone or a Westerner or anything else," said Team Canada hero Paul Henderson. "We were all Canadians. The series brought us all together. It brought an entire country together. It was Canada playing, not Team Canada. The political feel was always there, but as we got behind [in the series] it sure as hell became war and really got ramped up. I remember saying to my wife, Eleanor, if we don't win this series we're going to be known as the biggest losers in the history of Canada, the worst team ever put together. That's the difference between winning and losing. We were voted the team of the century!"

"Henderson has scored for Canada"—the five words legendary broadcasting pioneer Foster Hewitt shouted out in Luzhniki Ice Palace in Moscow.

The winning goal scored with thirty-four seconds remaining in the eighth and final game—capping off a remarkable comeback for the ages in the series and in that game—became a rallying point for a country, a defining national moment. As someone said years later, when it comes to hockey, you can't teach Canadian. Finally, Canada's best (those that played, anyway), proved they were the best, even if the margin was ever so slight.

For those old enough, the goal became Canada's "where were you?" moment. For not just hockey, but life. For Americans, their moments from around that time are typically the assassination of President John F. Kennedy in 1963, or when Neil Armstrong became the first person to walk on the moon in 1969. Ours was a hockey series and a goal. Henderson has scored for Canada.

"The people who are ten years younger than me and ten years older than me," said Peter Mahovlich, "will always remember where they were on September 28, 1972."

"Those games from 1972, they were a part of history," said Soviet goaltender Vladislav Tretiak. "Not knowing about them [for a Russian] is like not knowing about Alexander Pushkin [the greatest Soviet poet], or not knowing about Yuri Gagarin [the first person in space]. I know that everyone in Canada remembers that series. We also have an older generation, especially the older generation, who remember the games and where they were.

"In Canada, I know kids missed school to watch the games and how happy they were. In our country, too, people watched those games [in the middle of the night] and didn't go to sleep. And everyone who watched them remembers and passes their memories on to their children. And, of course, today's generation would also like to know what this miracle was all about."

The ultimate irony is that while Canadians exploded with excitement and pride and were quick to wave the flag and proclaim they were the best and hockey was indeed their game—in the end while one team was declared the winner on the scoreboard, the truth is there was no loser in the series. The late comedian Norm MacDonald once wrote that Cold Wars don't end in ties. He was right, but while the series may not have ended in a tie, both sides and the game ultimately won. Canada salvaged its reputation and the Soviets proved they were good enough to win. And the two hockey cultures would come together in the years ahead.

"In reality, no one can say they lost, because everyone won," said Tretiak. "We're still talking about the series. I think both teams—all the players, ours and the Canadians—are heroes."

And in the end, the game was changed forever.

"We opened that window, we practically broke through that window," added Tretiak. "These games are part of history and are unrepeatable. And as long as hockey exists, they will probably be remembered. Canadians will remember them and so will Russians. Why? Because this really was a sports jewel. Those games really were amazing."

When it was over, amidst the celebration in the Team Canada dressing room, Dryden was quoted as saying: "When we look back on this series in twenty years, it will have been the most important."

He was right. It still is, fifty years and counting.

1972.

CHAPTER 1

A Super Series Is Born

In July 1966, hockey power broker Alan Eagleson was entertaining at his cottage north of Toronto. The guest list included Canadian national team founder Father David Bauer; Carl Brewer, who had played seven seasons with the Maple Leafs but had regained his amateur status and was about to become one of Bauer's leaders and trusted defencemen; and the great Bobby Orr, no introduction necessary.

Hockey, as you would expect, dominated the conversation. But Canada's national game wasn't the only topic on the minds of the four sporting fanatics. At the time, the World Cup of soccer was being played in England, with the host country ultimately capturing worldwide headlines and national adoration when it defeated West Germany to win its first championship.

"I've read a dozen stories about all sorts of guys taking credit for the series," Eagleson said, recalling the beginnings of the 1972 Canada–Soviet Union series. "We were listening to the World Cup of soccer on the radio. I thought, 'Why can't we have a World Cup of hockey?' It wasn't just Russia and Canada then. I wanted to go far beyond that."

In due time it would happen, of course. But first things first.

What Eagleson had in mind in 1966 did not in the short term extend beyond a hockey showdown between Canada and the Soviet Union. Many more informal and formal gatherings took place after Bobby Charlton and his England teammates became national heroes at Wembley Stadium one afternoon that late July. And many more hockey executives, administrators, bureaucrats, and politicians became involved before Phil Esposito and Paul Henderson and others would become heroes in Canada in 1972.

The prospect of a hockey super series picked up steam on the political campaign trail leading up to the June 1968 federal election. New Liberal leader Pierre Elliott Trudeau promised to investigate why Canada struggled on the international sports stage and to find ways to solve the situation.

"Here's where you have to start: 1968, in Rossland, BC," former Hockey Canada secretary-treasurer Chris Lang told the *Globe and Mail.* "Pierre Trudeau is on the campaign trail and says, 'If I'm elected, I'm going to take a look at sport because I can't figure out why we're not doing well in international hockey.'"

Trudeau was far from being a sports nut, even though he captained his high-school hockey team at Collège Jean-de-Brébeuf in Montreal. But he did understand the importance of hockey to the country's overall psyche, morale, and pride.

Canada was in a major slump on the international scene. Senior clubs had represented the country at the World Championship and the Olympic Games until Father Bauer instituted the national team program in the mid-1960s. But Canada had not won an Olympic gold medal in hockey since the Edmonton Mercurys in 1952 in Oslo, Norway. The country's last World Championship victory was in 1961 in Switzerland with the Trail (BC) Smoke Eaters.

"Hockey is considered our national game, and yet, in the World Hockey Championships, we have not been able as amateurs to perform as well as we know we can," Trudeau said.

After Trudeau won the election to become Canada's fifteenth prime minister, he followed through on his campaign promise. His government commissioned a task force to study Canada's hockey failures internationally, specifically at the Olympics and World Championships. Charles Rea, an oil company executive who happened to be Brewer's father-in-law, and John Munro, the federal minister of health and welfare, headed up the endeavour.

Rea persuaded the prime minister to create Hockey Canada in February 1969 to develop solutions to Canada's poor international record at the time. Rea hired another oil executive, Charlie Hay, as the new agency's volunteer chairman. It was a separate organization from the Canadian Amateur Hockey Association, although the two hockey bodies merged in 1998 and became known as Hockey Canada.

The first significant deduction in 1969 as to why Canada had stumbled against powerhouses such as the Soviet Union and Czechoslovakia was that Canada was at a disadvantage having to play just their best amateur players. Canada's strength was in the NHL, and without its best players, championship victories would continue to be hard to come by. Meanwhile, the Soviet Union and Czechoslovakia had state-sponsored national teams that spent months together training. They were amateurs it seemed in name only.

"The task force decided between February and July of 1969 that Canada was fundamentally playing with a handicap," Lang said. "The Russians were using their top twenty players. Our top five hundred players were all in the NHL, so we were essentially using players 501 through 520, and that's why we kept losing."

Hay swiftly forged a relationship with Eagleson, the newly minted head of the National Hockey League Players' Association (NHLPA), who still maintained his position as the most powerful agent (Bobby Orr's agent) and a massive influencer in the game.

Eagleson accompanied CAHA secretary-manager Gordon Jukes and Air Canada employee Aggie Kukulowicz, a former player who acted as their interpreter, to the 1969 World Championship in Stockholm. They met with all the top hockey nations to express Canada's increased interest in the international scene, what the country's best players wanted to achieve, especially if the International Ice Hockey Federation would allow professionals to compete in the World Championship and Olympic Winter Games.

The IIHF and Hockey Canada agreed to a year-long trial in which Canada would be allowed to employ up to nine non-NHL professionals for tournaments such as the World Championship, which Canada was slated to host in 1970 in Montreal and Winnipeg. The first step under the agreement occurred at the prestigious Izvestia Tournament in mid-December 1969 in Moscow (*Izvestia* was Russia's daily newspaper of record until its demise in 1991. The hockey tournament has been known in recent years as the Channel One Cup.)

Canada put together a lineup fortified with five pros and finished second in the six-country, round-robin tournament to the host Soviets. The Canadians actually tied the mighty Soviets, 2–2, and their only defeat was a 4–0 loss to the Czechs.

The excellent showing from Canada, with its handful of professionals, didn't sit well with the IIHF or the International Olympic Committee, however. On January 4, 1970, the IIHF convened an emergency meeting and decided to scrap the provisional use of professionals. Hockey Canada was upset, and so was Munro. His recommendation to Hockey Canada and to the CAHA to pull its participation from future IIHF events was enacted, which also meant Canada would not host the 1970 World Championship.

Canada wound up not playing in the World Championship from 1970 through 1976 and did not enter a team for the 1972 and 1976 Olympic Games. But this development in 1970 didn't deter Trudeau, Eagleson, and Hockey Canada officials from their pursuit of a series with the Soviets. And, after the October Crisis in the province of Quebec, later that year, the prime minister needed an event to bring the country together.

The Front de libération du Québec (FLQ) had perpetrated bombings and robberies between 1963 and 1970. In October 1970, the FLQ kidnapped British trade commissioner James Cross, as well as a Quebec minister of labour and immigration Pierre Laporte, also the province's deputy premier. Laporte's body was later found strangled in the trunk of a car at the Montréal Saint-Hubert Longueuil Airport. The prime minister invoked the War Measures Act, deploying one thousand soldiers from the Canadian armed forces. Cross finally was released on December 3, 1970, after fifty-nine days of being held hostage. The Canadian troops withdrew a few weeks later.

Trudeau needed something big to unify the country. So he turned to hockey, which was and continues to be so much of the identity, fabric, and heritage of Canada. The hockey rink had always been a place to escape. Trudeau turned also to the Soviet Union. He wanted to build Canada's political relationship with the Soviets anyway during the Cold War, and his government knew of their desire to promote their way of life through sports, particularly hockey, on the big stage, such as the Olympics.

More signs that the Soviet Union was open to a possible showdown with Canadian pros came in May 1971 when Trudeau took a twelve-day trip to Moscow and other parts of the country to strengthen political relations between the two nations. Trudeau met with Soviet premier Alexei Kosygin, the country's number two under general secretary Leonid Brezhnev. A few months later, in October, Kosygin spent a few days in Toronto and visited Trudeau in Ottawa, where he was actually attacked by a protester, and there was more hockey talk.

Several weeks after Kosygin's visit, and after the Soviets celebrated another championship at the 1971 Izvestia Trophy tournament in December, Canadian Embassy diplomat Gary Smith came across an eye-opening newspaper column.

"One of my jobs was I had to read the government newspaper *Izvestia* every day," Smith told the *Globe and Mail*. "One night, this was December 1971, there was a very interesting column by someone calling himself the Snowman. The Soviets had won the Izvestia tournament again, and he wrote that it was now time to play the Canadian professionals. When I saw that, I knew that you didn't just write something like that in a Soviet paper. This guy must have some official authorization."

Smith found out the author of the column was a reporter named Boris Fedosov. Smith invited Fedosov to the Canadian Embassy in Moscow for a consultation that also included embassy employee Peter Hancock. As a result of this get-together, next on the guest list to the embassy was Soviet Union Ice Hockey Federation general secretary Andrei Starovoitov. Smith's feelings about the Russians' keenness for a super series between the two countries were bolstered from these meetings. He sent word back to Ottawa through Robert Ford, the Canadian ambassador to Moscow at the time.

Soviet hockey was on a roll. The Big Red Machine had reeled off nine consecutive World Championship titles between 1963 and

1971. The Russians also celebrated gold-medal victories at the 1964 Olympics in Innsbruck, Austria (Canada was fourth), and Grenoble, France, in 1968 (Canada won bronze). They would win again in the 1972 Winter Games in Sapporo, Japan, less than two months after the Snowman's dispatch.

The Soviet victory in Japan was significant. As the Snowman pointed out in his December 1971 column, the Big Red Machine craved a new challenge, and a third straight Olympic gold only hastened the necessity.

The closing ceremony of the 1972 Winter Games was on February 13. The 1972 World Championship in Prague was less than two months away. Officials from Canada and the Soviet Union would assemble to negotiate an arrangement for a super series during the tournament.

They met at the Hotel International in Prague. Sitting on the Canadian side of the table were Hay, Gordon Jukes, and CAHA president Joe Kryczka, a lawyer. Sport Canada director Lou Lefaive also was in Prague, advising the Canadian contingent. Starovoitov represented the Soviets, while IIHF president Bunny Ahearne and vice-president Fred Page, a Canadian and former CAHA president, were also in the room.

On April 18, 1972, an agreement was signed to play eight games, four in Canada and four in Moscow, in September, contested under IIHF rules and with amateur on-ice officials. In a strange turn of events, the Russians failed to close the deal on a tenth consecutive World Championship victory. They lost to the host Czechs 3–2 and tied Sweden 3–3 in their final two games of the double round-robin, six-country tournament, finishing 7-1-2, three points behind Czechoslovakia (9-0-1). The two games were played after the announcement of the super series.

Still, the news of the eight-game super series was met with enthusiasm in both countries. The NHL, however, was not amused.

"So they announce this series, and the minute they do, [NHL president] Clarence Campbell holds a press conference in Montreal to say there will be no such series because 'we will not permit our players to play,'" Eagleson told the *Globe and Mail* on the fortieth anniversary of the series. "The owners said they were worried about giving up their players, their assets, without anything in return. I got Clarence and the owners onside by guaranteeing that every player would have a signed NHL contract and by guaranteeing that part of the profit would go toward the players' pension fund."

Toronto Maple Leafs co-owner Stafford Smythe also helped calm his fellow owners' bluster. As a patriotic Canadian, he wanted this series to happen. He first managed to get the ownership groups in Montreal and Vancouver onside. Smythe then convinced Chicago Blackhawks owner Bill Wirtz and his Detroit Red Wings counterpart Bruce Norris about the importance of the series, conveying it was the first step towards putting together a version for hockey of the World Cup that soccer enjoyed. The hockey version would include an American side. Of course, this was Eagleson's original concept and came to fruition in 1976 with the inaugural Canada Cup.

There still was, however, plenty to figure out for the 1972 series. Where would the games be played in Canada? Who would coach? Which players would be selected? Ticket sales and television rights also had to be ironed out. Heck, what would the Canadian team be called, and who would design the team sweaters?

"This is when Eagleson shot to the fore, fast becoming the leader and public face for all plans," Hockey Canada board member and journalist Douglas Fisher wrote in the *Toronto Sun*.

Eagleson had a business connection to the ad agency Vickers and Benson. He asked creative director Terry O'Malley to come up with a sweater design. O'Malley enlisted the services of a transplanted Englishman, John Lloyd, an art director who knew little about hockey. The country quickly fell in love with Lloyd's design of a large Maple Leaf on the sweater's front and the word "CANADA" above the numbers on the back. In those days, the players' names on the backs of sweaters did not exist. This was a stride in that direction.

O'Malley also convinced Eagleson to find a better team name than the NHL All-Stars. This team, after all, represented Canada, although in truth it eventually didn't represent all the best Canadian players or all the NHL players. O'Malley and his employees brainstormed. On the shortlist were Dream Team and Team Canada, two names put forth by a copywriter from Detroit by the name of Terry Hill. Although the Dream Team was tempting, O'Malley chose Team Canada because the former seemed a little too cocky and not the Canadian way. Dream Team, of course, would become a prominent handle two decades later for the United States Olympic basketball team. On the practice sweaters, at least, it was Team Canada Équipe, fitting for a bilingual country. On the game sweaters, it was simply Canada across the shoulders on the back.

The television rights were sold to a group that included Bobby Orr Enterprises and Maple Leafs co-owner Harold Ballard for $750,000, outbidding McLaren Advertising, the rights holder to *Hockey Night in Canada*. The Orr-Ballard group cleared $1.2 million in profit, selling one-minute commercial time for between $12,000 and $15,000. Eagleson was the secretary of Orr Enterprises, and partnering with Ballard made for strange bedfellows. Al and Hal became hockey's Odd Couple.

"We're hustlers," Eagleson told the *Globe and Mail* in 1972. "We'll be able to sell the advertising. The $750,000 is the profit. The arrangement is that the first $100,000 comes to Hockey Canada [for developmental projects], and the balance is split between Hockey Canada and the National Hockey League Players' Association. Each [Hockey Canada and the NHLPA] then contributes $25,000 for its use in international hockey."

Eagleson hired Harry Sinden as the head coach for $15,000 and John Ferguson as the assistant coach for $10,000. The latter had only recently retired as a player, in 1971. Eagleson even struck a deal with Air Canada to fly more than three thousand Canadians to watch the games live in Moscow.

Montreal, Toronto, and Vancouver were obvious locations for three of the games because those cities had the only NHL teams in Canada at the time—the Canadiens, Maple Leafs, and Canucks, respectively. Winnipeg became the fourth location because it had lost out on the chance of co-hosting the 1970 World Championship due to the snafu with the IIHF over the use of professional players.

When Winnipeg was chosen, Eagleson and Hockey Canada could not possibly have known what would play out that off-season with Bobby Hull bolting from the Blackhawks to sign with the upstart World Hockey Association's Winnipeg Jets, becoming the game's first multi-millionaire player.

Even though part of the agreement between Hockey Canada and the NHL prohibited using WHA-bound players, Sinden initially named Hull to his roster of thirty-five players on July 12. Immediately, Campbell and Wirtz voiced their outrage and threatened to withdraw all of the players from the series.

Fisher, now acting Hockey Canada chairman because Hay fell ill, issued a statement that Hull would not play for Team Canada.

Fisher's words whipped up the country into a fervour. Canadians demanded Hull suit up for Canada. Trudeau didn't miss a beat in backing the uproar. He summoned Fisher to Ottawa for a briefing on the messy matter. Fisher arrived on Parliament Hill to find an aggressive mob of reporters.

"The session inside was strained," Fisher recalled. "We were not mutual admirers. Trudeau gestured to stacks of messages. Most demanded, he insisted, that Hull play. If Hull could not, some people wanted him to block the Soviets from coming.

"The prime minister thought we should go ahead and play Hull. Surely the NHL, noting national outrage and government support for Hull, would back off. I insisted they would not. We had no series if Hull dressed. The Americans were not Canadian patriots. Their war with the WHA for 'stealing' players was mean and getting meaner.

"The prime minister needled me about my cautious Canadianism, but I think the lawyer in him made him agree neither of us had the authority to breach Hockey Canada's deal with the NHL management and players. So I went forth to tell irate reporters that playing Hull meant no team of substance, so no Hull."

The Hull matter eventually subsided. Four players from the original roster—Hull, Gerry Cheevers, J. C. Tremblay, and Derek Sanderson—were dropped. It was time for the memorable and dramatic series to make its historic mark. But it didn't unfold quite the way many Canadians had expected. The NHL stars didn't run roughshod over the so-called amateurs. It was quite the contrary.

Former national team players such as Billy Harris, who also coached abroad, and Brian Conacher, who both played with the Maple Leafs, and brothers Herb and Gerry Pinder, had warned before the series that the Soviets were better than many thought.

"With the Nationals, we played against both the NHL and the Russians many times and believe me, we did better against the NHL than the Russians," Herb Pinder told the *Montreal Gazette* at the time. "I know people think former members of the Nationals are prejudiced about this series, because if the NHL does badly, then it makes the Nationals look better. Time of year is a big factor. The Russians will have an edge in conditioning regardless of how hard Harry Sinden works his players. They shoot hard and they don't waste shots. The Russian goaltending isn't as bad as we like to believe."

That scouting report was far more accurate than most. It also reminded that the Soviets would not be taking part in a series like this, especially with the potential political and social fallout in the fiftieth anniversary of the Soviet Union, unless they were prepared and confident they could compete and win. There was too much at stake. They may have been hoping to learn and grow and all the other rhetoric, but they came to win, or at the very least throw a mighty scare into the Canadians and prove they truly belonged at the front of the world stage, make no mistake. And so they did.

"Our expectations were based on the fact that we often played in Canada against amateur teams," said Soviet goaltender Vladislav Tretiak. "Of course, we also watched professionals play. We liked some of the games, we didn't like the others, but regardless the level of professional hockey was very high. We were the Olympic champions and we very much wanted to play against them. And especially our [former] coach Anatoly Tarasov, who had been dreaming for years for such an encounter. We were the best in Europe and the world. But across the ocean there were other hockey players, who were considered the strongest in the world. They would say they would defeat us by a double-digit margin and they would destroy us physically.

"Generally, there was this kind of mocking attitude, and that's why such a series of games couldn't be arranged for many years. But thank God it finally did happen. Thanks to Alan Eagleson, who did so much for this, and to our own hockey federation and sports ministry. We were representing all of Europe, not just the Soviet Union, because we were the champions. Therefore, these games were very important. Of course, we were very worried, we didn't know what would happen. We had great respect for Canada as the birthplace of hockey. We went there and just wanted to show our game."

That game was impressive. The Soviets shocked and awed and rattled the Canadians' "it's our game" attitude and their imagined supremacy on opening night, and went on to win twice and tie once on Canadian ice before heading home to Moscow. The sounds of booing fans followed Team Canada as they departed their home country, which felt betrayed and let down by its hockey heroes—just as Team Canada felt betrayed and let down by Canadian fans and media. All could agree, this wasn't how it was supposed to have played out, at least not in the minds of Canadians.

"It was history," said Soviet forward Boris Mikhailov, "where two great hockey powers of that time played against each other, with the strongest players from Canada and the Soviet Union. Each of the teams wanted to prove that it was the best at the moment . . . They thought they would have an easy time with us, they were mistaken big time. We taught them a lesson, that's it."

And as much as all of that may have hurt, it's also what made the series great.

Yes, for hockey, it was a question of who was the best. But it all became as much about politics and real life as about the game. Hockey became a metaphor for the other, the vehicle through which supremacy in so many different aspects would be proven. It was us versus them, our politics versus theirs, our ways of life competing. During the Cold War sports became about celebrating who and what you were, a melding of competition and nationalism. Propaganda couldn't hide what was happening on the playing field. You won, or you lost.

There had been other international sporting events that, because of the political climate in the world back then, took on a different perspective and scope. The 1972 Olympic men's basketball final was a summit of a different kind. The Americans hadn't lost in the Olympics since basketball began play at the 1936 Berlin Games. They had won seven straight gold medals until the Soviets surprised in a wildly controversial game, 51–50, in 1972 in Munich.

That game and upset came on September 9, one day after the Canadian leg of the Summit Series, in Vancouver, had concluded with a similar shock level. Another Soviet win in the fifth game left the Canadians with no margin for error, but incredibly, with an unwavering resolve, they would somehow prevail against all odds, achieving the unthinkable in a series that already had seen the unthinkable. How much more could there be?

"We knew this was something special then," Eagleson recalled. "But not even we could visualize what would come out of all this.

"We made an eight-hundred-thousand-dollar profit from that series. That was it. I thought it was the start of something interesting, but I never thought it would become the business that it has over the years. International hockey has put in excess of twenty-five million dollars of new money into hockey, money that wouldn't have been there otherwise. It has been very important for the players' pension plan, but it has also had its rewards for the fans. It opened up the hockey world, and we've seen some outstanding hockey as a result."

Eagleson played a massive role in opening the door to international hockey for Canadian professionals, as did others, including Trudeau, who, burdened with prostate cancer and Parkinson's disease late in life, lived until September 28, 2000, the twenty-eighth anniversary of the exciting conclusion of the series, before passing away at the age of eighty.

Indeed, the 1972 Summit Series, as it became known, changed hockey forever.

CHAPTER 2

A Dream Team and Nightmare

Ultimately, the great Bobby Orr didn't play a game in the Summit Series, but he still managed to have a profound influence on its outcome. Great ones often do that. They somehow find a way to make a difference.

Orr, the Boston Bruins superstar, who was the most valuable player and best defenceman in the NHL the previous five seasons (and three more to follow), had much-publicized and much-lamented chronic knee problems. In fact, in the spring of 1972, he was again suffering, but still managed to help lead the Bruins to a Stanley Cup championship and win the Conn Smythe Trophy as the most valuable player in the playoffs.

But doctors determined after the final that Orr required another surgery on his wounded left knee, which took place in Boston on June 6. According to reports, Orr had been advised that he shouldn't aggressively test the knee on ice until the fall, about the time the Summit Series was set to begin, but privately he hoped that he would be ready sooner than that.

So despite that grim outlook, Orr was still named to the bloated thirty-five-man Team Canada roster and eventually did test the knee midway through training camp, arriving on August 23.

"I tried skating three weeks ago and it was no good," Orr told reporters. "There was too much soreness in the left knee. But, on Sunday, I put in an hour of skating and shooting [at his Orr-Walton sports camp] and there are no ill effects. So, I may as well do my skating with the guys at Team Canada camp. At the same time, I can step up therapy I should be doing anyway."

Orr suggested, if all continued to progress well, that he might be ready to play in the final four games in the Soviet Union. Alas, that didn't happen, but Orr remained with the team throughout the series, and his presence was noticed and welcomed.

"Bobby tried to play," said Maple Leafs winger Ron Ellis. "My respect for Orr was always great, but even more after that series. He couldn't play, but he stuck with the team. It was very helpful to our morale to have him around. He could have been sitting at home, but he stuck with us all the way."

"Anytime you lose a Bobby Orr that's a big blow," said Rangers defenceman Rod Seiling. "He's maybe the best player to ever play the game. You can't replace him. So we started off one key man short."

Not that any of the players truly doubted they wouldn't still win without him, especially when Orr made sure that the next best player, the NHL's most prolific scorer and reigning scoring champion—66 goals and 133 regular-season points—was on the ice at Maple Leaf Gardens when training camp opened on Sunday, August 13. But it took some convincing to get Phil Esposito there.

"The first call I got asking me to play I said no, that was from, I believe, Eagleson," said Esposito, who spent his summers in his hometown of Sault Ste. Marie, Ontario, running a hockey school with his brother, Tony, the brilliant goaltender with the Chicago Blackhawks. "We were at the hockey school and I got called off the ice to talk to Eagleson. I said I didn't want to play. The second phone call I got was from Harry Sinden. I said no again because Tony was adamant he didn't want to do it. Tony said, 'Don't you put me in that position, I don't want to do that.'" Playing would have meant closing down the summer hockey school and losing that income. "I said, okay, brother, I'll tell him no. And I told them no again.

"The third phone call I got was from Bobby Orr. Now, I wasn't going to turn down my teammate and my friend. Bobby called and said, 'Phil, I can't play, my knee is bad. We really need you and your brother.' I said 'Bob, geez, I have to give up my hockey school. I've got to give all these people their money back.' He said, 'I understand, but we need players. It's just going to be a fun time anyway.' That's what he said. A fun time, like an exhibition all-star game. I said, 'Bob, I don't know, let me talk to Tony and I'll call you back.'

"So, when we got off the ice after the next session, I told Tony, 'I gotta go. I'm going.' And he said, 'Are you shitting me? You promised me.' I said, 'Tony, I gotta do it because Bobby asked me to do it. Not Eagleson, not Harry—Bobby. He's my teammate, he's my friend and I'll do it for him. If I asked him to do something, I would expect him to say yes to me. I would.' That's the truth, I did it for Bobby Orr—not for Eagleson, not for the country, not for anybody. I did it because Bobby Orr asked me.

"We had two weeks left in the hockey school, so we had to figure out how to give back all the money. Gene Ubriaco [a former player], who was also with the school, went crazy and said, 'How could you do this to us?' I said, 'I don't know what to say to you, Bobby asked me so I'm going.' I told Tony, 'If you don't want to go, you don't have to.' He said, 'How the hell am I going to stay away if you go?' He was right. He had no choice. Let's not forget, Tony had won the Calder Trophy [rookie of the year] a couple of years earlier, when he had fifteen shutouts, which is still the record [for most shutouts in the regular season]. And he had just won the Vezina Trophy. Quite frankly, I'm sure glad he did come because we would have never won that series if it wasn't for my brother, Tony. He stopped the bleeding a couple of times."

While it took a lot of arm-twisting to convince the brothers Esposito to sign up, convincing Harry Sinden had been easy. He was officially introduced as head coach on June 7 during NHL meetings in Montreal, and given a $15,000 salary. He had led the Bruins to a Stanley Cup victory in 1970, their first in twenty-nine years, but had been out of hockey for a couple seasons. He had asked the Bruins for a modest raise after his Cup win, but was denied, so on principle Sinden decided to leave and take a job with a home construction business in Rochester, New York.

"Like always, the fight was over money," said Sinden, who grew up in Weston, Ontario, a suburb of Toronto. "I left a job for a difference of five thousand dollars and today they leave for a difference of five million. I never did want to leave the Bruins, we'd just won the Cup, but three days later, I left. That's another story. It's funny, but when I got the call from Al [Eagleson], strangely enough it coincided with the company going bankrupt. I was probably going to be looking for work shortly. I was at Cape Cod vacationing when I got the call. We drove back, I went to my office, and they took the keys to my car. I had to take a cab home. So, I was out of the business at that time. When I got the call from Alan, let's just say it was good timing."

In some ways, Sinden was a surprise choice, given he had been on the sidelines for two seasons, but in some ways he wasn't. He had only coached in the NHL for four seasons, all with the Bruins, but in that fourth season, with the likes of Orr and Esposito and a strong supporting cast, they did bring that elusive Stanley Cup to Boston. As well, from the first day of training camp until the day the airplane touched down in Montreal and Toronto when the series was over, it was a fifty-day commitment for players, coaches, trainers, and management. And one much more stressful and intense than originally thought.

Not many coaches employed in the fourteen-team NHL at the time (about to expand to sixteen teams that upcoming season) would necessarily have wanted to make that kind of commitment, or would even have been allowed to by their team owners, because NHL training camps would already have been well underway by the time the series ended. In fact, not many of the owners were enthused with the concept of the series to begin with.

"It did surprise me to be asked," said Sinden, who turned forty midway through the series. "But then again, I was also available. A lot of coaches weren't because their teams were going to start up training camps. From a timing standpoint it worked out perfect for me."

In addition to his NHL experience, Sinden had competed internationally as a player, winning a silver medal with the Kitchener-Waterloo Dutchmen in the 1960 Winter Olympic Games at Squaw Valley. A defenceman, Sinden was also the captain of the Whitby Dunlops, who defeated the Soviet Union in the gold medal game at the 1958 World Championships in Oslo, Norway. So he knew the Soviets, how they played, how they thought—and how good they were. As with everyone else who had seen the Soviets play, or had played against them, however, it was one thing to know how skilled and well conditioned and prepared they would be, it was another to contemplate how that would measure up against the mighty NHL players. Even Sinden, as respectful as he was, never envisioned what would unfold in the series ahead.

In a somewhat surprising move, Sinden selected former Montreal Canadiens winger John Ferguson to be his assistant coach. Ferguson, who was tough and talented and had won the Stanley Cup five times, had retired in 1971 after eight seasons with the Canadiens. Sinden had even offered to add Ferguson to the playing roster, but he declined, preferring instead just to coach.

"The thinking was to find the right liaison between me and the players because I only really knew the Boston players, and Fergie had such high respect amongst all the players in the league for a number of reasons," explained Sinden. "He came highly recommended by Alan Eagleson and a couple of others. I had never met John personally, although I certainly knew far too much about him as a player [the Bruins and Habs being archrivals]. I looked forward to working with him. He was new at it, so he was very eager—attentive and very helpful."

And Ferguson brought an intensity that would soon be much needed by Team Canada.

When he was introduced as head coach, Sinden said he would select thirty-five players—a number he couldn't live without and ultimately a number he couldn't live with—to attend training camp in Toronto. He also said it would be difficult to not include on that roster Chicago Blackhawks star winger Bobby Hull, who at the time was still being wooed by the upstart World Hockey Association with hockey's first multi-million-dollar contract. At first, Sinden said Hull would not be invited, then soon after said he would, "wherever he is."

After Ferguson was hired, he and Sinden sat down and put together their invite list, which included four potential WHA players—Hull, goaltender Gerry Cheevers and centre Derek Sanderson of the Bruins, and defenceman J. C. Tremblay of the Montreal Canadiens.

Interestingly, when the Summit Series was first announced, Hull said he wasn't interested in playing. Then again, he was asked shortly after the Blackhawks had been eliminated from the Stanley Cup playoffs and well before he did sign with the WHA Winnipeg Jets. Hull argued the schedule was already too long and the players didn't need to be playing in a high-pressure series in the fall. His attitude would change after he signed with the Jets on June 27. Regardless, on July 12, Dan Proudfoot reported in the *Globe and Mail* that Doug Fisher, who was the chair of the Hockey Canada executive committee, said the agreement with the NHL to allow the players to participate stated that no player was eligible unless they were signed with an NHL team before August 13, the opening day of training camp.

There were a variety of theories as to why Canadian players who signed, or were about to sign, with WHA teams would be excluded, including litigation and insurance coverage. And the NHL wasn't keen on showcasing "rival" talent. There was a stir across the country from fans outraged that Hull wasn't being allowed to play—"To Hull with Russia" was the rallying cry—but the bottom line is, the original thirty-five-man roster was revised to delete the four WHA players. The NHL with its inner workings with Hockey Canada saw to that. Eagleson, a lawyer by trade and as brazen as they came, thought about naming Hull to the roster with the hope that public opinion might sway the NHL. No chance.

So, Bruins goaltender Eddie Johnston replaced his partner Cheevers; Maple Leafs defenceman Brian Glennie replaced Tremblay; and Blackhawks centre Stan Mikita replaced Sanderson. And there was no Hull, replaced in name by Rick Martin.

"Yeah, I think it mattered," said Ellis. "If we'd had some of them, like Hull, it might not have gone to eight games to decide the outcome. We would have welcomed them with open arms."

"I didn't really care one way or another," said Maple Leafs winger Paul Henderson. "We didn't need them, we had enough firepower.

Even to this day I believe that. The only guy who would have changed anything would have been Bobby Orr, who was hurt. Bobby Hull? We had lots of goal scorers. That didn't concern me. In fact, I'm glad he wasn't there, he's a left winger like me."

Indeed, had Hull been included, then perhaps the eventual series hero might not have been invited, even though he had almost declined the invitation himself.

"My wife, Eleanor, and I did have plans that summer," said Henderson. "We had planned a trip to Europe. But when you stopped to think about it, it was 'I've got to do this, I've got to represent my country.' We hemmed and hawed for a bit, but it quickly went by the wayside."

Beyond the WHA issues, there was considerable speculation that Eagleson, a prominent player agent in addition to being a major influencer of the series, had a loud voice in the invite process, heavily promoting his clients, something that wasn't lost on the players and others around the team. It was just another divide of sorts that had to be overcome.

"We had a long list that we pared down to thirty-five, which is an awful lot to try to manage," said Sinden. "I can remember Fergie and I, we had some help, we'd often call some other coaches and managers around the league, get their opinions, but we eventually narrowed it. We got some turndowns, too, out of necessity for the players."

A few of those rejections included Rangers centre Walt Tkaczuk, who was running his own hockey school in the Kitchener, Ontario, area, and Canadiens defenceman Jacques Laperriere, whose wife was pregnant and experiencing complications. Rangers goalie Ed Giacomin was coming off knee surgery and declined, while Bruins defenceman Dallas Smith simply couldn't leave his family farm. A lot of players back in the day either had summer jobs, hockey schools, or worked on their family farms. With Laperriere a late scratch, his Montreal teammate Guy Lapointe was added to the roster, deciding to attend even though his wife was pregnant, due to give birth sometime during the series.

"At the beginning, we weren't quite sure if it would just be NHL players, or whether we could take some WHA players, or if it was just Canadians—who was it?" said Sinden. "Our list was pretty long. When they sorted it out and it was just NHL players, we lost Bobby Hull and a few others. It took a while to get through it. We had several meetings before we knew where we were going. But it's a nice choice when you're looking at players of that calibre.

"I felt we had to be a team, not an all-star team. There were some political appointments and I'll leave it at that. But they were all good players. We didn't think it would really matter, they were all so good. But I knew enough about the Soviet team that we would have to have a good team effort to beat them. I'm not so sure anyone else was quite aware of that as I was. We had that in mind, as you can see by the lineup. We added people like J. P. Parise, Wayne Cashman, Ron Ellis, Bobby Clarke—hard-working checking players. We knew we needed a real team atmosphere to survive, or at least I did."

In the end, Sinden was able to name ten of the top eleven players in the NHL's most valuable player voting to the roster—Orr, Dryden, Phil Esposito, Jean Ratelle, Vic Hadfield, Tony Esposito, Bobby Clarke, Brad Park, Rod Gilbert, and Gilbert Perreault. The only one missing—Bobby Hull. Even the prime minister approached NHL president Clarence Campbell to try to get Hull included, but to no avail. He also had eight of the top ten scorers from the previous season, Hull again the notable absence; Bruins winger Johnny Bucyk from that list was not invited, one of a few decisions that was widely debated. Others overlooked included Maple Leafs centre Dave Keon, who was very disappointed, Bruins (and Esposito's) winger Ken Hodge, and Canadiens centre Jacques Lemaire.

"I did put the roster together by potential lines, trying to balance each line out with all the good players available to us," said Sinden. "We sat down, Fergie and I, and looked at what the lines would look like—the twenty-man roster, not the thirty-five roster."

In addition to the thirty-five-player list, Sinden invited three junior graduates: goaltender Michel "Bunny" Larocque, selected sixth overall in the 1972 entry draft; defenceman John van Boxmeer, selected fourteenth (both picked by the Canadiens); and winger Billy Harris, the number one selection overall by the expansion New York Islanders. Those three were invited for the experience, but also to give Team Canada—a name Sinden preferred—four goaltenders and two full teams for intra-squad games at the training camp, since there wasn't any team to have exhibition games against. The plan was to have two-a-day workouts at Maple Leaf Gardens, with a scrimmage in the morning and a practice in the afternoon.

Thirty-five, while a necessity, also quickly became an encumbrance. Truth is, Sinden really didn't have any other choice, not if he wanted intra-squad games and scrimmages. But to get to that number, to get some players to even commit—which says a lot about the mindset—Sinden had to make promises he ultimately couldn't keep, though they seemed innocent enough at the time. In terms of managing egos and pride, thirty-five was too many.

"A lot of players wanted to go, felt they should go, but were reluctant to go because at the beginning they thought it was going to be a little bit, let's say, not quite as spectacular as it turned out to be," said Sinden. "So, I promised everybody they would play a game in the tournament. If you're looking at that lineup, you wonder if you'll ever get to play. So, to persuade them I guess, to give them some comfort,

I promised them they would all play at least one game. Ultimately, I couldn't live up to it, but it probably helped to get thirty-five players (from ten different NHL teams) on board."

It wouldn't have been possible back then, not with the tight time-lines of the tournament, and not with the egos, but years later Canada's world junior team found a better way, by having a pre-selection camp to whittle down the numbers for the main camp. Of course, they were able to play university teams as tune-ups. But back then it was the first ever, and the circumstances were different. Had the series been a romp, as many predicted, thirty-five would have worked out fine. Who knew?

Incredibly, three of the final names added to the roster were Henderson, Ellis, and Clarke—all three of whom would make enormous contributions—although Sinden doesn't recall it being quite that way. Henderson and Ellis were selected because they were two-thirds of an excellent line in Toronto, good offensively and very responsible defensively. And Clarke, who was three years into his NHL career with the Philadelphia Flyers, was a hard-nosed centre—equal parts skill and nastiness—coming off a terrific season, having put up eighty-one points. He was selected ahead of, for instance, Keon, who had battled through injuries the previous season and was unsigned, though he was healthy in time for 1972. That selection also led to considerable debate amongst the management team.

"It was just assumed the top players would be going," said Clarke. "Of course, they weren't taking players from the WHA. So that eliminated a few. The rest seemed easy to pick. The Bruins were easy choices. The Rangers had some good players. The Canadiens, of course, there were a lot of automatics. They filled in some of the roster with some young guys like Gilbert Perreault and Marcel Dionne. I was in a similar situation. My understanding is I was the one chosen because Walter Tkaczuk couldn't go."

"When they announced they were going to invite thirty-five players, I thought there was a possibility, I was at the peak of my career," said Ellis. "I got the call, they explained a lot to us and said everybody would play at least one game in the series, and to be honest that would have been enough for me, just to represent my country in one game. As it turned out I was able to participate in all eight."

"I wasn't surprised," said Henderson. "I thought they might even pick our line. Ronny and I played with Norm Ullman [with the Leafs] and we could play against anybody. All three of us were good offensively, but all three of us were very responsible defensive players. I had scored thirty-eight goals, and as I looked down the list of left wingers I really felt—my assets were my speed and shot—that I would get selected. But nobody knew for sure, and I sure was happy they chose me."

What Sinden and Ferguson envisioned was Clarke being a younger, more aggressive version of Ullman, though neither Henderson nor Ellis quite saw it in the beginning. Of course, Clarke had often been underestimated in his career. As a teenager, he was diagnosed with type 1 diabetes. Despite that, Clarke played on and was a star with his hometown junior Flin Flon (Manitoba) Bombers. But because of the diabetes, many teams worried that Clarke might not be able to endure the rigors of the NHL, even though doctors assured them that if he took proper care of himself he could.

Clarke, who was just five-foot-ten, 165 pounds, fell to the second round of the 1969 draft, selected seventeenth overall by the Flyers. He quickly became an outstanding player, dangerous offensively, a top defensive forward, and he played with an edge. He turned twenty-three the day Team Canada opened training camp.

While some needed coaxing and promises, others jumped at the opportunity. Chicago defenceman Pat Stapleton, who was from

Sarnia, Ontario, was supposed to have knee surgery that summer, but he called it off because he wouldn't have been able to skate until the beginning of October. Instead, he worked out with thirty- and forty-pound weights to strengthen the knee so he could play.

"I was in Scarborough and I got the call toward the end of June, beginning of July," said defenceman Brad Park. "It was Harry calling inviting me to play. I asked, what about the wives? I said if my wife [who was pregnant] could go to Moscow, that's all I wanted because to have that experience, during the Cold War, going to Russia was such an enticement. I wanted to play just for that, just to see another culture. They were a mystery. I never thought about how they'd been beating up the Canadians, the teams they had played in World Championships and Olympics. That never crossed my mind. I wanted to go to see something very few people ever get to see."

Park was a key addition to that lineup, especially with Orr unable to play. Park was the next best thing. Quite literally. Selected second overall in the 1966 NHL draft, the Toronto native debuted with the Rangers in 1968. Similar to Orr, Park was a good skater, talented offensively but also a very good defenceman. But he was always second best to Orr, which isn't the worst billing a player could receive. Three years in a row leading up to the series Park was runner-up to Orr for the Norris Trophy as the NHL's best defenceman.

Interestingly, Park and Orr had fought several times during their careers, and Park and Phil Esposito never really saw eye to eye, but then the Rangers and Bruins were huge rivals. Funnily enough, on November 7, 1975, Park, Ratelle, and Joe Zanussi were traded to the Bruins—for Esposito and Carol Vadnais. Small world.

Others had still different reasons for wanting to play.

"I was anxious to play because representing your country is a real honor and I had the privilege to do that in '64 with the Olympic team with Father Bauer," said Rod Seiling. "Being selected in some respects also stood you apart from some of the other players in the league. We all have egos, we all like to be appreciated, recognized for what we do and how we contribute. I looked forward to it."

That 1964 Canadian Olympic team finished with five wins and two losses, in a three-way tie for second place with Sweden and Czechoslovakia. For whatever reason—Seiling and the Canadians believed it was underhanded—the tie-breaking formula was changed mid-tournament.

"In '64, it was Canada versus the Soviets in the final game [of the medal round]," said Seiling. "The winner of that game wins the gold medal and we're actually up by one point going in. Bunny Ahearne [head of the International Ice Hockey Federation] gathered his minions together and changed the tie-breaking formula. If things had been left the way they were to start the tournament, we win a medal [bronze]. But he flipped it in such a way that when we lost, we didn't get a medal. It's hard to fathom how a team can be playing for the gold medal and not end up winning a medal. But he did it. He was a part of '72 as well."

The Soviets won the gold in 1964. Meanwhile, Ahearne was unintentionally helpful in the Summit Series coming to be when he and others balked at the Canadians briefly being allowed to use a handful of professionals internationally. That strengthened the resolve to create a super series. Ahearne was also outspoken in his criticism of the Canadian professionals after game 1 of the Summit. He never liked the idea of the pros playing against the so-called amateurs.

"The politics of sport," said Seiling.

There were some players pleasantly surprised when they were invited, but it spoke to Sinden and Ferguson trying to build a balanced team.

"The person who was most responsible for me was John Ferguson," said Peter Mahovlich. "We played together in Montreal, and when Harry asked him to be an assistant coach, he said he would agree if he could have two players, Serge Savard and me. Of course, Harry probably would have picked Serge anyway. But Fergie knew what we were all about and that we were team players."

Lapointe was another player whose wife was expecting, but he still decided to go.

"It was a tough decision for me," said Lapointe, who was just twenty-four in 1972. "But I figured it was a great chance to play for Canada. To be playing with this team after only two years in the NHL, what an honour."

Lapointe's son, Guy Jr., was born while the team was in Sweden, the day before their first exhibition game.

"I think I missed the first eighteen days of my son's life. He was born on September 15."

CHAPTER 3

Willing, but Not Ready

Training camp was meant to get the team ready to play, but Brad Park saw a slightly different story behind the scenes over those three weeks.

"I can't say it was a training camp dedicated to conditioning. It was in Toronto and I lived in Toronto. My wife was pregnant and overdue, so I stayed at home, not at the team hotel. I'd roll into the rink the next morning for practice and look at some of the guys who'd been out the night before and, well, they'd had a good time! Can't say no one took it seriously because professional pride was at stake."

But . . .

"I used to say, the closest I'm getting to the ice is my drinks," said Phil Esposito. "The ice in my drinks. There's a picture somewhere of Wayne Cashman and me in our long johns trying to do exercises, it's fucking hilarious. We were so bad. I've never been able to touch my toes, never—still can't do it. The times were different back then. Remember, we thought it was going to be like an all-star game. You try, but you don't try. You make sure you don't get hurt."

Of the many challenges confronting head coach Harry Sinden and his assistant John Ferguson when Team Canada assembled for the first time on August 13 at Maple Leaf Gardens, getting his players' attention, getting them to take this series with the Soviet Union seriously, even just a little more seriously than many were, was certainly a major one.

"The problem we had, it was not a serious training camp," said winger Yvan Cournoyer. "We took it very loosely. During the training camp, I had a hockey school running in Montreal. I was going to Toronto to practice, then I'd come back to Montreal, then back to Toronto, then back to Montreal . . . We weren't very serious about it. When everybody is like that, you don't take them seriously, it's not good. And thirty-five players was too many. I don't know if they were even the best in the NHL, but I think Eagleson had a little say in that, a few clients."

"Some of the guys had time to prepare, I didn't," said defenceman Guy Lapointe, who was a late addition to the roster. "When Jacques Laperriere decided not to play [due to the health of his pregnant wife], that opened up a spot for me. When people ask me about 1972, it's usually about why did Canada get off to such a slow start? I tell them we got together for about three weeks in August for a training camp, but nobody took it seriously. Players would leave for a couple of days because they had hockey schools to run. The Russians had been training together for ten months."

Beyond that, there were other mental obstacles to overcome. First, there were some players, such as Phil Esposito and his brother, Tony, who were led to believe the series was going to be "fun," an "exhibition," and they really didn't want to be there in the first place. They were all giving up a large chunk of their summer, and in the case of the Espositos also revenues from their hockey school. They were essentially doing all of this for minimum paid expenses.

"The off-season is precious for a player, a seventy-eight-game schedule is a tough row to hoe," said Sinden. "They look forward to summer. To give that up was a heckuva commitment. And their reputations were on the line. I just don't think they recognized that in the beginning, but eventually they did."

"Tony wasn't happy," said Phil Esposito. "Even flying down on the airplane heading to training camp, we had a few drinks, he said, 'You fucked me, you got me involved in this. I don't want to go to Russia. I hate Russia.' I laughed, I did. I said, 'Tony, how bad can it be?' He said, 'I don't even know if I'm going to be playing, you think I'm going to go through all of this and not play?' I said, 'I don't know, who the hell knows?' I said, 'Tony, apparently there are going to be thirty-five guys, and I was told everybody is going to get a game. We've got eight games in the series, so everyone's going to play and it's going to be like an exhibition, like an all-star game.'

"But who the hell wanted to do that?" continued Phil. "I'm an NHL player. I don't give a damn about a stupid exhibition series with the Russians in which we had everything to lose and nothing to gain. Who wanted it? I didn't care about it. I probably wouldn't have even watched it. That's the truth. I didn't care. I was caring about my team, the Boston Bruins. Tony was caring about the Chicago Blackhawks and we had training camp coming up and it was the first time I was making a half-decent salary. I didn't want to get hurt. There were no guaranteed contracts back then. What happens if you get hurt? You think Boston cared about Team Canada?"

A second challenge was to get the players to stop reading—actually, believing—their press clippings, most of which suggested the Canadians would easily win all eight games, or close to it. More reserved journalists thought the Canadian squad might spot the Soviets a win or two. A few former players and coaches who had experience with the national team and international hockey offered cautionary advice, but mostly they weren't heard—or listened to.

"If we would have known more about the Russians, we would have had a better training camp," said centre Red Berenson. "The media, the fans all said, 'These Russians won't have a chance against these NHLers.'"

Sinden, in trying to figure out how to get his players in the proper mental state, showed them an old black-and-white movie.

"It was a video of the 1958 championships in Oslo in which I played, and I wanted to show them both the glory of winning for your country and how difficult, even in those days, the Soviet team could be," said Sinden. "Well, it became a bit funny. The quality of the movie wasn't very good and I don't think the speed was right. Anyway, there were a lot of funny incidents as I showed it. I really wanted to get to the award-winning part of it, where I could touch on the pride of being a Canadian—but they had a few laughs along the way. As a matter of fact, I had to shut the movie off. They were looking at it as a kind of a comedy. I can understand why now. Of course, I was in it and I fell down a couple of times and there would be a big cheer from all the guys watching. It was an attempt at doing what I thought was the most difficult thing to do, to get everybody prepared for a pretty tough tournament."

Turns out, it *was* the most difficult thing to do.

Another big challenge was physical conditioning. The NHLers were used to enjoying their summers, a steady diet of beer and golf for most. Of course, there were some who worked hard on their farms or at other pursuits, but nothing to truly prepare for a hockey series. Back in the day they would report to camp in September (some team's invite letters to training camp reminded players to bring their golf clubs), play upwards of a dozen exhibition games, and get themselves into "game" shape. Needless to say, in mid-August very few were in "game" shape, some not even remotely close. The Soviets, meantime, had already been in intense training for weeks, make that months (some suggest these "amateurs" didn't stop training all calendar year).

For Team Canada, the regular season had ended on April 2, the Stanley Cup was awarded to the Bruins on May 11. So it was three months from Cup celebration to Team Canada training camp, four and a half months for those who missed the playoffs. Not an insignificant amount of time to be away from the ice.

"We had guys who came to training camp, who hadn't skated since the season had ended," said Cashman. "Many guys just went to training camp to get into shape, and we had six weeks of it back then. We didn't have that much time to get ready for this series. It was a short training camp and they had to bring in a lot of players. There was no other team at that time in the summer to scrimmage against. So we had to bring in enough players to have two teams and that caused a lot of hard feelings for the players who [eventually] didn't get to play."

In fairness to the players, there weren't a lot of training options at the time. Dry-land training existed in some places, but it really wasn't a thing then. And summer ice time was scarce to say the least. Some players lived in smaller towns and remote communities with no access to training facilities.

"You have to remember, there was no dry-land training, there was no summer training, there was no summer ice," said defenceman Rod Seiling, who was from Elmira, Ontario. "Compared to today's player, even if you had wanted to, it would have been nigh impossible to have trained. We only got the call in July and you're reporting a month later. I have a farm. Normally I'd be off my farm in early September to go to training camp and things would be done and put away. I would run, but there was nothing else to do and nowhere to do it. In those days, NHL players went to camp and played themselves into condition. It was a marathon. It was a dozen exhibition games, and if you were lucky you got the odd night off. You wouldn't expect [Harry's training camp] to be any different."

"I can tell you there was no serious skating in the summer of 1972," said Berenson. "Our sport was deep in tradition—stuck in the mud. There were a lot of good things that came out of that series. The Russians were in such good shape."

The final challenge for Sinden was not just the size of his roster, but from where the players came—meaning, he had put together a group of thirty-five (which would prove to be as unwieldy as it was necessary) from ten different teams, and the simple truth was, on the ice a lot of them were bitter rivals who didn't like each other very much, if at all. That was typical for the times, and much different from today. In the NHL of the 1970s, there wasn't much fraternization amongst players on opposing teams.

"You had the Boston group, the Rangers group, the guys from Montreal, the Chicago players, we weren't friends," said Berenson, who at age thirty-two was the fourth oldest player on the team behind Frank Mahovlich, Bill White, and Gary Bergman. He was also one of only a few with international experience, having played with the Belleville McFarlands winning the 1959 World Championship in Prague. "It was a real challenge to become a team. Harry and John did a good job of bringing us together. But it took time. Once we realized it wasn't Boston versus the Rangers anymore, and that it was us against the Russians, we were better."

"Unlike today, players on one team did not talk to players on another team," said Peter Mahovlich. "That's just the way things were back then. So you had the Boston Bruins—Wayne Cashman, Bobby Orr was around, there was Don Awrey, and, of course, Phil. They sort of stuck together. We had six players there with myself, my brother, Guy Lapointe, Kenny Dryden, Serge Savard, and Yvan. We stuck together. The Rangers had five players. Chicago had five. So it wasn't easy to come together."

"We never liked anybody on the opposition," said Rangers winger Vic Hadfield, who was coming off a career-high fifty-goal season, tied for second with Bobby Hull behind Esposito's sixty-six. "Don't forget most of us were from the days when there were only six teams. Back then, it wasn't like it is today with all these charity events and golf tournaments. Everybody is buddy-buddy. You can see it in the warmups. I can remember when we would go to Montreal for a game. We would fly up but take the overnight train back to New York with the Canadiens. They would be in a car at one end, and we would be in a car at the other end. There would be a restaurant car in between. Nobody ever went to eat because we didn't want to run into one another. Part of it was out of respect, but we didn't like each other."

So it took some time and a few beers, ironically, to achieve harmony within the dressing room, at least to some degree.

"We knew each other a little bit from Player Association meetings and stuff like that, but we didn't really know each other that well," said centre Bobby Clarke. "It took some time. What probably helped us a lot, and it's probably what we shouldn't have been doing, was at night everybody would get together and drink some beer and talk hockey— things hockey players like doing. It wasn't like, 'Oh man, I've got to get to bed at nine p.m. because we've got a big series coming up.' It was more like, 'Let's go out and have a beer, and have a good time.'"

"They probably didn't like each other when they were on different teams," said Sinden, "but they were now on the same team, and that was an interesting aspect of that whole group of players, how quickly during our time at training camp they realized that they were going to have to behave on that team as teammates, as they did on their own NHL teams. That, to me, was startling the way that worked. It took some time, but we didn't have any dissension or animosity, that I know of, from one player to another. We had some from the players to myself and management."

It was only decided partway through training camp that the players, who originally had not been promised any money, reportedly could earn as much as $5,000 each off gate receipts from the three intra-squad games, but that number would likely be much smaller.

"We only told them about it the other day, long after they'd agreed to play for their country for nothing," Sinden told reporters midway through camp. "It could be as low as fifteen hundred dollars per man, or as much as five thousand. But it's much more likely to be twenty-five hundred or so. They play the Russia-Canada series for nothing, but I insisted we owe professional athletes something for using their valuable services in other games."

Most of the players remember only receiving $1,500 for their troubles, while there were later newspaper reports suggesting that they received upwards of $2,000 to $2,500. Whatever the money, it really wasn't an issue. Some were there because they felt they had to be, and some wanted to be part of the spectacle regardless, though few had any idea of what they were really signing up for. One group that took training camp seriously from the very first day were Bobby Clarke and Maple Leaf wingers Paul Henderson and Ron Ellis, three of the final picks to the roster, who were put together as a line early in camp by Sinden. Ultimately, they were the only line to remain intact from start to finish in the series.

"Initially, we were disappointed," said Henderson. "There were seven left wingers, seven right wingers, seven centre ice men, so Ron and I knew we would play together. So we looked through and we thought at best we're the fourth line. If we can get Stan Mikita, we might be the fourth line, but if we get Bobby Clarke we're definitely going to be the seventh line. We get to training camp and we're with Clarkie."

But what the three of them shared was an intense desire to prove themselves, make the team, and get more than just the one promised game in the series.

"We wanted to prove to ourselves and the rest of them that we could play," said Henderson. "We got to camp, and the first practice the three of us were together. I distinctly remember we went out afterwards and had a beer—I didn't know Clarkie at all then—and I remember saying I really wanted to play in the game in Toronto. My mom was still alive, my dad had died, I really wanted to get into that game. So let's get serious and show them that we can play. Why don't we work our arses off and see if we can get into the lineup. Nobody had to motivate Clarkie, that's for sure. Drop the puck and he would do anything to win a hockey game. So I think the three of us were probably in better shape, but we worked our rear ends off in practice. We were trying to prove ourselves."

"We clicked right off the bat," said Clarke. "We had complementary styles of play. Henderson had speed, and he could shoot the puck. Ellis was a tremendous defensive player. I was a puck chaser. We also knew that if we didn't work our asses off, we would be part of the group who only would play once in a while. We played well from the start and they couldn't take us out."

"Bobby Clarke, in my mind, was a young Norm Ullman," said Ellis. "Good passer, good on the faceoffs, great forechecker. So we didn't have to change our way of playing. Other players had to make big adjustments with new line mates—we didn't have that. The other thing that is so important is to play the Russians you have to play strongly in both ends of the rink. That was the way we played in the

NHL. We could all skate and we played in both ends of the rink, that's how we had to play."

During daily scrimmages, during practices, and during the Red-White intra-squad games the line was certainly noticed and effective. In the first intra-squad game, played before a crowd of 5,571—who paid regular-season prices at Maple Leaf Gardens in eighty-degree heat—all three ended up with two points, with Ellis and Clarke scoring goals.

"Better than any all-star game I've ever seen," Sinden told reporters of his White team's 8–5 win. "The shooting was great and the conditioning, well, I was surprised to see them going as well as they were in the last five to eight minutes of the game."

Their hard work continued. In the second game, Henderson had a goal, Ellis an assist. In the third game, Henderson had two goals, Clarke a goal and assist, and Ellis an assist.

"The three of us decided, let's give it our best shot, and things started to fall into place," said Ellis. "In the scrimmages we were starting to play well, and in the Red and White games we sort of dominated a little bit, scoring goals. We played our way onto that team."

"You know the old story, we were underdogs to get on the team," said Henderson. "We had fifteen future Hall of Famers on that team. We knew at best we were going to be the fourth line, but we worked our arses off. Then we played the Red-White games, and the last game our side won 6–2; I got two of the goals and Clarkie got a goal and we didn't have any scored against us. As it went on, it was evident we were as good as there was out there, and it was just because we were underdogs. When you start off with [Frank] Mahovlich and Cournoyer and Esposito, then you come back with Gilbert, Ratelle, and Hadfield, then you've got Perreault and Martin and whoever else. We were underdogs, but once we got our foot in the door it worked out well. We got serious, where a lot of guys really didn't. There were four or five guys I don't think they worked up a sweat the whole training camp."

Sinden still believed his training camp was tough enough physically, but he admitted there were challenges with the timing and pulling the team together, and also getting the team mentally prepared. Even though Sinden and others knew the Soviets would be good, conditioned, and prepared, no one really knew how that would measure up against the Canadians, the NHLers. Whether it was going to be "fun" and an "exhibition" or not, deep down everyone knew the series was still about bragging rights, about staking claim to global hockey supremacy. But Sinden's biggest challenge was convincing the players it might be more difficult than they thought.

A scouting expedition to Moscow didn't help the cause.

Team Canada sent a couple of the Maple Leaf scouts, Bob Davidson and Johnny McLellan, to the Soviet Union. McLellan had been coach of the year in the NHL two seasons earlier with the Leafs, and he played for the Belleville McFarlands when they beat the Soviets in the 1959 World Championship in Prague. Davidson was the Leafs' head scout, and both were very well regarded in the game. Their best-laid plans quickly unravelled and became a nightmare, Soviet style. In fairness to both scouts, they were only able to spend four days there and saw just one intra-squad game and a single exhibition match between the Leningrad Army squad and the Soviet Selects. In the one game they saw that involved twenty-year-old goaltender Vladislav Tretiak, who had won gold at the 1972 Olympics, his team lost 8–1. He allowed all eight goals and was not terribly impressive. Little did the scouts know that Tretiak was getting married the next day and apparently had enjoyed himself a little too much the night before.

The scouting trip was essentially a waste of time. There were no player lineups to match numbers to names, though they probably would have been messed up by the Soviets anyway. The Soviets were masters of deception, and they had struck again, ensuring the scouts never saw the full measure of the Soviet team. The scouts reported what they saw, and the players believed what they read.

"The scouting reports were not good," said Cournoyer. "We were told they didn't have a goalie, that Tretiak wasn't very good."

"What made it difficult is from what we were told, it was an industrial league–type team that was going to represent the Soviet Union," said Hadfield. "The report came back they can't skate, their equipment is ragtag. But this was typical Russian bullshit. We didn't know what we were about to get into."

The scouting report certainly could have been misleading, but it also begged the question: Was anyone watching the 1972 Olympics, or World Championships, or any other major tournaments before those? It was really a collision of factors—the scouting, the press clippings, ego, the time of year, the lack of interest amongst some— that conspired against Team Canada in the beginning.

"You see what you know you're going to see," said Dryden of the scouting trip. "That's the lesson of anything. That's how we all are in things. Those guys are experienced scouts, and as experienced scouts what do you do? You watch somebody again and again and again. Well, they didn't have the opportunity to see these players again and again and again. Also, what is it that they are used to in terms of scouting? Well, you see guys up against their peers; that's why you want to watch them in a playoff series, or in big games, and see how they do against others that are really good.

"They were seeing them against others who played the same way as them. They can pick out who is better, one player or another, but to try to transpose that observation and judgment to NHL players, that's a different story. The scouting job that they had to do was a job that scouts don't usually do. They don't scout that way. They scouted the way they had the chance to scout, and when you scout that way you don't see what you need to see and pass on what needs to get passed on."

"Training camp was enough physically to get them ready," said Sinden. "But to get them ready mentally, they had to play against the Soviets and see what they were up against."

Next stop, Montreal—where seeing would be believing.

Labor Day '72: Unions struggle to improve image

By ROSEMARY SPIERS
Star staff writer

METRO WEATHER
Mostly sunny and cool.
High upper 60s, low near 45. Pollution Index 1 at 7 a.m. Details page 2.

The Toronto Star

Holiday edition

ESTABLISHED 1892

July-paid circulation Mon. to Fri. 493,073, Sat. 685,107   ***   Monday, September 4, 1972—34 pages   Mon.-Fri. 10¢; Sat. 25¢; Home delivery 75¢

Not even Superman could keep egg off our faces

By MILT DUNNELL
Star staff writer

LARRY SEFTON
Runs steelworkers' affairs

Should be questioning

Possible effects

See LABOR, page 2

- Labor's next big objective will be to organize the white-collar workers. Page 5.
- A veteran labor leader looks back on 50 years of union progress. Page 4.
- The origins of Labor Day. Page 21.
- Ottawa's labor shrinks don't wait for strikes. Page 13.

Party leaders mix hockey and politics

By JACK CAHILL
Star staff writer

Montreal bar fire toll 37 2 sought

MONTREAL (P-Reuter)—

See MONTREAL, page 2

Lawrence calls police to emergency meeting

EVERYONE'S AFTER HIS ONE VOTE

HAMILTON (CP)—

It's a desperate situation for Team Canada tonight

By FRANK ORR
Star staff writer

See TEAM, page 5   See LEADERS, page 1

See LAWRENCE, page 2

GOALIE ALL ALONE—Team Canada goalie Ken Dryden, of Montreal Canadiens, gets the feeling close-hand that he's alone against the Soviets when his teammates seem to desert him in this goal attack by Soviet players Aleksandr Yakushev (left) and Evgeni Zimin (No. 11). Dryden saved the shot but seven others passed him as Soviet team beat Team Canada 7-3 in series' opener in Montreal Saturday.

At Montreal museum

$3 million in paintings stolen by hooded trio

Special to The Star
MONTREAL —

The Toronto Star

- Mark Spitz, the 22-year-old fitness dentist from California, is hoping to extract an unprecedented seventh gold medal in swimming at the Munich Olympics today. He's already set six world records. Page 11.

- Drawing 25,000 persons—the season's biggest turnout to the CNE Grandstand—singing stars Sonny and Cher last night endeared the audience with their easy bantering and charm. Page 22.

MARK SPITZ
Olympic golden boy

With no Sunday newspapers, hockey fans in Toronto waited a day to be reminded of the shocking opening-game loss and other shocking real-life news that transpired in Montreal. (Courtesy of the *Toronto Star*)

CHAPTER 4

Game 1—A Shocking Start

The Montreal Forum, situated at the northeast corner of Avenue Atwater and Rue Sainte-Catherine West, had opened in late November 1924. It was rich in hockey history, home to so many great moments, witness to so many Stanley Cup champions, the incredible Canadiens teams of the late 1950s, the infamous Richard Riot, and the stage for some of the best players ever. People even insisted it had its ghosts. But it hadn't seen anything quite as haunting as what was coming.

The Forum always seemed to have a special feel and energy to it on a game night, as if it had its own pulse and personality. But somehow, on a Saturday night, a hockey night, it was even more special. Full with 18,818 fans and dignitaries, including the prime minister, the feeling was like no other on the hot and steamy opening night of the Summit Series—Saturday, September 2.

"The Forum was an electric place for a midweek game against the St. Louis Blues, let alone a Saturday game against the Boston Bruins, let alone a playoff game against the Bruins," said goaltender Ken Dryden, 1972 rookie of the year with the Montreal Canadiens and a Stanley Cup champion in 1971. He knew how energized that building could be. "But then you get to a game like this, it was an exploding place."

There was a wide range of moods and emotions in the building that night. For some there was tension, there were nerves, there was trepidation, there was excitement and great expectation. And for some it felt like just another game.

"I don't know if you can write this or not," said Phil Esposito, "but my girlfriend at the time, who later became my wife, flew up to Montreal that day. Let's just say we spent the afternoon having some fun. There wasn't a sense of urgency, not for me anyway. I thought it was going to be like an exhibition game. You know you're going to get into it a little bit. But these guys had never faced pro players before, although I always considered them to be pros because they were getting paid, except they were in the goddamn army. But they were getting paid. For me, there was no sense of urgency."

That would soon change.

The weeks of buildup and suspense were finally over, and the series that for years had never seemed possible was about to happen— finally, best versus best—although not without a few scares in the hours leading up to puck drop.

A day before the series was to begin there was the potential for a delay, if not postponement, although that was highly unlikely. A Montreal man had obtained a court order allowing him to seize the Soviets' equipment until their government paid the $1,889 in damages he had been awarded for his car being destroyed by a Soviet tank during the 1968 Soviet invasion in Prague, Czechoslovakia. Apparently, the prime minister's office had gotten involved, and according to Aggie Kukulowicz, a Winnipeg native who was a sports representative with Air Canada and the official interpreter during the series, Alan Eagleson settled the issue by writing a cheque for $2,200.

Then, on game night, just a couple hours before puck drop, the Soviet team was nowhere to be found in the arena. Turns out they'd been late leaving their hotel, then got stuck in traffic. They eventually arrived and carried their own equipment bags into the rink.

"I remember going down to the team bus a couple of hours before the game, and I was the only one sitting on the bus," said athletic trainer Rick Noonan, a Canadian who at the time was working for the University of British Columbia athletic department. The Soviets had travelled with a masseuse but asked for a trainer to be assigned to them for the games in Canada. Hockey Canada chose Noonan, who had won a couple Memorial Cups with St. Michael's College and the Toronto Marlboroughs and worked for Father David Bauer and the national team. He knew the Russians and they knew him. He had met the Soviets on the tarmac in Montreal.

"I think the game time was around seven-thirty and it was already six-thirty. I know the Forum was only a few blocks away, but we had to get going. I went up to the team dining area, and there were all the officials, coaches, and players, drinking black coffee or Coca-Colas and eating pastries. They needed only fifteen minutes to dress and were out there in time for the warm-up. Some Canadian players liked to be at the rink two or three hours before the game, but I learned later that the Russians didn't want to expend too much nervous energy. That's why they arrived at the rink closer to game time and it was that way for all four games in Canada."

Inside both dressing rooms there was a measure of nerves and pent-up energy, both teams wondering just how good the other really was. The Soviets later admitted they were nervous, that the scenario had suddenly become quite real and the only place they could deal with those emotions was on the ice.

"There was no fear," said winger Alexander Yakushev. "But there was a sense of nervousness. That's because it was the first time we were playing against Team Canada with professionals, whom we had seen very little. And we hadn't played many games with such a big audience watching and certainly not in Canada."

The night before the game, as a group, they had gone to the cinema to watch a movie, *The Godfather*. Interestingly, earlier in the day legendary goaltender Jacques Plante, who had starred mostly with the Canadiens and was working on the French television broadcast for the series, visited with twenty-year-old Soviet goaltender Vladislav Tretiak, whom he had met a couple years earlier. Plante had predicted Team Canada would win all eight games. Perhaps fearing the youngster might be a little apprehensive (and about to be thrown to the slaughter), he offered some hints, through an interpreter, on how to play the Canadian shooters.

"I first met him in 1970 when he was playing with the St. Louis Blues," said Tretiak. "We had a practice on the same rink as the Blues. I went into the dressing room to take a shower and suddenly [Soviet coach Anatoly] Tarasov runs in and says, 'You are taking your shower while Jacques Plante is out there on the ice? Go take a look at how he is practising.' I parked myself behind the net just to watch his movements. He noticed me. He gave me his stick.

"Then, of course, before game one he came into our dressing room. This was very unexpected for me. Normally, no outsider would be allowed in, but they must have let him in out of respect. He started speaking to me in English, but I didn't understand anything. So he started drawing. It was obviously difficult to understand anything, but just the fact that he came to see me, I don't know why he did it. Perhaps he thought they were going to get twenty by me, or there was a kind of fraternal feeling. I should have asked him. But the very fact that he showed such respect and came to see me—that made me happy. I was very grateful. As I was looking at him, I could see a famous great goalie. What a great guy. Canadians probably weren't pleased, though."

The Canadians, other than Esposito perhaps, felt equal parts nerves and excitement themselves that night in the Forum and were perhaps collectively a touch overconfident, ignoring the advice of some pundits who reminded the nation that the Soviets might be better than advertised. Team Canada, on orders from coach Harry Sinden, had gotten its first glimpse of the Soviets the day before at practice at the Forum. But the players saw what the scouts had noticed: the equipment and the skates were of poor quality, and they prepared in a different way than the Canadians, focusing on different facets and skill sets of the game. In interviews after, several of the Soviet players said they sensed a "confidence and arrogance" about the Canadians. The Soviets remained to watch them practice afterwards.

Canada, of course, had its roster issues with the exclusion of Bobby Hull and three other World Hockey Association players, but the Soviets had some roster issues of their own. Vsevolod Bobrov, a former star player, was named the Soviet national coach, replacing the legendary Anatoly Tarasov after the 1972 Olympics, which the Soviets won. Tarasov had expected to continue as coach, but Bobrov took over for the World Championships, in which they were defeated by Czechoslovakia. Boris Kulagin, who scouted most of the Team Canada training camp in Toronto, was named assistant coach.

"Tarasov tried for so many years to make this series happen," said Tretiak. "So obviously he was disappointed that he didn't get to go. Bobrov was a good coach, once a professional player himself, and he did a lot for hockey. He deserves a lot of credit, especially for the games in Canada . . . but it really wasn't difficult for the coach to motivate us for the games in Canada because each player wanted to prove something."

The Soviets left off their thirty-one-player roster two prominent players, defenceman Vitali Davydov and forward Anatoli Firsov, who ironically was regarded as the Bobby Hull of Soviet hockey. Both Soviet players were said to have injuries, although there was speculation they had differences with the coaching staff.

Bobrov had played against the Penticton (BC) Vees in the 1955 World Championship. Remembering how that series played out physically, especially for him, Bobrov had his players take boxing lessons during training camp to prepare for Team Canada.

Despite the criticisms of the Canadian pre-tournament scouting entourage, who only saw a couple games during the *Sovietsky Sport* tournament and one national team practice in Moscow and one in Leningrad, the Canadians were well aware of how skilled and well conditioned the Soviets were. In particular, Team Canada knew of their best forwards, Valeri Kharlamov and Alexander Yakushev; both, along with Tretiak, were future members of the Hockey Hall of Fame. They had also heard about forward Boris Mikhailov, who was, best put, the Soviet's Bobby Clarke, meaning he would do anything to win. Needless to say, by game time both teams were anxious and ready.

"We were like caged animals," said Paul Henderson. "We just couldn't wait to get out there and get them. We just wanted to thump the hell out of them, show them once and for all, that they wished they never came over here. We knew they were good, but we had so much firepower we felt we would just overwhelm them."

"There were nerves, sure," said Dryden. "I think what I was really feeling was excitement, that whatever the feelings were through August in Toronto, that's one thing. But then a day or two away is the first game, the anticipation builds, the buzz gets louder. All of a sudden it's there, and then once you're in the arena, the sound and energy of the arena, whatever nerves you're feeling get turned into energy. That's truly what I was feeling."

For the Canadians, the game plan was relatively simple. As Henderson had said, they were going to use their firepower to subdue the Soviets. They would play an NHL-style game on NHL-sized ice and apply offensive pressure, shooting on the supposedly weak Soviet goaltender as much as possible. They were only allowed to dress seventeen skaters, so the coaches decided to dress a dozen forwards—four lines—and five defencemen. It would prove to be a huge mistake, one of many on this night.

"The only thing that bothered us going into the first game was how hot it was," said defenceman Brad Park. "It was like ninety degrees in Montreal. It was hot and humid. The day before, we arrived in Montreal and we had a practice. Afterwards, we went and sat on a patio having a beer and sandwich, the weather was beautiful. We were gung-ho. Our attitude was let's go out and take care of business. We'd seen them practise and watched the drills they were doing—a lot of criss-crossing, play making, three-on-three scenarios in tight spaces—which were entirely different than what we were doing in practice at the NHL level. Their uniforms looked shabby, nobody had anything new. The Russian-made stick didn't look so good. Meanwhile, we all have new gloves, pants, sweaters, we're outfitted to the tee."

In deciding who would play in that first game, Sinden rewarded training camp and intra-squad game performances and opted for some proven combinations. Dryden was given the nod in goal, although some thought Tony Esposito had a better camp. But Dryden was playing in his home building and he had prior international experience, though not an especially good record against the

Soviets. On defence, Sinden opted for Park with Gary Bergman, Rod Seiling and Don Awrey, and Guy Lapointe as the fifth man.

Up front, Esposito started the game with two Montreal Canadiens—Frank Mahovlich and Yvan Cournoyer—on his wings. The GAG Line—Goal-A-Game Line—from the New York Rangers would remain intact, Jean Ratelle centring Vic Hadfield and Rod Gilbert. Red Berenson would centre a third line with Peter Mahovlich and Mickey Redmond, and the fourth unit would be Clarke between Henderson and Ellis, a line that had been together from the first day of training camp and had been the team's best.

The Forum was hot and full on this night, so the quality of the ice was a factor. The air was also heavy. Indeed, by the second period the ice was soft and there was a fog hanging over it. Prime Minister Pierre Elliott Trudeau, who a day earlier had called an election, was on hand to drop the puck during the ceremonial faceoff and watched the game in a seat behind the penalty box. Just prior to the series, Sinden and a few others from the delegation had driven to Ottawa to meet with the prime minister and present his eight-month-old son with a mini Team Canada sweater. That son's name was Justin. Former prime minister Lester B. Pearson was also in the stands, as well as Conservative leader Robert Stanfield and lawyer and businessman (and future prime minister) Brian Mulroney. You could have held a political convention in the Forum. Even the anthem singer got caught up in the moment, at one point singing: "Team Canada we stand on guard for thee . . ."

Typically with a ceremonial faceoff there is zero intensity. The puck drops and the home team softly pulls back the puck and gives it to the dignitary. Not this time. Esposito won the draw with the enthusiasm reserved for the real opening faceoff, then had to chase after the puck, back to the Canadian blue line, to retrieve it. When he brought it back to Trudeau and the delegation at centre ice, he said something that made them all laugh.

"I knew this faceoff was symbolic," said centre Vladimir Vikulov. "I didn't know why, but I really wanted to win it. At the last second, I decided not to fight for the puck. I thought it would look strange."

"I made sure I won it, that's for sure," said Esposito, whose temperature had gone from ambivalent to very interested. "I didn't want them to even win that faceoff, because all of a sudden it started to become pretty intense, because we saw them, and what really blew my mind is when they were practising they had rickety skates, their gloves were torn, but all of a sudden everything looked brand new. And it was game on. I don't know what I said to Trudeau, I probably said something like 'Here's a puck for your collection.' Or 'Puck off!' I'm not sure."

But everyone smiled and laughed. And those smiles would remain for a while longer, but only a short while longer.

Just thirty seconds into the game, Park slipped in from the point and fired a pass through the defence, which Frank Mahovlich deflected. The rebound bounced up in the air, and Phil Esposito tapped it in, cutting the tension in the Forum and on the Team Canada bench. Henderson actually took the first penalty thirty-three seconds later, but the Canadians killed it off and at the 6:32 mark, Clarke cleanly won a faceoff in the Soviets' zone and Henderson scored from the top of the circle. The rout was on. The scouts were right. Except . . .

"There was a little bit of apprehension at the start," said Peter Mahovlich, "then bang-bang it's 2–0 and we thought it's going to be 10–0 before you know it."

"We scored on the first shift; it was a confirmation that 'oh, we knew this would happen,'" said Berenson.

With an early 2–0 lead, it's possible the confidence many of the Canadian players carried into the series was gusting to overconfidence. But there was also a realization happening that no matter how good their start was, the Soviets were good, really good. And the lead and the play wasn't lopsided.

"Phil scored right off the bat, I scored at the six-minute mark, but I remember I came back to the bench and I said to Clarkie and Ronny, 'Boys, this is going to be a very long series,'" said Henderson. "Everybody on the bench knew six minutes into the game that this was a very gifted team. Their physical conditioning was just incredible."

"When it's 2–0, I don't know that you think," said Dryden. "You're playing. If you're thinking, then you're not absorbed. I do remember between the first goal and the second goal that we scored that it was kind of routine action. I do remember having that feeling. There was a kind of flow of play and evenness of play of two regular opponents playing against each other. This wasn't the rink being tilted on its end with the first goal being scored, then a second, and they were scored early in the game and pretty close to each other so that it meant we were just this incredible wave and it was in our favour. No, it wasn't. In between the goals there was kind of a game that was going on. It wasn't just this overwhelmingness of us at the beginning. Yes, it was right up to the first goal, but in the time between the first goal and the second goal it wasn't."

There was, if not a sense of dread, then a serious concern amongst the Team Canada players—maybe, too, among the fans in the Forum and the estimated 12 million watching on Canadian television. It was estimated that, worldwide, 100 million watched that game.

"The Soviet players were stoic, they showed little emotion," said Noonan. "When they fell behind 2–0, there was no anxiety or panic. You couldn't tell if they were ahead 2–0 or down 2–0 in games."

It was about midway through the opening period that the Soviets started to relax. Afterwards they admitted they had never been in an atmosphere like the Forum that night, even though they were welcomed by polite applause during the introductions. Of course, there was more sympathy than animosity then.

"I was especially nervous when they were introducing the Canadian players before the game," said Yakushev. "There was cheering for two minutes after every name. Those nerves were very much present during the first few minutes."

"To be honest, when they scored two quick goals, there was a feeling they would tear us to pieces," said Mikhailov.

"On the other hand, we believed in ourselves because we were multiple times World and Olympic champions," added Yakushev. "There was no fear, just excitement which paralyzed us during those first ten minutes."

Once they found their legs, the pinpoint passing started, the circling with the puck in the neutral zone began, until it was just the right time to enter the Canadian zone, a way of playing that was foreign to Team Canada.

"Obviously, the start was great," said Esposito. "But then a few things happened. We started getting penalties in the second period, and once that happened it was over. We just couldn't keep up to them. It was different for us with the recoiling, going back, and circling. We had never seen that before. It was a great learning experience, and we soon found out we would have to adjust. As the series went along, Harry and Fergie did a great job in making us adjust."

But for the rest of game 1 that learning experience would be painful. Yevgeni Zimin, who took a pass from Yakushev, was the first Soviet to beat Dryden, a dozen minutes into the first period.

"The most important goal in my hockey career was the first goal of the series," Zimin later said. "I shall always remember the red light shining behind Ken Dryden's back in the first period in Montreal."

"After Zimin scored the first goal, we found our game and destroyed Team Canada ourselves," said Mikhailov.

Late in the period, nine seconds after defenceman Alexander "Rags" Ragulin, a veteran of three Olympics and nine World Championships, was sent to the penalty box, Vladimir Petrov tapped a rebound past a fallen Dryden to score short-handed. After twenty minutes the game was tied. But it was feeling more like a loss in the making.

"The first two goals went in so quickly and easily for us, you thought we were playing a senior team or something," said Clarke. "Then, all of a sudden, by the end of the first period we knew we were in trouble. They were flying. They were the far better team in the first game."

"At the end of the first period it's 2–2," said Park. "We had only dressed five defencemen, so we're going every second shift. At the end of the first period Gary Bergman and I were sitting in the dressing room and we're sucking wind. Bergy looks at me and he says, 'What do you think?' I said, 'We're in trouble.' We knew it right then. They were much better conditioned than we were. In the NHL, we always played five defencemen, so technically it wasn't a problem, but at this stage of the series you're not in mid-season form. You're sucking air."

The Soviets, too, had thought this first game might go differently. After the game, Soviet coach Bobrov was quoted as saying he told his team to essentially brace for a Canadian onslaught, but if they fell behind by a goal or two to maintain their poise. And so they did.

Despite the feeling of impending doom, Team Canada had other chances in the first period to alter the flow of the game. When they were up by two goals, Esposito was stopped by Tretiak in close.

The Canadians missed on a couple more chances, and Esposito had another opportunity late in the period when it was tied.

"It started off well and maybe that was a problem," said Ellis. "Maybe because of our quick start we got a little complacent and couldn't get the momentum back. But they certainly proved to the world that they could play the game. I recall, we came off after a shift and we're up 2–0 at the time, we're sitting beside each other and we're huffing and puffing. Even though we're up 2–0, we knew we maybe didn't prepare properly the way they had and we had better get our act together."

"They had Montreal Surprise written on their sticks," said Awrey. It was a Finnish brand of hockey stick. "It was like they knew. They were a surprise to us. They were ready, we weren't."

Ellis, who was assigned to check Kharlamov, was almost lost for the series when he was injured during the first period.

"The puck was between me and a Soviet player," said Ellis. "I was going for it and I got tripped from behind and I fell forward and the back of my neck hit the player's thigh. When I first got hit, I thought I had broken my neck. That's all I can remember. I think I was out very briefly. I was able to get off the ice and get through that game, but I really hurt my neck badly, I really wrenched it.

"Once the adrenaline was gone, I woke up the next day and I could hardly move my neck. I thought I was done for the series. I told the trainers. That's when Harry approached our line and basically said we need you guys to shut down Kharlamov. And he looked at me and said, 'Ron, can you skate?' I said 'Yeah, I can skate.' So we took that role on. Being the right winger, I played against Kharlamov. What an exceptional player. That was a very important role for us and I took it seriously. We kept the injury quiet, but I'm still suffering from it today."

The importance of neutralizing Kharlamov was hammered home in the second period when the slick winger scored two minutes in and again midway through to give the Soviets a 4–2 lead heading into the third period. It was obvious the Soviets had adjusted to the smaller ice surface and the nerves were completely gone.

"Between periods you could hear a pin drop," said Team Canada trainer Joe Sgro. "Everyone was in shock."

"We ran into a team that was in mid-season form," said Seiling. "And it showed pretty quick. By the end of the second period, I hadn't missed a shift. I'd played every other shift on defence and I felt like I was skating on my knees. We only dressed five defence and that took a toll. It didn't help that we were hitting everything that moved on the other side, and you tire yourself even faster. What energy you had quickly disappeared."

"By the end of the second period, we were looking around at each other in disbelief because we knew they were just starting to wind up," said Berenson. "We were whipped. I mean physically whipped. The spirit was there, but the legs, heart, and lungs weren't there."

Despite the shock, despite the fatigue, Team Canada was a determined team to start the third period, but Tretiak proved the scouting reports wrong, making several great saves, again on Esposito and Frank Mahovlich. But the Canadians persisted, and at 8:22 Clarke redirected in an Ellis shot to make it 4–3. Clarke, as feisty a player as you will find, had set a tone of sorts in the second period when he upended Soviet centre Alexander Maltsev with a slew foot and whacked him over the head with his stick. Fortunately, all the Soviets wore helmets. Only a handful of Canadians did. But as skilled as these two teams were, they both played with a vicious edge.

"It was a war," said Esposito.

Despite pulling to within a goal and having several near misses, or several great Tretiak saves, five minutes after Clarke's goal Mikhailov made it 5–3, and fifty-seven seconds later, as the Canadians began to slow, Zimin scored again. Yakushev made it 7–3 in the final two minutes and Dryden was hearing Bronx cheers.

Game over. Series on. No handshake.

The dejected and shocked Canadians, claiming they were not aware of the international protocol, immediately left the ice. The Forum remained deathly quiet. And a nation was in shock.

"After the game, the guys got out of their equipment, showered, and left the rink in a hurry," said Sgro. "Everything was dead. It was a rude awakening. That night was really tough on the players and the coaches. It was a slap in the face."

"It's a genuine shock," said Dryden. "It's not shock as in mouth open and eyes wide shock, it's the kind of stunned shock of you don't quite know what you feel and what has happened. It was more that than anything."

Turns out the pundits were right, after all. The series opener was an exercise in flexing muscle, an exhibition of great speed and skill, the proverbial cakewalk. It just wasn't the one almost everyone had imagined. Instead, it was the one every Canadian feared, the worst nightmare they could imagine. This one game shocked the hockey world, and no matter what happened the rest of the series, the Soviets had proved they could play and they could win. And in some ways, it wasn't the score that shocked the most, but how easily it came to be.

"I remember thinking afterwards, 'I am glad I am not the coach because the game plan didn't work and we're going to have to make changes,'" said Henderson. "And what do you do? It was a sickening feeling. Oh my God, we were going to have such a good time, we were going to enjoy each other, win the games. It just changed overnight."

"It created shock across the country," said Ellis. "It was just not the way it was supposed to be."

Next stop: Toronto.

CHAPTER 5

Shock and Awe

Even on the best of nights, even after a great game, Ken Dryden never slept well. Imagine the sleepless night he experienced after the Soviets had administered a 7–3 beating on Team Canada in the series opener, in his home rink.

"I don't sleep after games," said Dryden. "I'm always someone awake three in the morning, four in the morning . . . When you wake up, you hope that it didn't happen. Until you go out into the outer world, there's nothing around you to tell you that it did happen. You know it did, but you hope it didn't. And it's only when you get to the arena that you know for sure that it happened and then you have to deal with it."

And dealing with it means coming to the realization and the admission that this is going to be a tough series, that your worst fears, which you never really admitted to, have come true—the Soviets are for real.

"At a certain point that certainly kicked in," said Dryden. He spoke from experience, as the last time he'd played the Soviets, a few years earlier, with the Canadian national team, he'd been beaten, 9–3. "And when it happened, each player starts to feel it and they might feel it at a slightly different time. They might feel it after a shift that they're out and up against these guys and thinking, 'Boy this is not quite what I expected.' Maybe it happened when the Soviets scored their first goal. For each player it would come at a certain moment, and that's a tough moment to feel."

In some ways, that moment left most of Team Canada feeling numb the next day when they gathered in Toronto for a closed practice, to try and regroup physically and mentally in preparation for the second game, which felt like a must-win game, one in which they had to prove themselves. An element of doubt, however strong, had intruded upon the Canadians, while the Soviets were very much believing.

"Going into that first game, I thought it would be much more than just an exhibition," said coach Harry Sinden. "I knew them from before. We watched them work out the day before the series started in Montreal, and they staged a strange workout that seemed to be for our behalf. We couldn't really tell much about them, except that their individual skills were so high. In that first game, they beat us in every facet of the game, it wasn't close. But it took that game, to get the hell beat out of us—that went an awful long way towards getting our guys mentally ready for a tough tournament."

That game said more to the players than the coaches ever did, or could.

"We had a charter back to Toronto after the game," said Sinden. "There were a few seats up front where Fergie and I sat. We talked about a few things, then I said I was going to go back and talk to the players. They were as much in shock as everyone else was. I told them we were going to be on the ice at eleven the next morning at Maple Leaf Gardens. If we were going to do this properly, we had to do it together, we had to take that loss as a group and not pin it on anybody—that type of a talk."

When the game was over in Montreal, while they were sitting in the coach's office next to the dressing room trying to understand what had just happened, and maybe get a grasp on what lay ahead, Sinden and Ferguson had a couple visitors stop by. Two legendary NHL general managers, Tommy Ivan of the Chicago Blackhawks and Sam Pollock of the Montreal Canadiens, offered some encouragement and a message: "There are still seven games to go." It was a simple message, yet profound.

They may not be the seven games you had once envisioned, but there was still time, don't quit on yourselves. That was the message. There was much work to be done and in a big hurry, and it wouldn't be easy. As you might expect, some emotions were raw. Brian Conacher, the former Maple Leaf and Canadian national team member—and one who had warned that the Soviets were going to be good—had said on the television broadcast essentially that the Canadian team had to come together, that it needed a leader and a different approach. Ferguson, intense on and off the ice, saw Conacher at the rink and asked him if he was a "Commie lover." Sports columnist Trent Frayne, who had praised the Soviets for their puck handling and skating skills, had a similar experience with Team Canada organizer Alan Eagleson. Fair comment was tough to swallow.

The country's pride was wounded. The author Morley Callaghan once wrote that hockey was "our own national drama." And now it really was. The shock of it all left everyone confused. The media that had forecast a shellacking the other way jumped on the team as well, most seemingly forgetting their own previous projections. A headline in the *Globe and Mail* said: "Canada Mourns Hockey Myth." A few of the French-language papers proclaimed: "*Une Leçon*" ("A Lesson") and "*Le Canada Écrasé*" ("Canada Crushed").

"We really didn't know how big an event it was," said winger Wayne Cashman, who did not play in the opener. "But after that first game, it brought to our attention what was going on here. It was no longer true we were playing a bunch of amateurs. We were playing a well-fit, well-organized, well-coached hockey team."

"We were tricked," said winger Vic Hadfield, "but that was the Russian way."

As much as the loss had gotten the players' attention, the coaches still had to make sure they tended to a wide range of emotions, from their own shock at the loss to the anger and disbelief of a country. They also had to ensure they weren't leaning on any excuses because so many of them were feeling duped—either let down by their scouts, or set up by the Soviets, or both—and maybe just a little worried. Sinden had to make sure that whatever doubt might have crept in didn't become overwhelming and debilitating. And while they thought of themselves as Team NHL, that mentality would soon have to change to Team Canada, and with it would come an even greater pressure.

"I knew how good they [the Soviets] were from watching them play against the Czechs and the Swedes and from playing against them on the Canadian national team," said Dryden. "I knew they were really good in that context. But I didn't know how good they would be against the best. None of those players on the Czechoslovakian team, or the Swedish team, with the exception of Ulf Sterner, had played in the NHL, and when you didn't play in the NHL, the assumption was you didn't belong in the NHL. As good as any of those players were, they weren't good enough.

"And on the national team, even the Father Bauer teams, in the end only a couple of players would have played in the NHL, and most didn't have prominent careers in the NHL. All of a sudden, you've got Team Canada, where it's all of the best of the NHL, there they are. I knew enough to be cautious, but I didn't know enough to say to anyone else, or even quite to myself, 'Wait a minute here, these guys are really good, we don't have a clue how good they are, and we're falling into a trap of our own making.' No, I didn't feel strongly enough that they were that good in the context of Team Canada."

"At the end of the game you're disappointed, you're frustrated, and you know that Canada has been let down dramatically, all those things," said defenceman Rod Seiling. "And you know you're helpless. It's almost like you've been set up. A feeling of what have we gotten ourselves into?"

Two new things for Team Canada, that by and large were not felt heading into the series, were a genuine fear of losing and a profound respect for their opponent. And when you are supposed to win, losing is that much tougher to swallow. Players will often say that until you have that fear and respect, it's difficult to raise your game to the level required to overcome your opponent.

"You need the opposition to get the best out of yourself; you need to be challenged, and they sure as hell did that for us," said winger Paul Henderson.

"When we started, we were not prepared, nobody was in shape, nobody was taking them seriously," said winger Yvan Cournoyer. "We didn't respect them at all. We had scouting information that they had a bad goalie, they had bad skates and bad equipment, all of that. But they were winning Olympics and World Championships. We should have been more careful. The first game, we didn't know anything about their style, how they liked to control the puck, go around the net, the interference, we didn't expect any of it. They had a different system than us. I don't know if we had the best defencemen in the league, our defence was not that quick, not that fast, but the Soviets were a pretty speedy team. We had a problem.

"I remember in 1967, when Toronto beat the Montreal Canadiens in the Stanley Cup final, we didn't respect them. We thought we were going to win easy. But it taught us no matter if you have a good team, or a better team, if you don't respect the other team you have a chance to lose. After that we were scared to lose, and maybe that helped us to win more Stanley Cups. But's that exactly what happened in the series: we didn't respect the Soviets at first, we didn't know what happened. Luckily, we had seven more games to try to figure them out."

Beyond all the emotional challenges, on the ice Team Canada still had to deal with conditioning issues, and that would simply take time. They also had to be concerned that the Soviets were every bit their match skill-wise, and could handle and move the puck as well as, if not better than, the Canadians at this stage. It was a mighty challenge ahead. And the Canadians also had to deal with the mounting criticism, the likes of NHL president Clarence Campbell publicly questioning Sinden's roster selections for the first game. Some of the media coverage was harsh. Even loudmouth Maple Leafs co-owner Harold Ballard weighed in, calling the first game a national disaster. In typical carny fashion, Ballard also said he would pay $1 million for the rights to the flashy Russian winger Valeri Kharlamov. Not too many years later, Ballard wouldn't let Soviets into his building.

As Dryden noted in his book *Face-off at the Summit*, Bunny Ahearne, the president of the International Ice Hockey Federation, was also quoted as saying: "I told you so. The moral of the story is that you don't have to be a Canadian to be a top-class hockey player. I don't think the Canadians will wake up. They're too small-minded. Now they'll start to think up alibis." TASS, the official Soviet news agency, wrote that the "myth of the Canadian pros' invincibility" had been shattered.

Beyond simple pride, there was no shortage of "bulletin-board" motivation for the Canadians. But where Sinden and Ferguson really had to go to work was on the ice. The respect and fear, pride and emotion would all come into play. Hate, too. But they had to figure out how to neutralize the Soviets, to deal with their deft passing and speed.

"A lot of what I'm saying now is probably in retrospect," Sinden said, "because I think we felt it would be very important to make sure we had a really strong offence and we didn't spend enough time considering how difficult it would be stopping them.

"When we got back to Toronto, Fergie and I had a meeting and we wanted to change the style of play a little bit, to compensate for the Soviet team. We thought we could do it at practice the next morning, and I think it had some effect on the following night [game 2 in Toronto]. But what probably had a bigger effect was the respect our team had gained for them in that opening game. They took the loss and said we're just going to have to be better, and they were."

At the beginning of a very subdued practice, Sinden addressed the team for about ten minutes at centre ice, trying to lift their spirits. It was certainly a much different mood than when they were last on the Gardens ice, just prior to the tournament, feeling pretty good about themselves. Now Sinden had to erase the doubts and introduce changes to the game plan, which were designed to put more pressure on the Soviets with a stronger forecheck, to try to slow them down and turn the game toward a more traditional Canadian style—meaning much more physical. The appropriate roster moves would be made.

As for the Soviets, there were rumblings a few bottles of vodka might have found their way into the dressing room post-game, certainly back at the Queen Elizabeth Hotel.

"After the game, of course, there was euphoria," said winger Alexander Yakushev. "No one expected that we would win by such a score. It was all fantastic, we were in a great mood. It was so great that, psychologically, we were in seventh heaven."

"After the first game the fans cheered us and booed Team Canada," said winger Boris Mikhailov. "There was this excitement in the dressing room—that we can not just play with these guys, we can beat them!"

While the game finished at roughly 6:30 a.m. in Moscow, many Soviet fans celebrated the win in a big way. For them, it was as big as any win that could follow. They had made their statement.

"It wasn't just another series anymore," said Frank Mahovlich, "it was *the* series."

"I remember thinking when that first game was over, well, it's game on," said defenceman Brad Park. "Now it's re-establish, make some changes. We chartered back to Toronto that night, I got to the hotel, and I called my wife, Gerry, at about two o'clock in the morning, and she said, 'You better get here quick.' We lived in the east end of the city, so I jumped in my car and drove out to the hospital, Scarborough General, and my first child, James, was born. [Forty years later James was his dad's guest when Team Canada was invited back to Moscow for a reunion.] It was a whirlwind twenty-four hours for sure. It sure took my mind off the devastation of the game, which was probably good. And I didn't have to go to practice the next day, I'd been up all night."

No doubt many of the Canadian players had spent a restless, fitful night after game 1, not just Dryden.

METRO WEATHER
Cloudy, chance of shower Wednesday. Low near 50, high 65-70. Pollution index 3 at 11 a.m. Details page 2.

The Toronto Star

four star edition ★★★★

ESTABLISHED 1892   July paid circulation Mon. to Fri. 493,073, Sat. 665,107   Tuesday, September 5, 1972—72 pages   Mon-Fri. 10¢; Sat. 25¢; Home delivery 75¢

Terror in Olympic Village: Games suspended for 24 hours

MUNICH (Reuter-AP-UPI) — The 20th Olympic Games, thrown into chaos by an Arab guerrilla attack on the Israeli team quarters, were suspended today for at least 24 hours.

The suspension was announced by Avery Brundage, retiring president of the International Olympic Committee (IOC), and Willi Daume, president of the West German Olympic Organizing Committee.

It came just hours after Israeli Premier Golda Meir asked for the Games to be called off until nine Israeli competitors being held hostage by Arabs are freed.

Five Arab terrorists armed with submachine-guns and explosives stormed the Israeli quarters in the Olympic Village early this morning, and shot and killed at least one Israeli.

They then seized nine members of the Israeli team as hostages and threatened to kill them if 200 Arab terrorists held in Israel were not released.

Hans Klein, press chief of the Olympic Organizing Committee, said he wasn't sure whether or not the Games would resume tomorrow.

"For right now they are off, for today and this evening; maybe in the future we will have to change this," Klein said.

Never before in their history have the Games been suspended once they have started.

The Olympic peace has been broken," Klein said, reading the Brundage-Daume statement, "by murderous acts and violence. As a token of our involvement, all events of the afternoon will be cancelled."

The statement ended last night and the track and field athletes had a day off before the last four days of competition.

Mrs. Meir, speaking slowly and softly on a nation-wide radio broadcast, said: "We have instructed the chairman of the Israeli

The trouble came on a day when the Olympic sports program was confined mostly to minor sports.

There were basketball semi-finals, boxing quarter-finals, the grand prix de dressage stage in the equestrian team event, fencing, soccer semi-final round, handball, volleyball, weight-lifting, wrestling and yachting.

The swimming ended last night and the track and field athletes had a day off before the last four days of competition.

Olympic Committee and the Israeli ambassador (in Germany) to demand suspension of the Olympic Games and not to go through with them as long as the Israelis are not released."

Mrs. Meir did not say whether Israel was willing to go along with the guerrillas' demands and free imprisoned Arabs in exchange for the lives of the Israeli athletes.

Israeli policy has been to never give in to such terror.

The 74-year-old grandmother politician said she was confident that the German and Olympic authorities were doing everything they could to free the Israeli athletes, coaches and Olympic officials.

"It is inconceivable that the Olympic events should carry on uninterrupted as if nothing has happened while our citizens are under threats of murder inside the Olympic Village," she said.

Mrs. Meir said she had received a message from Chancellor Willy Brandt of West Germany, "expressing shock at what has happened and promising to do anything possible to prevent further violence."

She continued: "This crime is a most vile violation of the international order in which the spirit of sport had appeared to have

overcome all international difficulties and differences and in which the Olympiad had become a symbol of friendship and unification of nations and races.

"That is why this crime is as conspicuous by its brutality."

Brundage, who will be succeeded by Ireland's Lord Killanin after the Munich Games, warned last month, that "political blackmail" can kill the Olympics.

He said he was "heart-sick" at the decision Aug. 22 by the IOC to expel white-ruled Rhodesia and avoid a mass black African boycott of the Games.

GOLDA MEIR
A 'vile' crime

OVER THE TOP TO PUT THE GAME AWAY — Peter Mahovlich, No. 20, shepherds puck around the form of Soviet goaltender Vladislav Tretiak to score Team Canada's third goal last night and put the game beyond the reach of a Soviet comeback. The puck can be seen deep inside net. Canada won game 4-1 and evened the eight-game series at 1-1. Next game is tomorrow in Winnipeg.

An eye-popper of a hockey game showed just how good it can be

By MILT DUNNELL
Star sports columnist

Israeli trainer killed by Arab guerrillas 9 athletes held hostage

MUNICH (AP-UPI)—Five Arab terrorists armed with submachine-guns and explosives stormed the Israeli quarters in the Olympic Village today, killed at least one member of the Israeli team and held nine more hostage in their living quarters.

The terrorists, members of the Black September Movement, demanded the release of 200 Palestinian guerrillas held in Israel and an airplane to make their getaway.

WILLY BRANDT
Appeals to Arabs

MOSHE WEINBERG
Israeli trainer killed

Star man at scene: A bizarre setting made by a madman

By TRENT FRAYNE
Star staff writer

Liberal ex-minister Claude Wagner joins Quebec Conservatives

By PETER DESBARATS
Star Ottawa editor

16 men, 4 women are named to Ontario Press Council

From our Ottawa bureau

OTTAWA — Two Toronto residents, J. H. Smith, retired chairman of Canadian General Electric Co. Ltd., and Dr. Lita-Rose Betcherman, former director of the Ontario Labor Department's women's division, were among members of the public named today to the Ontario Press Council.

JOHN HERBERT SMITH
Retired industrialist

LITA-ROSE BETCHERMAN
Women's rights advocate

121 killed across Canada

A Toronto woman died who died 130 feet beneath Georgian Bay yesterday while exploring the wreck of a 19th-century vessel was among at least 121 persons who died accidentally across Canada during the three-day Labor Day weekend.

● Details, page 41.

CHAPTER 6

Game 2—A Must-Win Scenario

It was never going to be just another hockey series and now it really wasn't. After one game the expectations and disappointment of a nation weighed heavily on Team Canada, not to mention their own pride and reputation. And put simply, the second game of the series was one they absolutely had to win. It felt like the series hinged on it.

Team Canada had been humbled and embarrassed 7–3 by the Soviet Union in the series opener. After Toronto were stops in Winnipeg and Vancouver before staring down four games in Moscow. Falling behind by a couple games might not be mathematically insurmountable, but it wouldn't be easy to overcome, and in this case especially so without the cloak of invincibility and superiority they'd had heading into the series.

"In retrospect, it was a must win," said coach Harry Sinden. "We didn't just lose a squeaker in Montreal, we got clobbered, and we had to make up not only for the loss, but for the kind of embarrassment we caused the country at that point. That was prevalent in the players' minds."

But it's amazing how pride, character, and fear of losing can be such powerful motivators. As a sign a fan held up in historic Maple Leaf Gardens on Monday, September 4, read: "It's our game and we're going to prove it." That was the mission statement for Team Canada.

"After game one, it was a sickening feeling," said winger Paul Henderson. "In defence of everybody, Harry [Sinden], too, you just can't put a team together, a team has to come together. There are different roles to play."

Towards that end, for the second game, Sinden overhauled his roster, making eight lineup changes, almost half the lineup—in part because he had made that promise to all the players that they would play at least one game, but mostly because the lineup and the strategy obviously hadn't worked in the opener. It wasn't like they just had some bad luck and lost; they were thoroughly beaten. The plan was to use a smarter and more punishing forecheck and to have more attention to detail defensively, with a stronger backcheck. The Canadians had played a more wide-open game in the opener, hellbent for offence. It was time to tighten things up. And get physical, a game the Soviets weren't used to playing.

"We were going to try to physically intimidate them as we went along," said defenceman Brad Park. "That worked. The hockey was very skilled, but also very chippy. There were times when we were very belligerent and intentionally so. As I told the Russians at a reunion a few years ago, when we were having breakfast with [Russian president Vladimir] Putin, I said before game one we didn't know your names. After game one we knew your last names. After game two we knew your first names, and by the time we got to game four we knew where you lived. That's how intense our learning experience was."

The first lineup change was in goal with Ken Dryden, who had allowed all seven goals in game 1, replaced by Chicago's Tony Esposito, with Boston's Eddie Johnston serving as the backup. Sinden, who had dressed just five defencemen the first game and watched his defence wilt, this time dressed six. Out were Don Awrey and Rod Seiling; in were the Montreal Canadiens' Serge Savard and the Blackhawks pairing of Pat Stapleton and Bill White.

"At the morning skate, getting ready, I realized we were going with six defencemen," said Park, who remained in the lineup as did Gary Bergman and young Guy Lapointe. "Six defencemen was very good news. And with the forwards we added, we were going to be a much more physical team."

Up front, Sinden took out the Rangers' high-scoring GAG (Goal-A-Game) Line of Jean Ratelle, Rod Gilbert, and Vic Hadfield, who he thought had some speed issues in the opener, and the seeds of roster discontent started to grow. Sitting out wasn't a popular option for any player, regardless of what was at stake. Players love to play and they all have egos. In the case of Hadfield, who was from nearby Oakville, he had family hoping to watch him play. It was the start of a bad relationship with Sinden. Red Berenson and Mickey Redmond were also taken out, replaced by Chicago's Stan Mikita, Boston's Wayne Cashman, and Minnesota's J. P. Parise and Bill Goldsworthy.

"Part of it was to be more aggressive, and we changed the lineup a little bit to do that," said Sinden. "We felt then, like I still do today, that when people examine the skill set of a player—can he shoot, can he skate, can he pass—they always leave out, can he check? To me that is a skill set that is strong in all good players. That's probably something we didn't do, or think about, in Montreal, and we started to feel that we had to do that part of the game a lot better. To do that we put in a couple of players who were noted for that—Parise and Cash. We played Ronny Ellis and Bobby Clarke together, who are so great at that. So our checking game really improved. If I was scouting today, it would be the number one skill set I would look for. The players seemed to understand that after getting the hell beat out of them!"

Another forward who could check and do all the other things, Peter Mahovlich, didn't think he would stay in the lineup for game 2. But the coaches liked his penalty-killing skill. They knew the more aggressive style for game 2 would mean the Canadians would likely be taking penalties, and assistant coach John Ferguson had been insistent on Mahovlich being named to the thirty-five-man training camp roster for that reason. It turned out to be a great call on both fronts. The Soviets, meanwhile, only made two changes.

If nothing else, the Canadians were far better prepared for this game, far more intense. Game 1 scared them straight and had gotten their attention—heck, it got the attention of a country—and they knew just how important game 2 was. Winger Yvan Cournoyer was convinced then and now: lose that game and lose the series.

"It certainly felt that way," said Dryden. "I think we went into that second game with that feeling of desperation. But I never quite imagined that anything but a final game is the final game, so this game doesn't determine everything. You just would have to find a different answer in Winnipeg if Toronto hadn't turned out the way it did. There were a lot of moments that it would have been easy to say, "If we don't win tonight [in Toronto], we're going to be behind in the series and we're not even in Moscow yet."

Most nights, Maple Leaf Gardens could be a quiet, reserved building. The fans were certainly knowledgeable, but typically not boisterous. There might be a measure of tension in the air, or even a stifling pressure, an excitement, but now the question was no longer how good were the Soviets, but how good could the Canadians quickly become?

The sellout crowd of 16,485 gave Team Canada a rousing ovation when they first stepped on the ice, but the players admitted to feeling tense. Unlike the opener, when the mood had been much lighter leading up to the game (and for at least the first six minutes or so), on this night it was all business. During the pre-game introductions, the Canadians stood grim-faced, heads down. While pride was driving the players, so, too, was another emotion.

"For myself, it was anger," said Bobby Clarke. "I was angry with my own performance. I was angry our team was inept. I always used anger as a motivator. We had to reach a lot deeper into ourselves to win that game. The Russians were better at that point. They were better conditioned and better at everything. We had to reach down and find what we could. We got some spectacular plays. The one by [Peter] Mahovlich, for the short-handed goal, was one of those plays. It gave us a tremendous lift."

In addition to making personnel changes, Sinden also shook up the forward lines, putting Esposito with Cashman, his Bruins line mate, and Parise. For Esposito, it was like being back with his big line in Boston, which included Cashman and Ken Hodge. Sinden admitted that Esposito worked better with two forecheckers on his wings and they shouldn't have gotten away from that. Mikita, meantime, centred Frank Mahovlich and Yvan Cournoyer. The Clarke-Henderson-Ellis line remained intact, assigned to check the Kharlamov line.

The first period, while intense and physical, just as the Canadians had hoped and planned, was also quite tedious and slow. There were constant delays on faceoffs, both teams apparently figuring they had the last change, neither giving way—and the officials seemingly oblivious to the gamesmanship. Both goalies, Vladislav Tretiak and Tony Esposito, were very sharp to keep the game without a goal after one period.

"Tony stole the game for us," said brother Phil. "He did."

Indeed, both Esposito brothers had a profound influence on the outcome. It was Cashman who helped get the puck to Phil, who then beat Tretiak to open the scoring at 7:14 of the second period on a delayed penalty, a lead that would hold up until the final period. Esposito later claimed he had taken a stick to the head after he scored. He had already declared it was "series on after game one." Now, in his mind, it was war.

Brian Conacher, the colour commentator on television, had said during game 1 the Canadians needed someone to pull them together, and it quickly became evident that Phil Esposito had drifted from being disinterested in the beginning to the uncontested team leader.

The Soviets' frustrations were starting to boil over the deeper they got into the game, figuring the officials—Americans Steve Dowling and Frank Larsen (there were only two officials under international rules)—were letting the physical Canadians get away with too much rough stuff. In the final seconds of the second period, Soviet defenceman Gennady Tsygankov received a slashing penalty, and Kharlamov, while arguing with the official, bumped into him and was assessed a ten-minute misconduct.

"The way the officiating came about for the series was negotiated," said Dowling, who was from Winchester, Massachusetts. "There were no Canadian officials and no Russians as officials. It would be Americans in Canada; Europeans would referee the games in Russia. The series was run under international rules, not NHL rules, which meant the officiating was limited to two officials on the ice and they were both called referees. They handled all of the duties of the referee and the linesmen. So you're a referee and a linesman, you're picking up the puck, you're dropping the puck, you're calling offsides, icings, you're calling penalties, you're conducting the game.

"It was fairly unique the way they selected those to work the games in Canada. There were four of us, two from the east coast and two from Minnesota. Of those four, I'm the only one living, which only goes to show you what refereeing can do you to your longevity. The other three guys [Larsen, Gordon Lee, and Len Gagnon] had international experience, the Olympics. I was twenty-six years old and they were in their forties. At the time, Ian "Scotty" Morrison was the referee and chief of the NHL, and sitting on his desk was a contract I was going to sign during the '72 series. That would have made me the first American referee in the NHL since Bill Chadwick started in 1949. I was known to the people who selected the officials. I was working some games in the American Hockey League. I was refereeing and officiating in the professional style versus the style of the other seven referees in the series, who only had international experience. They refereed the way it's done in an Olympics, which is fairly, properly done, but without a lot of violence and physicality, and that aspect of it came into play.

"The first game in Montreal, the Canadians came in and they were fully anticipating they were going to win all eight games, this was just going to be an exercise. I was at that game, I was a goal judge. At the end of the game in the Montreal Forum, five minutes after the game was over, nobody had moved. The entire stadium was frozen because they had lost. I'm thinking, watching the finesse in the first game, that the Canadians were not going to go for this, so game two was going to be a game of physicality. Scotty Morrison came in before game two and said, here's the lineup changes, look who's in the lineup now—look at Parise, Cashman, Goldsworthy—they weren't there in Montreal, so you've got your work cut out for you.

"Well, game two progressed in that manner, it was a lot more physical. But there weren't a lot of penalties because the game was called in a manner that was not the Olympic manner, it was the North American manner, which upset the Russians because a lot of physicality was going on and they were used to penalties. That brought in some frustration, and that played itself out in the game."

Years later, Soviet forward Boris Mikhailov, who was a nasty player himself, admitted the Soviets weren't familiar with the Canadians' physical style of play, adding that it was obvious in game 2 that they had come to respect the Soviets.

"The main thing our coaches told us was that the Canadians were playing rough and that we had to be patient," said Tretiak. "So we were patient. The NHL rules are still different from international rules. That's why we couldn't find a common approach. It was very difficult to officiate these games."

As the physicality evolved over the game, the Canadians were short-handed five times, the Soviets three. Kharlamov had the misconduct. So incensed were the Soviets with how the game was being officiated that after the second period, in which both teams had three minor penalties, the head of the Soviet delegation, Andrei Starovoitov, barged into the officials' room, yelling and complaining and knocking over chairs. It was Cashman who seemed to be the target of most of their wrath.

"I remember Fergie coming up to me before the game," said Cashman. "He said, 'We realize where we are at with these guys in terms of conditioning. Maybe we can slow them down a little . . .' I knew what he meant by that. He wanted me to be physical."

When the series shifted to Winnipeg for game 3, in which Lee and Gagnon were officiating, the Soviets asked Sinden to not let Dowling and Larsen work the fourth game in Vancouver. The two teams had previously agreed to the officiating rotation. But Sinden hadn't been told about the antics in the officials' room in Toronto, and he agreed to the change. This proved to be a portent, as officiating would become an even bigger issue and controversy when the series shifted to Moscow, and Sinden would come to regret his understanding nature.

The Soviets opened the third period shorthanded and angry. To make matters worse for them, on the power play, Park, with a beautiful pass, sent Cournoyer in on a breakaway and he scored to make it 2–0 at 1:19.

Penalties continued to be a discussion point. Clarke was called for slashing Mikhailov, and on the ensuing power play Yakushev flipped a puck over Tony Esposito to cut the lead to one at 5:53.

The young forward Yevgeni Zimin assisted on the goal. He played well in both games, but was not seen in the series after that second game. There was some speculation he had suffered a shoulder injury, while others believed he was too creative and unstructured a player and the coaches were unhappy with his game. But there were also rumors that he was hoping to defect, which never did happen.

After that goal, the tension was already building when, twenty-one seconds later, Stapleton was called for hooking. This wasn't the first two-goal lead of the series for the Canadians, and it felt like they might be on the verge of blowing another.

Peter Mahovlich deserved to be on Team Canada. He had played in the 1971 NHL all-star game in Boston, the East team coached by Sinden. In fact, fifteen members of Team Canada played in that game. But he still believes it was Ferguson who got him on the roster. Regardless, he was an excellent penalty killer, and penalties would be a big factor in the series. Mahovlich doesn't have any memorabilia from the games, but he does have several incredible memories, including one in the third period of game 2.

"They made it 2–1, then we got another penalty called on us," he said. "Harry came over to Phil and me and told us that we would start the penalty kill. Phil said to me, 'Instead of just throwing the puck down the ice, let's try to hold it, get into the neutral zone and throw it around a little bit,' because they were so good at keeping the puck. Of course, Phil does a great job on the draw. He wins the faceoff. He was coming out of our own zone. I was coming off the left side, and instead of shooting the puck down the ice, he bounced the puck off the boards to me.

"I looked for Phil, to move it back to him, and then I thought about sending the puck back to one of our defencemen. Well, I faked a shot into their end and then found myself one-on-one because I didn't see where their other defenceman was. I had a plan to carry the puck in deep, but their defenceman was on his tippytoes, so I decided to drive it to the net. I did and scored a goal. I said to Harry when I came off, 'Sorry about that. I meant to kill a little more time off the clock.' He looked at me and smacked me in the head, and said, 'Good job.'"

So emotional were the Canadians that they emptied the bench to celebrate.

"Oh, what a beautiful goal," said Park. "He faked a shot, their defenceman [Evgeny Paladiev] gets up on his tippytoes, which is a natural thing, Peter pulls it around him then dekes around Tretiak, while falling over him. A few years later, he tried to do the same thing on me, but I didn't completely go for it. But I know the feeling. It was two great dekes, but it felt like it was happening in slow motion."

"To this day, I think it's one of the greatest goals scored in Maple Leaf Gardens, the whole history of it, one of my all-time favourite goals I've ever seen," said Henderson. "I remember thinking, if they score on the power play, we were up the creek in a lot of ways, we're in big trouble. That goal changed the whole momentum of the game. That was the turning point. That saved the game for us."

And maybe the series. You can't have the heroic final goal of the series in game 8 without Mahovlich's goal in game 2.

The Soviets couldn't score on the remaining power play time, and at 8:59 Frank Mahovlich scored to seal an impressive victory, three goals in the third period with an overall 36–21 edge in shots. For Team Canada it was a much better team effort. The decision to dress six defencemen and put a greater emphasis on defensive play was smart. Savard was a terrific addition on the blue line. And their physical play did impact the Russians' speed and composure.

Final score: Team Canada 4, Soviet Union 1.

"As a coach, you try to guide the players and make sure they don't get off track," said Sinden. "They were so ready for that game after getting blown out. They were embarrassed, no question."

As they departed the Gardens ice, the Canadians were given a standing ovation and Phil Esposito declared on national television, "This is even bigger than winning the Stanley Cup as far as I'm concerned. This is as excited as I've ever been in my life."

What a difference a few weeks, and an embarrassing loss, meant to Esposito's mindset.

"I felt that way, too, that it was bigger than winning the Stanley Cup," said Sinden. "The pressure that was mounting, it was very political, that tournament. The pressure on us to maintain our prestige . . . it became more than a game."

For one night, at least, the players could feel excited, satisfied, and, like most of the country, relieved.

The front-page headline in the *Toronto Sun* the next morning read: "WE DID IT!" Between the letters you could feel the sigh of relief.

"I always said, if we didn't win that game, I don't think we could have come back and won the series," said Cournoyer. "After losing the first game, everybody was saying, it's almost impossible, what are we going to do? But we won that game, so now we know we can beat them. That's why it was such an important game."

On this night, it was the Soviets who left the ice frustrated.

"That game put us in our place," said Mikhailov. "We understood that we had to be ready for every game, which is what we did after that."

"It was very difficult to get up for the second game that same way [as the first game]," said Yakushev. "And, sure enough, we didn't look as good during that game in Toronto. On the other hand, Team Canada also didn't expect such a result in game one. So they really did get up for game two and looked like a totally different team."

The Canadians, meanwhile, were confident that if they could continue to pull together and improve their conditioning, they could win the series. Or even just the next game. But it was going to be tough. There was no overconfidence. It was a nice win, but it hadn't come easy, and they knew it.

Just before leaving the dressing room, Sinden offered a cautionary message to his team.

"I remember I told them to enjoy the victory, but don't gloat over it," he said. "Enjoy tonight, savour it, but we've got a lot of games to play."

And there were different challenges ahead in Winnipeg, where they would play under the watchful eye of Bobby Hull and a fan base that hadn't forgotten or forgiven.

$17 million Massey Hall planned for Metro Centre

By SID ADILMAN
Star staff writer

Plans were to be announced today to demolish Toronto's 78-year-old Massey Hall and build a new one for $17 million as part of the $1 billion Metro Centre development.

The new concert hall will be ready by October, 1976, unless s o m e t h i n g goes wrong with the directors' plan to sell the old one on Shuter St. for $1 million and move to a city-donated site at Simcoe and Front Sts.

The scheduled presence of two cabinet ministers and other federal politicians at a press conference late this afternoon has prompted speculation that Ottawa will help pay for the move.

Massey Hall's directors were expected to insist that the existing building be wrecked.

This would end a move by Sam Sniderman, the Yonge St. record dealer, who wants to buy it and keep it standing for concerts that wouldn't compete with those in the new hall.

Sniderman told The Star he knew nothing of the directors' plans and would not discuss them until they were announced.

Metro Centre is a development first proposed four years ago by Canadian National and Canadian Pacific railways to redevelop 200 acres of railyards north of the Gardiner Expressway between Yonge and Bathurst Sts. It would provide office space for 50,000 people, housing for 20,000 and would encompass new head office and production quarters and studios for the Canadian Broadcasting Corporation's English network.

Scheduled to be at a press conference called for after today's board of directors meeting, are Edward Pickering, co-chairman of the Massey Hall Committee, W a l t e r Homburger, managing director of the Toronto Symphony which would be the building's prime tenant—out at no rent—External Affairs Minister Mitchell Sharp, and Donald Macdonald, federal minister of energy, mines and resources.

The presence of Sharp, Macdonald and other Toronto area MPs being invited by Pickering suggests that federal money will be allocated to help build the hall. Massey Hall has received n o g o v e r n m e n t grants or other financial support in the past.

The new Massey Hall would seat 2,800, slightly

See NEW, page 3

METRO WEATHER
Friday showers and cooler. Low near 60, high in the low 70s. Pollution index 4 at 11 a.m. Details page 2.

The Toronto Star

four star ★★★★ edition

ESTABLISHED 1892 | August paid circulation Mon. to Fri. 494,287, Sat. 683,249 | Thursday, September 7, 1972—88 pages | Monday-Friday 10c; Saturday 25c; Home delivery 75c

Great Soviet goalie robs Team Canada of win in game 3

By MILT DUNNELL
Star sports columnist

WINNIPEG — With only 13 seconds remaining in a game that had the hockey fans of two continents reaching for the tranquilizers, Alexander Nikolavich Maltsev whipped a shot from a soggy spot 20 feet to the left of the Team Canada net.

Tony Esposito, the shutout king of big league hockey in North America, reacted slowly. His view was screened by the mass of sinew and bone that was churning and wrestling, bobbing and weaving, almost to the edge of his goal crease.

At the final flicker of an eyelash, Tony spotted the puck and made the save. His brother, Big Phil, most prolific shooter in a league that once was considered to tower higher than Mount Everest over any other circuit in the world, was checking Maltsev.

They sensed knockout punch

Phil had frozen in his stance, toe to toe with the Soviet star, as the shot was delivered. Maltsev also had stopped dead in his skate tracks. Both players sensed this could be the knockout punch.

When Tony smothered the puck, the mask of horror on Phil's face changed to a wide grin. He looked Maltsev in the eye and gave him a friendly pat on the shoulder.

The Russian shook his head and smiled. It was an exchange of thoughts without words. Maltsev was saying to Phil: "Comrade, you could have won but you almost lost."

Phil was saying to Maltsev: "Friend, we should have won but we're damned happy to settle for a draw. Twice, you were two goals down. Don't you know when you're licked?"

Goalie picks off 'winner'

Vladislav Tretiak, the skinny Soviet goalie, continues to be the single most persistent factor in what now looms as a Canadian loss of the series.

He picked off what would have been the winning goal by Paul Henderson in the third period.

Henderson didn't even shoot when he could see the white of Tretiak's eyes. He waited until he could see the fillings in his teeth. Tretiak made a stab and grabbed the puck, which was perfectly fired.

When Soviet coach Vsevolod Bobrov was asked what Tretiak will do with all the rings he is receiving for being picked as outstanding Soviet player, Bobrov replied:

See GREAT GOALIE, page 2

- Soviets and Team Canada lift hockey to new heights of excellence, page 16.
- New line's young legs earn Russians a tie, page 17.
- Soviet hockey players' personalities are warming up, Toronto trainer discovers, page 17.

CP photo

GOALIE'S CATCHING STYLE.—Vladislav Tretiak in the Soviet goal catches a hard drive from Team Canada's Paul Henderson in the third period of game that ended in a 4-4 tie in Winnipeg last night. The game, third in the eight-game series, demonstrated again Tretiak's masterful ability to keep the Canadians at bay.

German rescue bid 'absolutely correct' Israeli leaders say

TEL AVIV (Reuter-AP-UPI)—The 18 grieving survivors of Israel's Olympic team flew home today just hours after the Israeli government said it fully supported the West German effort to save nine Israelis held hostage by Arab terrorists in Munich on Tuesday.

Foreign Minister Abba Eban called the German decision "absolutely correct and perfectly in order," adding: "We have made it clear that Israel does not give in to blackmailers, that to give in to them is to increase their spirit, their resources, their sense of success and to make the increase of this activity inevitable."

After a day of terror unprecedented in Olympic history, 17 persons were killed Tuesday after a shootout between West German police and the eight terrorists. Nine Israelis, five terrorists and one policeman died in the bloodbath. Two Israelis had been killed earlier in the day, when the terrorists had scaled a fence and invaded the Israeli quarters at the Olympic Village.

After an emergency cabinet meeting yesterday, Premier Golda Meir said she noted "with appreciation the decision taken by the authorities of the federal G e r m a n government to take action for the liberation of the Israeli hostages and to employ force to this end."

THREATENED TO KILL

The terrorists had threatened to kill one hostage every two hours unless Mrs. Meir's government freed 200 Arab commandos imprisoned in Israel.

Flags flew at half staff at Lod Airport today as the Israeli team arrived home with the bodies of 10 of their dead comrades. President Zalman Shazar and cabinet m e m b e r s were gathered for a funeral service, although the victims are to be interred at separate funerals in their home towns.

11th VICTIM TO U.S.

The body of the 11th Israeli slain in Munich, that of weightlifter David Berger, was to be flown to Cleveland, his former home

See ISRAEL, page 4

- Egypt blames West Germany for killings, page 4
- Gun drawn on Canadian pole vaulter, page 4
- Toronto man mourns slain nephew, page 4

Thousands honor slain Israelis across Germany

By ANTHONY MURRAY
Special to The Star

MUNICH — West Germany has been swept by a wave of pro-Israeli sentiment in the wake of Tuesday's slaughter of 11 Israeli athletes and team officials after Arab terrorists invaded Israel's quarters at the Olympic Village.

Relations between Bonn and the Arab world, recently improved after years of lying fallow, have been thrown back to a new low.

More than 120,000 workers at the country's six Volkswagen plants laid down their tools yesterday for several minutes of silent homage to Israel's dead Olympians.

Thousands of Germans filed in mourning through the streets of Dusseldorf, Munich and West Berlin.

In Frankfurt, schoolboys gathered near the city's Jewish monument demanding that all Arabs be thrown out of the country.

To erase Nazi image

The Olympics, seen by West Germany as a chance to erase some of the bitter memories of the 1936 Games in Berlin, staged in stark militaristic fashion by Adolf Hitler at a cost of $650 million, have been a humiliation for Chancellor Willy Brandt.

Brandt, speaking on television on Tuesday, said "The joyous Games are over. In the coming days we will have to prove ourselves anew."

Unlimited amounts of money were offered in ransom for the Israelis held hostage by Arab guerrillas and prominent German politicians offered to change places with the hostages to save the host country's reputation. Both offers were refused.

The Palestinian terrorists have lost any credit they may have had. And Brandt's government is bitter over the passivity of many Arab capitals during the dramatic attempts to save the Israeli team members.

Sought Arab support

From the moment the gun-wielding terrorists, members of the Black September organization, burst into the Israeli quarters in the Olympic Village at dawn Tuesday, West Germany sought to enlist Arab governments in the rescue effort.

While German officials tried desperately on Tuesday night to bargain with the Arab gunmen for Israeli lives, Brandt made a personal telephone appeal to Egyptian Premier Aziz Sidky to help prevent bloodshed.

But Bonn government spokesman Conrad Ahlers later revealed that the Egyptian reaction "had not been very helpful."

As a result, political leaders here began to abandon the delicate balance which Bonn had struck between the Arab nations and Israel.

Does it sound familiar?

Soviet sailors in Toronto amazed at Canada's skill

While millions of Canadians continued marvelling last night at how well the Russians play hockey, 41 visiting Soviet sailors were saying exactly the same things about Team Canada.

They arrived in Toronto with the same "nobody-told-us" feeling most of us have.

Six unlucky crewmen had to steer the freighter Archangelsk into harbor while the others sat glued to the television set in their darkened lounge.

"I don't know any longer who will win the series," said one.

Last night's 4-4 tie disappointed them almost as much as Canada's win in the second game Monday. But they were confident all will go well for the Russians when the s e r i e s moves to Moscow.

One sailor predicted a four-game sweep on their home ice. Another conceded Canada one of the games.

"It's very hard to say," cautioned their first officer, Alexander Chernyshev. "There are too many variations in the game to tell who will win."

They had all expected their boys to win the first game and were shocked at losing the second.

"We were over-confident—it must be so," said one.

Sound familiar?

Several of the sailors noted that the Canadians' checking has been rougher since the first game, but they had no complaints.

Chernyshev said hockey has probably become the most popular Soviet sport, and the series has been mentioned in every newscast from home that they've heard on their short-wave radio.

He said the Czechoslovak team, which beat Russia in the hockey finals this year, could also beat the Canadians.

He commented on the rules preventing Canadian professionals from playing in the European league:

"Pros and non-pros, it's the same thing—if they play hockey it doesn't matter. The Canadians should be allowed to play."

HOT TIMES BECOMING A HABIT

George Hamberge is 78, and he's sick and tired of dashing out on the street in his pyjamas, but thinks it's time to move again.

Six years ago someone set four fires at night in the house where he lived on Huntley St. in the Jarvis-Bloor St. area.

He moved to another rooming house on Pape Ave. and three years later he was out on the street in his pyjamas again, watching the house and his possessions go up in flames.

He moved back to Huntley St. because the house had a new owner—but early today he was back on the street after smoke filled his room from a basement fire.

MacNaughton named to succeed McKeough for 'a brief period'

Premier William Davis today put a temporary patch on his ailing cabinet with the appointment of Charles MacNaughton as provincial treasurer to fill the vacancy left by the resignation of Darcy McKeough.

Davis made it clear at the swearing-in ceremony in the suite of Lieutenant-Governor W. Ross Macdonald that MacNaughton's appointment would be for only "a brief period of time."

Appointment of MacNaughton, 61, who served five years as treasurer between 1966 and 1971, is regarded as a holding action until Davis completes work on conflict-of-interest policy guidelines for the cabinet.

He promised the guidelines within two weeks when he accepted McKeough's resignation yesterday over his involvement in a Chatham subdivision while he was minister of municipal affairs in 1969.

The premier is also expected to be faced with the departure of Allan Lawrence, provincial secretary for justice, to run as a Conservative in the riding of Northumberland-Durham in the federal election Oct. 30.

Davis hinted the Law-

See MacNAUGHTON, page 3

Brandt fears attack on Jews

BONN (AP) — Chancellor Willy Brandt's government said today it has received information that Jews in West Germany may be the targets of mailed bombs this weekend, during Rosh Hashanah — the Jewish new year.

1,200 Ontario elevator repairmen go on strike

About 1,200 elevator installers and repairmen went on strike against five major elevator companies across Ontario today, and union leaders expect the strike to spread to a national walkout over the weekend.

The strike followed the breakdown last night of talks between the International Union of Elevator Constructors and the Canadian Electrical Manufacturers Association.

The union has signed interim agreements with 27 Canadian elevator servicing companies, which are continuing to operate. James Hughes, business agent for the Toronto union local, said the five struck companies—Otis Elevator, Turnbull, Montgomery, Armor and Westinghouse — a r e all American-owned operations and the main strike issue "is that we are not going to be dictated to by American companies."

E. M. Tuff, chairman of the employers' negotiating committee, said the five companies do the majority of elevator installing and repairing in Canada.

"Things can go wrong but elevators are a dependable piece of machinery and we expect to keep them operating with the use of supervisory personnel."

Tuff put the number of disputed issues at 235, and said they include wages, fringe benefits, work jurisdiction, union security and hiring procedures.

The union leader said that the management bargaining team, two of whom he said are U.S. citizens, are trying to get the elevator technicians to agree to terms of a contract signed in July between the companies and U.S. members of the union.

"They are trying to ram American conditions down our throats," he said.

These conditions included exchanging the present formula by which the union members are paid. Under the old contract, the men get the average of the first top construction trade rates, which in Toronto comes to $7.25 an hour.

Hughes said the Canadian members want adjustments in this formula, to bring it more up to date, but that the companies are insisting on an entirely new and very complicated wage formula, which has been developed in the U.S.

Tuff, however, said that during the last days of negotiating the companies made a final offer that was not on the U.S. formula but was an improvement on the Canadian formula.

He said the union is asking a "quite expensive" wage increase and that the companies "just couldn't go as far as they wanted us to go."

By the third game in Winnipeg, Soviet goaltender Vladislav Tretiak was making a huge impression and front-page headlines. (Courtesy of the *Toronto Star*)

CHAPTER 7

Game 3—To Hull with Russia

And to hell with Team Canada.

That was the undercurrent for game 3 in Winnipeg: the tale of too many players who wanted to play in the series but were denied, and for entirely different reasons.

There was Bobby Hull, the former Chicago Blackhawks superstar left winger who was on the original Team Canada invitation list but was removed because he had the temerity to sign with the Winnipeg Jets of the newly formed World Hockey Association for almost $3 million, money that was unheard of at the time. As much as this was Team Canada, a birth certificate meant nothing without a National Hockey League contract.

The outcry from hockey and Hull fans across the country, especially those in Winnipeg, was loud, even more so after Canada dropped the series opener. One enterprising fan even manufactured pins that read: To Russia with Hull. But again, this was an NHL-sanctioned production, in concert with Hockey Canada. The NHL owners and president Clarence Campbell turned a deaf ear. If you were not signed to an NHL contract by the start of training camp, you didn't play. Simple. It didn't matter how good you were. Not even the prime minister could otherwise convince Campbell, who had been president of the NHL since 1946 and at one time was a prosecution lawyer for the Canadian War Crimes Commission at the Nuremberg trials. He was a smart man, but also a stubborn man. And the chief organizer of the series and the lead man of Team Canada, Alan Eagleson, was also the executive director of the NHL Players' Association. Yes, the series was political in so many different ways.

So Hull sat in the stands at Winnipeg Arena, amongst a sellout crowd of 10,600, the huge portrait of Queen Elizabeth II that hung from the rafters at one end of the rink, and alongside the man who had signed him to the record-setting contract, Ben Haskins. Hull was one of only a few who had predicted before the series started that Team Canada would have its hands full with the Soviets—not out of bitterness, but from paying attention over the years and knowing what condition the NHL players would be in during the summer. Hull would finally get his chance to solve the Soviets himself two years later when the upstart WHA assembled a Team Canada of their own.

The fact Hull was a spectator and not a star in the series still didn't sit well with a lot, but not all, of the Team Canada players, especially with how the series was unfolding.

"We couldn't worry about Bobby by then," said Brad Park. "It was great to have the WHA when we were negotiating salaries, that's for sure. I went from making $45,000 a year to $250,000 a year. I was happy to see the WHA. Would I have loved to see Bobby Hull play? Yeah. But there were politics involved."

"I totally disagreed with us being called Team Canada," said Phil Esposito. "I made it perfectly clear in our meeting the very first day. And I think that's when the players started to rally behind me, because I asked questions: Where's the money going and why are we called Team Canada? If you don't let Bobby Hull or Gerry Cheevers or any of those other guys who are playing in the WHA play, why are we called Team Canada? They're Canadians. Why? I was told by Eagleson, listen, just keep quiet, this is the NHL Players' Association. Then we should be called Team NHL. Makes sense, doesn't it? It would have been so much easier with Bobby and Cheesy and guys like Gordie Howe and Davey Keon [who hadn't signed with the WHA]. We knew Orr couldn't play. That was a big frickin' deal."

Regardless of the name of the team, with each passing game playing for Canada mattered more and more to Esposito and his teammates. And just winning mattered more, even it wasn't going to be the cakewalk that had been predicted.

Then there were the Team Canada players who were saying to hell with Team Canada because they were disgruntled about either not playing enough, or not at all. Whether there was a rebellion, an uprising, or simply an undercurrent of discontent that turned into dissension is open to interpretation. Different players sensed what was happening in different ways. But there was definitely unrest.

By the time the two Team Canada planes touched down in Winnipeg, there were still a handful of players who had not yet dressed. And they weren't happy. As a few of them mentioned, they weren't invited to a tryout back in August; they were invited to play. True enough, but just two games in, they might have been a tad impatient. However, therein lay the catch for coach Harry Sinden. Had the series unfolded the way almost everyone had expected, with the Canadians comfortably rolling over the Soviets, then Sinden wouldn't have had a problem keeping his promise and turning over his lineup game after game, easily getting everyone ice time. But that wasn't the case, and it wasn't going to change anytime soon. Every player knew deep down that they had to shorten the roster. They just couldn't agree who should be on it.

"Team management knew we were an all-star team," said winger Ron Ellis, "but we weren't a team in the true sense of the word."

Inviting thirty-five players to training camp was a mistake; by now everyone knew that, too. But in many ways, it had been unavoidable. With no exhibition games during training camp, extra bodies were needed for intra-squad games. In hindsight, perhaps there should have been tryouts, but Sinden had to make the promise just to entice players to even attend.

"After the first game," said Phil Esposito, "I was walking to the press area with Harry, and I said to him, 'Harry, if we don't become a team, we're not going to win, and you're going to have to make some very tough decisions.' He said, 'Well, I'm going to change the lineup for Toronto.' I said, 'That's not my point. You're going to hurt a lot of people. I think you've got to pick twenty guys and let us become a team. If it's me, fine. If it's not, let me know and that's fine with me. But the only way to beat this Russian team is to become a team ourselves, and we're not a team. We're a bunch of individuals that played against each other—some of us like each other, some of us don't. But we've got to become a team, all of us together.' He said, 'Phil, we promised that everyone would play.' I said, 'You can let everybody play, but we're not going to win.'"

After the victory in Toronto, which was much more difficult than they would have hoped, won with as much equal parts guts and guile as anything else, Sinden decided he would not break up a winning lineup except to make one change. Centre Jean Ratelle was added to the roster, and Bill Goldsworthy came out. But Ratelle would be without his Rangers wingers, Vic Hadfield and Rod Gilbert, who had played in the series opening loss. Sinden spoke with both players—Gilbert said he understood the reasoning, Hadfield was not pleased, to the point that Sinden wasn't sure if he would even be on the flight to Winnipeg. He was. There were others who were unhappy, too, the likes of Jocelyn Guevremont, Gilbert Perreault, and Richard Martin.

"Okay, we lost the first game. I know I didn't play in game two," said Hadfield, who was coming off a career-high 50-goal, 106-point season and finished fifth in Hart Trophy voting and was thinking of returning to New York to join the Rangers in training camp. "You know everybody is going to get a shot at it. You suck it up, as much as you want to play. We all wanted to play. But you are respectful of their decision."

For context, by and large all thirty-five players were good teammates. They were competitors and wanted to win, and they wanted to be a part of that winning. To make a difference. Sitting in the stands watching was not part of their DNA. For most of them, growing up and even playing in the pros, they were one of the best players, if not the best player, on their team. They weren't used to rejection, certainly not used to sitting. No one wanted to disrupt the process, but the question was, how long could they tolerate it?

"There were different roles we had to fill and guys had to understand that," said winger Paul Henderson. "But you have all these future Hall of Famers, how the hell are you going to get them in the lineup? The guys who weren't playing were pissed off. No one wanted to sit out a game, and when we're losing, they're saying, put me in there. That's how I would have felt, but we had to become a team."

Playing time would continue to be a problem, but even with that aside, Team Canada hadn't pulled together as a group. So, against that backdrop, with a crowd unhappy their new hero in Bobby Hull wasn't playing, and coming off a difficult but uplifting victory, on September 6 the Canadians and Soviets met in game 3 in Winnipeg (which had been home to the national team in 1969–70). This was the third game in five days, and for a Canadian team still struggling with its conditioning and playing a taxing physical, close-checking style, it would take its toll.

There was a very poignant moment before the puck dropped. The day before, in Munich, West Germany, at the Summer Olympics, eleven Israeli athletes had been killed by eight Palestinian terrorists, who had somehow managed to invade the athletes' village. A moment of silence was observed in Winnipeg. Real life had intruded on a hockey series that had become in part a battle of two different ways of life, communism versus democracy, but was still a game. Democratic West Germany stood on one side of the Berlin Wall, Communist East Germany stood on the other. That was very real. And this series was insignificant next to that. It was a hockey series that mattered a lot, but it was still a hockey series.

"I certainly remember initially hearing about what had happened in Munich," said Peter Mahovlich. "It was a horrendous story."

As it turned out, Bobby wasn't the only Hull sitting in the stands watching game 3. His brother Dennis was there, too, even though he had previously been told that he would be making his series debut. Dennis had originally declined the invitation to join the team back in the summer, when it was ruled that Bobby couldn't play. But he was talked out of that decision by his brother.

"I said I wasn't going to play if they weren't going to let Bobby play," said Dennis, who also played for the Blackhawks. "That was my decision. But then I talked to Bobby about it and he said, 'Oh, don't do that. Go and represent the family.' I called Harry to ask him if there was still a spot on the team, and he said, of course. As far as sitting out those first few games, I was glad I didn't play the first game in Montreal. We got murdalized [that's the way he said it]. We did better in Toronto and won. They told me I would play in Winnipeg because Bobby was there and all that stuff, but just before the game they changed their minds. Bobby and I went out for dinner after the game, and he told me that sooner or later, I would get a chance."

One lineup change Sinden didn't make, straying somewhat from his original plan, was he kept Tony Esposito, who had played so well in game 2, in goal. Sinden had said from the beginning Team Canada would need two goalies to win the series and that he would likely rotate them. But desperate times . . .

"We had the two best goaltenders in the league at the time in Esposito and Dryden," said Sinden. "As the tournament went on, maybe right from the beginning, both Fergie and I felt that with the exposure the team was getting, the goaltenders, they kind of operate on their own. They get up for the game by themselves as opposed to a pair of defencemen who can go over the game plan between themselves, same as with the forwards. But the goalie mostly has to prepare himself. As the tournament went on, we felt it might be too much for one guy because of how serious the tournament was turning. To ask a guy to play back-to-back games, without having time to mentally recover from the last one, was tough."

But the decision was made to ride the hot hand in goal in Winnipeg. Tony Esposito received a huge ovation in the pre-game introductions, almost as loud as Bobby Clarke, who was born and raised in Flin Flon, Manitoba, an eight-hour drive north.

The Soviets, meantime, from all accounts, were enjoying themselves, taking in movies on off days and shopping. Blue jeans were a hot item.

"When we arrived in Winnipeg, they went to a John Wayne movie and then went shopping," said trainer Rick Noonan. "They all bought blue jeans because it was something they couldn't get back home. It was just like all the Coke they drank. It was a novelty for them.

They also took shampoo and soap from the hotels. Toilet paper, too. They also took the toilet paper from the rinks. If you've ever been to Russia, you know why they took the toilet paper in Canada.

"They had personalities on the team. Boris Mikhailov was always joking. Alexander Ragulin never stopped talking. The big defence-man, Viktor Kuzkin, was always the last player on the bus. That's because after getting dressed, he would sneak into the shower and smoke a cigarette. They seemed down to earth to me. They carried their equipment to and from the bus. There certainly was no star treatment."

They made a handful of roster changes, three of them on defence— Yuri Shatalov, Valeri Vasiliev, and Vladimir Lutchenko were added. But perhaps the most significant move was they put back together the "Baby Line," also called the "Kid Line," which was made up of three university students—Vyacheslav Anisin, Yuri Lebedev, and Alex-ander Bodunov. On the broadcast, Conacher nicknamed them the "Headache Line"—a play on the name Anisin and the fact they were a headache to play against. Those young legs would be important.

"Oh, man, we were coming off a win," said Phil Esposito, "but we still weren't in condition. In Winnipeg, I've never worked that hard in my life."

Nevertheless, the Canadians did carry over some of the momen-tum and strong play from game 2. J. P. Parise put a second rebound past goaltender Vladislav Tretiak just 1:54 into the game for an early lead. The game plan remained the same: a strong, physical forecheck and to slow down the Soviets. Canada went on the power play a minute or so after the goal, but a Frank Mahovlich giveaway put Vladimir Petrov in alone and he beat Esposito, the Soviet's second short-handed goal of the series. It was the type of mistake Sinden feared, knowing they couldn't give the Soviets extra chances. Canada took the lead again when Ratelle scored on a nice pass from Cournoyer at 18:25.

In the second period, Cashman, who was public enemy number one with the Soviets, and who was being watched like a hawk by the officials, continued his heavy work in the corners. Cashman centred to Esposito, who put Canada ahead 3–1 at the 4:19 mark. But as they had discovered on opening night, no lead was safe. And the Soviets' penalty kill was lethal. Kharlamov, who again was superb, scored their third short-handed goal midway through the period, getting past Park to beat Tony Esposito and once again cut the lead to a goal. But just fifty-one seconds later, Henderson used his speed to restore the two-goal margin, another one that didn't feel safe, not for a Canadian team that was still adjusting to the Soviets' transition game and whose conditioning remained a big issue.

It was after the Henderson goal that Soviet coach Vsevolod Bobrov starting using the Baby Line more often, and it produced great results. And headaches for the Canadians. A minute later, Lebedev made it 4–3, and Bodunov tied it late in the period, the two goals coming 3:29 apart. Two blown leads for the Canadians, who slowed considerably in the third period but somehow managed to preserve the 4–4 tie, with Tony Esposito again exceptional, making a big save in the final minute, and Park saving the day sweeping a puck off the goal line. Tretiak, too, kept his team in it when he was forced to make a big glove save on Henderson with four minutes remaining.

"That game really made a difference," said Ellis. "We had a lead and the Russians sent out a Kid Line we really didn't know much about. They scored two quick goals, there was no scoring in the third. My feeling is if we'd been able to win that game, and we should have, we would have gone into Vancouver with more confidence, and that Vancouver game might not have been the disaster it turned out to be."

"Good teams don't lose two-goal leads as we did," said Clarke. "We didn't play as good as we did in Toronto. We dug deep down into the basket, but there wasn't much to grab. We weren't ready to play at that level for sixty minutes."

After that game and the success of the Soviets' Kid Line, a few of the young Canadians, such as Richard Martin, had hoped Team Canada would put together a Kid Line of their own with Gilbert Perreault, who did play the next game, and Marcel Dionne. It's a what-if that never came to pass, but years later several of the players wondered if an injection of youth for the fourth game might have made a difference.

Cashman, who had taken a slashing penalty in the first period and wasn't quite as effective this game in riling up the Soviets, took another penalty midway through the third and was given a ten-minute misconduct that ended his night.

"I guess the American ref thought I was a bit too rough," said Cashman.

Henderson was named player of the game for Canada, while the twenty-year-old Tretiak, for the second straight game, was named the Soviets' best player, which prompted Bobrov to joke about the player-of-the-game rings his young goalie was accumulating. "He just got married," said Bobrov, "so he will probably keep one and give the other to his bride. And with the third, fourth, and fifth? His former girlfriends will be honoured."

A rare burst of humour, but then the Soviets had plenty to smile about with the way the series was unfolding—with a win, tie, and one loss.

The Canadians practised the next morning in Winnipeg before departing for Vancouver, and incredibly, there was more bad news on the horizon. During practice, a Red Berenson shot had caught defenceman Serge Savard on the ankle. Savard had been inserted into the lineup in the second game and had been excellent in both games he played. The twenty-four-year-old had played five seasons with the Montreal Canadiens, but bad luck and injuries had interrupted the past two. He had twice broken a leg and now X-rays showed he had a hairline fracture in his ankle. At first it was thought he was done for the series, but Savard decided to remain with the team and ultimately would return for game 6 in Moscow.

Although the Canadians were content—or maybe the better word is relieved—with the results of the last two games, problems remained. Before they left Winnipeg, there was more talk about discontentment.

"I have a vivid memory of Harry Sinden chewing me out at the Winnipeg Arena at the workout before flying to Vancouver," said hockey writer Dan Proudfoot, who was covering the series for the *Globe and Mail*. "And he chewed me out loudly because he was on the ice and I was up in the stands. He was pissed because of a story that day that was harmless except for a paragraph I actually hadn't written. The story described griping on the fifteen-minute bus ride from the arena to the hotel following the game-day skate for the players who weren't in the lineup that night for game three."

Proudfoot quoted an unnamed player looking out the bus window and yelling: "There's where we can go eat. The Black Sheep Restaurant."

From another player: "I know how we can get to play. Let's hold our own game . . . maybe we'll make some money."

"Fergie was grinning with every wisecrack," reported Proudfoot. "He said to me, 'Listen, this squad is really ready.'

"'Ready for what?' shouted another player.

"I quoted [Rod] Seiling and [Rod] Gilbert, both positive about having been replaced and saying they needed to be ready to return.

Richard Martin had been signing autographs with S following his name. He claimed it didn't stand for 'Substitute,' rather 'Sabres.' I also quoted Gilbert Perreault griping, Brian Glennie reasoning that Sinden would find it easier to get everyone in the lineup as the team improved in upcoming games.

"The piece ended with a quote from Ken Dryden: 'It would be serious if there was a real rebellion. But there's almost a good restlessness rather than true discontent.'"

None of that should have bothered Sinden too much. Players gripe and wisecrack. And the feelings of some were well known. What really bothered him, though, was the paragraph that had been inserted into Proudfoot's story.

"It revealed that Hadfield and Martin had wanted to leave the team after the Toronto game, but were talked out of it," said Proudfoot. "The headline read: 'Discontent grows, two team members threaten to quit.' Dick Beddoes, a columnist with the paper, had phoned in that information, but rather than make it a separate story under his byline the [copy] desk made it the twelfth paragraph in my story. So I got credit for the 'scoop' but a lot of shit from Sinden. Ferguson took me aside after Sinden's outburst and told me not to worry about it. My guess: he had been the one who told Dick about Hadfield and Martin."

Whoever was the source, the story was very real and true, and it refused to quit.

"You may get ten different stories from ten different people because of ten different perceptions," said Dryden, looking back. "I don't know. And goalies aren't the best judge of that because goalies are always a little bit separate from the rest of the team, so if there is a buzz that's going on, the goalie might not hear the buzz. I wouldn't have thought [there was dissension] only because we had won the game in Toronto. It was disappointing in Winnipeg. You're always looking for turning points. You create Toronto as a turning point, and by the middle of the second period in Winnipeg that turning point is playing out and then it doesn't. It's disappointing that something got away that you shouldn't have let get away."

That morning in Winnipeg, Dryden was told he would start game 4 in Vancouver in search of another turning point.

By JOHN SAUNDERS
Star staff writer

METRO WEATHER
Sunday mostly sunny. High near 70, low mid 60s. Pollution index 8 at 11 a.m. Details page 2.

The Toronto Star

• THE CANADIAN • COLOR COMICS • STAR WEEK

Saturday edition

ESTABLISHED 1892   August paid circulation Mon. to Fri. 494,287, Sat. 683,549   Saturday, September 9, 1972—242 pages   Monday-Friday 10c; Saturday 25c; Home delivery 75c

Two federal government officials have been suspended for buying shares of a Toronto company around the time the company was awarded $727,000 in industrial incentive grants, Jean Marchand, minister of regional economic expansion, confirmed yesterday.

The two Ottawa civil servants, whose names Marchand would not reveal, are understood to have been involved in negotiations which led to the awarding of the grants to Silver Mines Inc. in April. No federal money has actually been paid to the company.

Silver Shield, headed by Toronto promoter Norton Cooper, is building a silver refinery and a private mint at Cobalt, where the company has a small mine.

It was the subject of controversy in the Ontario Legislature earlier this year when Morton Shulman (NDP—High Park) called the scheme a "swindle" and said the provincial government had been "conned" into giving Silver Shield a $325,000 grant for underground development work.

WITHOUT PAY

Marchand said the two federal officials were suspended without pay more than a month ago.

"It relates to their purchase of the stock at a moment when it was not felt to be proper," Marchand said.

Secretaries at the offices of two men directly involved in recommending and administering the Silver Shield grant have been telling callers the two are "on vacation."

Marchand said a firm of outside accountants has been hired to investigate the Cobalt project and the grant. "If there is any improper behavior it (the grant) will not be given," he said.

'INTERNAL ACTION'

J. P. Francis, senior assistant deputy minister in the department, said the accounting firm's report has been received, but he refused to discuss its contents. He also refused to disclose the numbers and prices of shares bought by the two officials.

Francis said the suspensions were an "internal disciplinary action" related to the alleged sale of knowledge of a grant before it was publicly announced. He said he would not comment

See OTTAWA, page 2

Blacks in Metro:
Racism exists
but hope does, too

★ In the past five years the black population of Toronto has exploded. Now it is 40,000 to 50,000. Blacks face discrimination in many aspects of their lives from housing to schooling. Yet most of their leaders feel Toronto may yet set the world an example of harmonious race relations.

"I've never seen so many black people," Al Crawford grumbled as he wheeled his taxi up Bathurst St.

"Everywhere I go I see them. It makes me wonder.

"They want to stand out, you know. They're trying to push their ways onto the people here, and let's face it—the people won't take it."

Blatant racial bigotry, you'd say.

Except that Al Crawford is black.

He is one of the few Toronto-born Negroes with roots going back to colonies of former slaves in Nova Scotia. To him, all these new dark-skinned people are foreigners "who will make things tough for everybody."

They are the people who have flocked to Metro by the thousands to form a major new population bloc since 1967 when the federal government scrapped policies that had severely restricted black immigration.

Within four years 47,000 arrived from the West Indies, where unemployment can run as high as 30 per cent. Two-thirds of them settled in Toronto. Lesser numbers came from Guyana, Africa, the United States and the Maritimes.

No official records are kept on the basis of skin color. A survey conducted by York University's Institute for Behavioral Research indicates Metro now has 45,000 to 50,000 blacks. Peter Marcelline, a city of Toronto planner from Trinidad, puts the total higher at 60,000 to 75,000.

Using the lower estimate, the current rate of immigration will mean a black population of at least 150,000 by 1980.

If they meet hostility even from some blacks, what do these newcomers encounter among whites?

Could Toronto face the ugly racial strife we've seen in so many U.S. cities?

The Star has interviewed many authorities close to the black community, from conservatives to radicals, who have considered this possibility.

They were virtually unanimous in their optimism that Toronto can set the world an example in harmonious race relations.

However, as the article and three succeeding ones will show, the roads of discrimination and distrust are already here.

Blacks charge that Metro's police force is riddled with racists. They're at least partly right.

Their children are having trouble in school.

Warnings of strife are also issued regularly by

See TORONTO's, page 1

—Star photo by Harold Barkley

BOYS KNOW NO COLOR BAR: Jimmy Taylor, who is 8 and white, and Curtis Mercury, who is 10 and black, live in the same Sackville St. apartment and are buddies. But in Toronto's adult world color often does make a difference.

No public hearings
Metro approves
paving Spadina ditch
down to Eglinton

Metro Council yesterday approved paving the uncompleted portion of the Spadina Expressway between Lawrence and Eglinton Aves. — without holding public hearings.

It also chose the Spadina route for a rapid transit line instead of Bathurst St., as had been recommended by transit officials. The subway line would cost $155 million.

The decisions came 15 months after the provincial cabinet chose "people over cars" and ordered work on the expressway, scheduled to be built south to Bloor St., halted at Lawrence.

The roadbed for the expressway had been laid as far south as Eglinton and it was this "ditch" that council as a 17-0 vote yesterday decided to turn into a four-lane arterial road.

Some members of council —like Toronto Alderman David Rotenberg—maintain before talking to Gordon Carton, his minister of transportation and communications. Carton was unavailable for comment.

Proving the four-lane road would cost $1.5 million and use four to each direction would be exclusively for buses.

The council decisions were opposed by York, Metro's second smallest borough, which had demanded public hearings before any action was taken as moving the unemployment section of the roadway.

York Mayor Philip White said he would appeal directly to Davis to veto the decision to pave the "ditch" because it would dump thousands of cars and trucks into residential streets in his municipality.

TRANSIT ROUTE:

He said the borough would also fight the Spadina rapid transit route because the Ontario Municipal Board because it would cut into rapid parkland. Council voted 18-8 for the Spadina line along the route it was originally supposed to

While said moving the ditch means York would get all the heavy traffic from North York.

"Just because North York had a population of more than 500,000 and the borough of York has only 143,000, it doesn't mean they can push us around," White told council. They may feel that they are Canada but we're Canadian.

The decision to build a subway line along the original route was regarded as a major victory for North York representatives on council, led by Controller

See METRO, page 4

Russian Jews' lot
described as worse
than under Nazis

By DONNA DELSCHNEIDER
Star staff writer

Murray Freedman is a University of Toronto scientist just back from the Soviet Union who would like to return soon, but knows he may never be able to.

He believes Soviet Jews are worse off in some ways than Jews were in Nazi Germany and said to us on an interview with The Star yesterday, the eve of the Jewish New Year.

He says the Jews are worse off in Russia than they were under the Stalin because for the first few years of Hitler's rule they were free to leave the country.

"It's a basic fundamental right for a person to be able to leave his country if he wants."

He said the Soviet Jews remain optimistic nevertheless. They are convinced that their best hope for being allowed to leave is to make as much noise as possible.

He has smuggled filmed documents out of the country.

Freedman talked to The Star yesterday because he believes he must speak out against the plight of Soviet Jews.

He believes that the "real lot" the Kremlin is keeping educated Jews leaving the country as tax evasion from leaving the country. The Soviets recently educated Jews leaving the country but would release them from making profit from leaving Freedman's smuggled

MURRAY FREEDMAN
Burned his bridges

films are copies of dossiers on the background and the professions of some 30 people who have applied for exit visas dossiers compiled by one of the country's top scientists who is trying to get out.

Benjamin Levich, the scientist who compiled the dossiers, lost his job when he and his wife applied for exit visas.

Freedman a 37-year-old biochemist, had been so used to an international scientific conference in Moscow and he also visited Kiev and Leningrad.

He talked to many people young, old and in-between. But more university students he became friendly with and several professors, Jews and non-Jews.

3 of 4 Canadians in poll
favor banning all strikes

Three out of four Canadians polled in a random sample are in favor of banning all strikes, and settling labor disputes by compulsory arbitration.

Four out of five of these same people are in favor of disallowing strikes in the public service, and almost as many would be willing to buy products made by a company whose workers are on strike.

Their findings, bound to be disquieting to Canada's union movement, emerged in a mail-polled readers in The Canadian Magazine. Results of the poll, which tabulated the feelings of 27,603 readers, appear in The Canadian Magazine included in today's Star.

Among the surprises

turned up by the poll was among some members, refuse to buy the products of a struck firm.

Young people, in the age group from 18 to 35, whom most observers would expect to be more pro-labor than their elders, were similar in their attitudes; two-thirds of them would do away with all strikes.

This provocative attitude is the lead item in today's Canadian Magazine.

indications that even among some m e m b e r s, labor disputes by compulsory arbitration.

Dennison's feet favored

INGERSOLL (CP) — Mayor Gordon Henry thinks he'll be at a decided disadvantage at the 65th annual mayoral grape-stomping festival here Sept. 21.

Henry said he had a cool look at Mayor William Dennison's feet when he was in

the Toronto mayor's offices Thursday and told Dennison, "Looking at my feet, and then at yours, I'm sure you will carry a definite edge into the competition.

Ten mayors, vice-mayors and aldermen will compete in this year's grape stomp.

BODY-CASE
FREEZER
ON DISPLAY

The Metro police museum in the headquarters building on Jarvis St. will be putting on display a freezer that for nearly six months held the body of a woman along with vegetables and meat pies.

When David Todd was convicted of manslaughter in the death of his wife, Grace, and sentenced to 18 years' imprisonment last June the freezer was an exhibit in the trial.

It joins other displays that include clothing worn by bandits and police equipment in one nearly a century-old.

The museum is open to the public during Police Week each spring and to groups of 25 or more who make arrangements in advance.

Israeli, Syrian jets
fight at Golan Heights
both sides claim kills

BEIRUT (Reuter-UPI) — Israeli and Syrian jet fighters tangled in aerial combat near the Golan Heights yesterday and both sides claimed kills.

An Israeli military spokesman in Tel Aviv said Israeli jets had downed three Syrian Soviet-built MiG-21 planes and damaged a fourth as they flew to brush Israeli villages in the Golan Heights area. All their planes returned to base, the Israelis said.

But a Damascus Radio report claimed the Syrian jets had shot down two Israeli French-built Mirage jets in battle.

The Syrians admitted losing three planes in the encounter, but the Damascus communique added that the Syrian pilots were unharmed.

The Syrian air force successfully confronted the Israeli aircraft which attacked two Syrian villages in the Golan Heights, which overlook Israeli territory, was apparently in reprisal for yesterday's Israeli air strikes placed with guerrillas bases in Syria and Lebanon.

Israel retaliated with fury yesterday for the deaths of its 11 Olympic men in Munich, sending scores of warplanes into Lebanon and to within four miles of Damascus in

See ISRAELI, page 4

To Moscow--like Napoleon?
Canada loses its home series--amid a thunder of boos

By MILT DUNNELL
Star sports columnist

VANCOUVER — The march on Moscow commences in a thunder of boos, with Team Canada's bugle banners in disarray and coach Harry Sinden's all-stars in a lather of disgust over the ridicule heaped upon them by those they hoped most to please—the Canadian fans.

Team Canada is generally conceded

to be the greatest array of hockey talent ever assembled in this country.

It was touted as the biggest cinch since Mackenzie King.

Yet in four games on Canadian ice, the Canadians managed to win only one game—the tightly disciplined Nationals of the Soviet Union. Come Monday, the third ended in a draw.

Last night, as the last act escaped from the punctured balloon of a national ego, it had the musty round of disappointment, disillusionment and—across the wind—almost contempt.

Many of the 16,000 partisans who jammed the beautiful home of the Vancouver Canucks of the National Hockey League, booed the Good Guys, whom they had hoped to send on their way to Europe with a resounding victory over the comrades.

Bill Goldsworthy, whose two penal-

ties helped the Soviets to practically sew up the 5-3 win before the first period was half gone, was a special target of the abuse.

Boris Petrovich Mikhailov, the Soviet team's 34-pound forward, whipped two goals past Canada's goalie Ken Dryden, while Goldsworthy did penance. They were almost identical goals with the same Mikhailov, Vladimir Petrov and Vladimir Lutchenko, drawing assists.

After the second goal, the customers gave Goldsworthy the old razoo in brass. Their displeasure spread to other members of the team. Ken Dryden, whose weak ankles almost sluggish in the Stanley Cup series of 1971 when Montreal eliminated Boston, was given more to make routine saves.

Frank Mahovlich must have figured he was in Toronto where the freight

See THUNDER, page 3

The Toronto Star
Campaigning
by computer

● COMPUTER CAMPAIGN: Warren Beanish, Conservative candidate in Metro's Rosedale riding, will send "personal" letters written by computer to voters in the Oct. 30 federal election. Page 17.

● CORPORATIONS are giving more to the United Appeal this year than in the past as a result of one man's ingenious plan aimed at the 300 biggest firms in Metropolitan Toronto. Page 18.

● CONFLICT OF INTEREST: Exactly what principle forced the resignation of Provincial Treasurer Darcy McKeough? Star writer Walter Stewart examines Canada's confusing conflict-of-interest laws in insight, page 21.

Another loss and a thunder of boos, a sad story relegated to the bottom of page one. (Courtesy of the *Toronto Star*)

Game 4—"To The People Across Canada—We Tried"

Vancouver is a beautiful city, in a picturesque setting surrounded by mountains and an inlet that flows out to the ocean. When the sun shines it is spectacular. When it doesn't shine bright, the city can be a dreary place. That dreariness can last for days and be relentless on the psyche. There was certainly nothing pretty about Vancouver as the dark cloud that was Team Canada rolled into town for game 4 of the Summit Series.

But what ultimately turned out to be their low point—"It was hell," said Paul Henderson—also became a turning point of sorts, when afterwards they finally started to become a team. In an odd way, it was a "where were you" moment of a much different kind, perhaps the worst kind at the time.

The players didn't really know how the country was feeling about them—not before the game anyway—except for what they were reading and watching and hearing in the media, and to them it was brutal. But how the fans were really feeling, they weren't quite sure, although they had their suspicions. In Montreal, after the 7–3 opening night loss, there was stunned silence. In Toronto, after the desperate 4–1 win, there was a standing ovation. In Winnipeg, after they had blown a pair of two-goal leads and clung to a 4–4 tie, there was disappointment.

But when they got to Vancouver, they soon felt the mood of that city and by extension the country.

"The fans were on us ten minutes into the game," said Peter Mahovlich, who did not dress for the game and sat in the stands with those disgruntled fans. "It was horrendous."

Once again, coach Harry Sinden had made multiple lineup changes, some of which were out of necessity. But it again pointed to the issue of building a team. Defenceman Serge Savard was out due to the hairline fracture in his ankle, and defence partner Guy Lapointe had a charley horse. Neither could play, and that was a big loss. They were replaced by Don Awrey and Rod Seiling, who were rock-solid defencemen, but not fleet of foot, especially against a team as quick as the Soviets.

Up front, Wayne Cashman and J. P. Parise, who had supplied a physical presence, were taken out of the lineup, as were Peter Mahovlich and Stan Mikita. Jean Ratelle was also scratched, but his two Ranger line mates, the disgruntled Vic Hadfield and Rod Gilbert, came in, as well as young centre Gilbert Perreault and winger Dennis Hull. But there were two other changes that were significant. Ken Dryden, who hadn't dressed since game 1, replaced Tony Esposito in goal, while Bill Goldsworthy was added to the forward mix with strict instructions to be aggressive, but smart.

In many ways the group looked more like the lineup that got rocked in game 1, including the goalie, who was struggling to find his game and trying to adjust on the fly.

"I don't know if I was surprised," said Dryden. "How was I feeling? Not good. I've got to figure it out. This is a game that is played different, and the biggest difference is that they play a passing game and they play a side-to-side game. The NHL game is an end-to-end game, setting up the wingers for the big shot. So, for the goalie, it's coming out and cutting the angles. That's how you play because your equipment doesn't cover a heckuva lot of the net and you've got to cover the net in a different way.

"And the Soviets' play, it's not a shooting game, it's a passing game. If they pass from side to side, if you're a goalie and you're out any distance, you're going to have to move laterally, and it's a big distance you have to move because you're out. It was coming to grips with that and how to adapt to that. Being a bigger body, deeper in the net, helps, but all of your instincts are the opposite. Again, this isn't learning something over six months of a season, this is learning it for tomorrow."

Or for tonight.

During the warm-up there were actually smatterings of booing directed at Team Canada, and they would intensify sooner rather than later. Goldsworthy, well intended, still couldn't control his emotions, and he quickly put his fingerprints on the game and the outcome. Others would be equally complicit, just in different ways. Goldsworthy, who had played in game 2, took a needless crosschecking penalty eighty-four seconds into the game. Thirty-seven seconds later Boris Mikhailov deflected a Vladimir Lutchenko shot past Dryden. At the 5:58 mark, Goldsworthy took another bad penalty, and 1:31 later Mikhailov scored again, same play. Just 7:29 into the game the Soviets were ahead 2–0.

That's when the booing began in earnest, 15,570 strong, and the anger wasn't directed at the visitors.

"We got what we deserved," said Bobby Clarke. "We took a couple of penalties that made us look like angry kids. It made us look classless and inept."

"Now we're trying to play catch-up," said Brad Park. "When you try to play catch-up, it's one thing to play it in the last five minutes of a game, it's an awful thing when you're trying to play catch-up in the second period. We were starting to gamble because we thought we had to gamble because we thought we had to leave Canada with a lead in the series. Once you gamble, you can be taken advantage of, and that's what basically happened."

One of the few Canadians with fresh legs was Perreault, who was making his series debut, and possessed electrifying speed. He helped stop the bleeding early in the second period, scoring on an end-to-end rush, a goal he called the highlight of his limited series action. But just fifty-seven seconds later the Soviets restored the two-goal lead. Cournoyer then missed on a couple breakaways set up by Esposito, and the Soviets comfortably led 4–1 after two periods.

The booing continued and intensified.

"It was just a night that went wrong," said Dryden. "It pretty much started wrong, and then it was one of those nights that never righted itself. Even at certain moments when things could have shifted another way, they were going so far wrong that it just wasn't going to get righted. And the hard part of that is that when a night has that feeling, the players can feel it and the fans can feel it. So you're feeling it the whole night, and there's just a kind of sourness to it, and then how do you express your sourness? That's when the booing and other stuff starts. It's being booed by your home crowd. This is Vancouver, it's not like playing for the Canadiens against the Canucks and being booed because you play for the Canadiens. No, Vancouver was our home crowd. It hits you. People react differently to it, but you feel it and it hits you."

In the third period, Canada made it 4–2 when Goldsworthy tapped in a rebound off an Esposito shot at 6:54, but the crowd still booed. Team Canada did apply pressure, outshooting the Soviets by a whopping 26–6 in that period, but Tretiak was excellent. He wasn't supposed to start the game in Winnipeg, but his backup, Viktor Zinger, was ill and still wasn't ready in Vancouver. So here was Tretiak, the supposed weak link in the Soviet lineup, playing all four games—and playing very well in each of them. Perhaps the Canadians' frustrations were best seen when Frank Mahovlich, of all players, normally a mild-mannered sort, sat on Tretiak, who was out of his net, for what seemed like an eternity.

And the fans booed.

The Soviets went up 5–2 before Dennis Hull closed the scoring in the final minute. By the end, the Canadians outshot the Soviets 41–31, and throughout the night Dryden endured derisive cheers when he made a routine save. Despite the shot count, there were too many moments when the Soviets looked like the Harlem Globetrotters, controlling the puck with apparent ease, and that only enraged the fans even more.

"We were never in that game," said Sinden. "They took control early and that was it."

When it was over there were more boos, born as much out of frustration as embarrassment and anger, because the fans really weren't feeling much different than the Canadian players themselves. If not duped, then they'd been misled to believe that the Canadians were invincible, and maybe what was happening had less to do with the Russians' talents than it did with the Canadians' underachieving. Another miscalculation.

"I understand them booing us," said Park. "Hell, I might have booed us, too, if I wasn't on the team. They expected more from us, we expected more from us, so deep down inside, the frustration was building and building."

"It was the low point of my career," said Ron Ellis. "We played hard, we just didn't play well. We didn't execute well. The Russians took advantage of that. To be booed off the ice was something that will stick with me the rest of my life because we were trying. We finally had to realize this was a great team we were playing, well conditioned and well prepared. The journey from that point on was going to be very, very tough."

Tougher than it already was.

"Our line didn't have many scoring opportunities," said Henderson. "That night was the worst I'd felt, I was labouring, and a lot of us were." But as poorly as the Canadians played, they were still stung by the crowd reaction, and the media reviews, and they were feeling the pressure of the daunting task ahead—four games in Moscow. This series had become much bigger because it wasn't keeping to the Canadian script. In the beginning, they hadn't agreed to play for love of country, but rather because the series was the first of its kind and they were going to win it—easily. But now, they were indeed representing their country, their hockey heritage, and their political values. And their reputations were directly on the line. If it wasn't already, it was certainly becoming a war on many levels. But there was one Canadian who would not go quietly into that Vancouver night. The guy who hadn't wanted to be there in the beginning was now fully invested: the leader, engaged and pissed off. Phil Esposito was named the Canadian player of the game, and he was interviewed by Johnny Esaw post-game on national television. He gave a speech for the ages.

"To the people across Canada, we tried," said an emotional Esposito, sweat dripping off his face. "We gave it our best. For the people that boo us, geez, I'm really, I'm really, all of us guys are really disheartened and we're disillusioned and we're disappointed in some of the people. We cannot believe the bad press we've got, the booing

In just a few years, Canada went from a great national pride and optimism for the future in celebrating its centennial in 1967 to a horrible low in 1970 when the FLQ crisis led to violence, kidnappings, and the death of Quebec Deputy Premier Pierre Laporte, spurring Prime Minister Pierre Elliott Trudeau to invoke the War Measures Act. In the fall of 1972, Canada was in the midst of a federal election and national identity crisis. A hockey series was supposed to provide a desperately needed distraction.

The series was a clash of hockey cultures, which ultimately became one of its legacies: Canadians learning from the training methods of the Soviets, which at the time were wildly different, and the Soviets learning something about the Canadians' determination. Valeri Kharlamov (above) goes through Soviet drills with assistant coach Boris Kulagin prior to game 1 in Montreal. Team Canada players do some stretches (below), but were not prepared to play at such a high level. Conditioning would become a significant factor early in the series.

The scouting reports on twenty-year-old Soviet goaltender Vladislav Tretiak were not flattering, though in fairness the Canadian scouts only saw him briefly, and not at his best because of his impending nuptials. Legendary goaltender Jacques Plante (above), who had met Tretiak a few years earlier, perhaps fearing his young friend was being thrown to slaughter, offered some hints prior to the first game on how to play the Canadian shooters. The fears were quickly set aside as Tretiak proved to be a star of the series.

It was all smiles before game 1 of a series that was supposed to be a laugh—for Team Canada. Brad Park (top) shakes hands for a photo with Vyacheslav Solodukhin. Soviet players (centre, from the left) Yuri Blinov, Alexander Ragulin, and Valeri Kharlamov are in good spirits before puck drop. And Prime Minister Pierre Trudeau (bottom) poses with both teams for what everyone in Canada expected to be a joyful start to the series.

Game 1 began as so many expected, with the Canadians getting out to a quick 2–0 lead. Frank Mahovlich (top) had a hand in Phil Esposito's opening goal, thirty seconds into the game. The rout seemed like it was on, but deep down the Canadians knew better. On this hot and sweaty night at the Montreal Forum, the Soviets shocked the hockey world and all of Canada with a 7–3 win.

The series was a clash of many cultures, including coaching. John Ferguson (top), the long-time Montreal Canadiens rugged winger, was asked to play in the series, but had announced his retirement and preferred to be an assistant coach to Harry Sinden (bottom), who had left the Boston Bruins after a Stanley Cup win and a salary dispute. The Soviets were in a coaching transition, as well, with Vsevolod Bobrov (centre), a legendary player and athlete, taking over from Anatoly Tarasov, known as "the father of Russian hockey."

For some the contempt for the Soviets existed long before the shocking first-game result, but it was based on politics, not hockey. On the afternoon of game 2, protestors marched outside Maple Leaf Gardens (top) and pamphlets were passed out to passersby and fans calling for freedom for all nations enslaved by Russia. An organization called Canadians for Fair Play Committee was particularly pointed in their criticism of the USSR. To Team Canada it felt like the series hinged on the outcome of that second game, in which Peter Mahovlich (bottom) scored an incredible shorthanded goal to lead the Canadians to victory.

The **relief** after the game 2 victory was palpable, as the stars—(top, from the left) Phil Esposito, Peter Mahovlich, and Paul Henderson—met with the media, staying hydrated in their own way. Harry Sinden and assistant John Ferguson also explained the win and the challenge in a post-game press conference.

we've gotten in our own buildings, and if the Russians boo their players, if the fans, if the Russians boo their players like some of the Canadian fans, I'm not saying all of them, some of them booed us, then I'll come back and apologize to each one of the Canadians, but I don't think they will. I'm really, really, I'm really disappointed. I'm completely disappointed. I cannot believe it. Some of our guys are really, really down in the dumps. We know. We're trying. Hell, I mean, we're doing the best we can, and they've got a good team and let's face facts, but it doesn't mean we're not giving 150 percent because we certainly are."

Esaw: "I think, Phil, the disappointment is a natural thing because the whole thing was an unexpected thing. We all live with the National Hockey League. We've all been so proud over the years of how great we are—"

Esposito interrupted: "Fans expect it because of the press that said we're so good. Not one of our guys said we're so good."

Esaw: "No, no, this is the thing. This is the thing on behalf of the fans. I must say that, ah, probably, since everything is relative, we know how good you people are, but the people didn't realize how good the Soviet team was. And now we've found out how good they are, I think we can appreciate how good both teams are."

Esposito: "I'll tell you, we love, I mean, everyone of us guys, thirty-five guys that came out and played for Team Canada, we did it because we love our country and not for any other reason, no other reason. They can throw the money for the pension fund out the window. They can throw anything they want out the window. We came because we love Canada. And even though we may play in the United States and we earn money in the United States, Canada is still our home and that's the only reason we've come. And I don't think it's fair that we should be booed . . . we're going to get better."

The comment showed how far Esposito, and probably all of his teammates, had travelled emotionally from the beginning of training camp. Looking back, Esposito is no less emotional. He didn't watch the interview until several years after, but he remembered how disappointed and angry he was that night.

"My dad told me, 'People are saying what's wrong with your sons, they're awful, they're going to lose,'" he said. "Somebody put a sign on my dad's lawn: 'Losers.' Little things like that. I remember the press, the *Toronto Star*, the *Globe*, the *Vancouver* . . . the headlines said we were just awful. I never saw a lot of the headlines, but we were told this. Before I did the interview, there were three kids standing right over the Zamboni entrance, yelling at me 'Communism is better!' I wanted to throw my stick at them like a spear. The booing really was the topper to me and not because of me. I felt bad for the guys. Man, I felt so bad for Billy Goldsworthy. He took a lot of stupid penalties, there's no doubt about it, and we did. Everybody got wrapped up in 'this is a war,' and some of the guys took it literally. I did, too, but it was a war on ice for me. I didn't care about the political bullshit, at that time it was a war on ice.

"I remember after the game, we're in a bar—me, Cash, Goldy, and one other guy—and we got into pretty bad fisticuffs with a bunch of people. The cops got us out of there. We got back to the Hotel Vancouver, we were okay, but that's the emotion we were dealing with. I believe somebody said something and Billy Goldsworthy punched him and that started it. Man, what a time."

None of the Team Canada players heard the Esposito speech as he made it, but he shared the message with a few teammates afterwards, that he had told the fans how disappointed they all were in the booing.

"They basically threw the team under the bus," said Tretiak.

"There's no question that Phil was our leader and without Phil we may not have won," said Seiling. "All of us were frustrated. We were taking time out from our lives to represent our country. We were proud to do that, excited to do that, it was an honour. Then to have the country turn on us, I'm not even sure our own families were that supportive of us. To them we had let them down, we were a disappointment. They'd been sold a bill of goods that we would win all eight games, that this was a romp in the park, this was a series of exhibition games, that Canada was finally going to throw its best out there and they would wipe the slate clean and show the dominance that they expected and thought Canadian hockey represented. For us to be in the position that we were and to have the media on our back criticizing us all the time . . . and we were aware of it. You can't get away from it. You can't go anywhere, you can't go in your hotel, everything is negative, negative, negative. For Phil to come out, what he spoke was true, it was from his heart, it was on behalf of all of us, and there isn't a player on the team that would have disagreed with what he said. It came from the heart."

"We didn't hear the speech," said Ellis, "but we were aware of it. We knew Phil was being interviewed, but we really didn't know what he said. It was from the heart, and it was so important for Canadian fans to hear what Phil had to say. I've said it before: I always wondered what was happening the next morning at breakfast tables across our county, when people were saying, 'What did you think of Phil's interview?' I think people began to realize, maybe we should get behind our guys, because after the game in Vancouver no one wanted to be near us. No one wanted to identify with us. But I do think the fans, because of Phil, realized the Russians are good, our boys are up against it, let's get behind them. It was like, you're on a losing streak in Toronto playing for the Leafs. You don't go anywhere.

You don't go out for lunch, you don't take your wife to dinner. That was the same feeling. Just stick to ourselves. To get out of Dodge, to get out of Canada was probably a pretty positive thing for us."

"I never heard the interview, never saw it, never knew about it until after the series was over," said Park. "It had no impact on the dressing room. Even when we went to Sweden, I never heard it talked about. My parents didn't even say anything when I went back to Toronto [after the fourth game] to see my wife and baby before we went to Sweden. I don't think they ran it again the next day in the news. Of course, I wasn't watching the news, anyway—I was trying to find a hole to hide."

And so when the Canadians hit the departure lounge in Toronto, the unthinkable really had happened. That was the emotional baggage they were carrying overseas. They had hoped Vancouver would allow them to leave Canada slightly ahead in the series. Instead, the now not-so mysterious Soviets returned home leading, 2-1-1.

"I don't think worried was what I had on my mind," said Sinden. "Fergie and I both, we're thinking, what are we going to do? We've got to do something here. We've got to change something. We've got to change the attitude. We've got to change the lines. We don't concede to this, or let the players concede to it—which they didn't. But we had to do something."

To a man, the Canadians were glad to get out of not just Vancouver, but the country.

CHAPTER 9

A Stop in Sweden

The next morning after the debacle in Vancouver, still smarting from the long night before, Team Canada flew east for a couple days, before reconvening in Toronto to depart for two exhibition games and some practice time, spread out over eight days, in Stockholm, Sweden.

If they felt abandoned by the country after the four games in Canada, winning just once and tying another, and especially after the relentless booing out west, then that feeling was given an exclamation point when they got to the airport in Toronto.

"There wasn't anybody at the airport to see us off," said winger Ron Ellis. "No one. That said a lot. The fans weren't happy, and to a certain degree they had a right not to be happy."

As much as Team Canada was in disarray, struggling on the ice and, to some extent, divided off it, they were being pushed into becoming, in their own awkward way, a team. Out of a need for survival, an us-against-the-world mentality was slowly starting to develop.

"We had a meeting in which we said, listen, we don't have too many friends right now in Canada, we're kind of on our own, there were fifty of us. We called ourselves Team 50—the thirty-five players, the coaches, the trainers. We're going to have to stick this out together," said coach Harry Sinden.

So, after four games and a roller coaster of emotions, they had a common cause to rally around that would hopefully pull them together: adversity. They were losing a series they had been told they were supposed to win handily; the country wasn't happy and was letting them know it. Like a face wash with a smelly hockey glove, it gets your attention.

"Glad to get out of Dodge? Probably," said goaltender Ken Dryden. "That's probably a good way of putting it, where you're in part glad to get out of how you feel and you hope that by getting out of Dodge, you have a chance to feel something different. But, of course, you don't quite. You may be physically getting out, but you're still in Dodge."

"We had to get away from Canada," said winger Paul Henderson. "Hell, even our families didn't like us. Sometimes, you get on the road, you have more time with the guys . . ."

Just like when they were travelling in Canada, Team 50 was divided into two flights for the trip to Stockholm. The NHL owners didn't want all the players on the same plane, well, just in case of an accident. And no doubt the terrorist attack at the Munich Olympics was weighing heavily. One plane flew via Frankfurt, Germany. The second flew via Paris, France. Both flights had a considerable layover between legs, time enough to leave the airport and explore, or just sleep and read and shop.

"We were thinking that we had to get out of town," said defenceman Brad Park. "I'm thinking, 'We've got to get by ourselves. We're in a hole. Get out of town and have a get-together and get ourselves reorganized. I was on the flight through Paris. We had like an eight- or nine-hour layover. So a bunch of us jumped in cabs and we went downtown. I made sure I was with Guy Lapointe, who spoke French. It's like eight or nine o'clock in the morning and we're having rotisserie chicken and red wine at a café. I said, this is kind of interesting. But it was a good thing."

The flight via Frankfurt turned out to be a bit of an adventure when the brothers Esposito realized, after disembarking the plane, that they had misplaced their passports. Luckily, according to Dryden, the flight crew found them on the floor underneath their seats. One crisis averted.

In the original planning, the eight-day stopover in Stockholm was intended to be a bit of a mini-vacation for the players. They would practise and play a couple exhibition games to get used to the larger international ice surface; the rink in Moscow would be a dozen feet wider than North American rinks. Only a small handful of the players, such as Dryden and Seiling, had ever played on the big ice. It was also going to introduce them to European officiating, which still involved just two officials, but with decidedly different standards than in North America, not that they didn't see some of that back in Canada. But, given that the first four games didn't quite play out the way they had planned, Stockholm became a little more important. Having said that, the players still had their fun. Again, all thirty-five players (minus Frank Mahovlich, who nursed a knee injury in Toronto) remained with the team—though some tentatively. A lot of them still thought that number was too high, that the roster should have been pared before leaving Canada.

The first day of practice, which was also Sinden's fortieth birthday, involved two on-ice sessions—a practice and an intra-squad game. It was on the second day of practice, September 15, that Guy Lapointe's son, Guy Jr., was born.

"It was a tough decision for me obviously to play in the series and go overseas, but I figured this was a great chance to play for Canada," said Lapointe. "To be playing with this team after only two years in the NHL, what an honour."

Lapointe would miss the first eighteen days of his son's life, but he would have quite the story to share. In celebration, a bunch of the players gathered to toast the new arrival in the Lapointe family. And from reports of the day, there was no shortage of toasting and socializing amongst the Canadian players all week, which was part of the bonding process.

"Without a doubt it was the right time to get away" said Phil Esposito. "I remember Guy Lapointe's wife having a baby, some guys got a couple cases of beer, and we went into a park, not far from the Grand Hotel, and we just sat there and talked and drank."

"After practices and after the games we were all going out as a team to have a couple of beers," said Park. "We were more as a group. In Canada, you would go home to family, or guys with your [NHL] team. But in Sweden, we're going everywhere as a group. We drank a few beers and talked about anything and learned to like and appreciate each other, bond."

But apparently some were perhaps a little too enthusiastic with their bonding, and not all the players approved. Dan Proudfoot, hockey writer for the *Globe and Mail*, wrote about one unnamed veteran player despairing over the drinking and the all-nighters that were going on, that the team wasn't focussed. There was a report of four players heard yelling in the hotel at 5 a.m., well after the 1 a.m. curfew imposed by coach Harry Sinden. But Proudfoot in another story did posit the notion that, as he put it, the drinking wasn't a major factor. "Some of the best drinkers are among the team's best players . . . some who venture no further than the Grand Hotel lobby haven't been able to skate effectively."

"One day, we split the team and half went to a town and put on a hockey clinic," said Sinden. "We had a lot of fun. Guy Lapointe can be a character, so he did his bit and we all had a great laugh and we needed that. The fans had a good time, the players had a good time, and the ones who stayed back in Stockholm, they bonded, too. There's no doubt the week in Sweden was good for our team."

Indeed, there were no shortage of characters on the team, and one of the biggest jokesters was winger Dennis Hull, who carved out a career of sorts in retirement entertaining at banquets and golf tournaments.

"We were coming together as a team," said Hull. "We were getting in better shape after being together for almost a month. And we had some fun. I do remember going to a bar in Sweden after one game. It was called the Glass Bar. I'm a history buff. That's why I went to Brock University. I told the guys that the flag was up on the castle in Stockholm, which means the king is in residence. Of course, there was a huge wall around the castle with these holes, and water was coming out. I said the water coming out there, that's called the royal flush. Everyone laughed except the guy next to me. I said to him, 'Didn't you think that was funny?' He said, 'No, I'm the king.'

"Pat Stapleton and Bill White were the best at keeping the team loose. Guy Lapointe was pretty good, too. But I got Guy good in Moscow. After a good period, he would say in the dressing room, 'Let's keep playing, guys, don't get a big head, don't get a big head.' He then went into the washroom and I made his helmet smaller. So when he put it back on, it didn't fit."

Lapointe didn't wear a helmet at this time, but don't let that get in the way of a good story.

One significant piece of news that did come out of Stockholm was that Bobby Orr, who was recovering from knee surgery and hoped to play in Moscow, practised with the team, but his damaged knee swelled up. He had hoped to play in an intra-squad game on September 15, and skated in the morning, but only lasted a few minutes. Proudfoot quoted Orr as telling bystanders: "It's all finished." So he coached one of the intra-squad teams. That could have been a huge addition for Team Canada—in terms of what Orr could bring on the ice, even in a limited capacity. He would have been a perfect quarterback for their power play. And, psychologically, his presence would have impacted both teams in different ways.

The two exhibition games against the Swedish national team pretty much went the way of all the other best-laid plans. They were supposed to be exhibitions, nothing too intense, to help celebrate the fiftieth anniversary of Swedish hockey. But Team Canada's practices were intense, and so the two games would be, too. Though they were hardly Picassos—far from it.

In the first game, in which Tony Esposito played in goal, the Canadians did not play well, although with good goaltending they prevailed 4–1. It was a chippy game on both sides, the Canadians physical, the Swedes using a little more stickwork. The game was also an introduction to officials Josef Kompalla and Franz Baader of West Germany, who would gain ignominy, at least in the Canadians' eyes, later in the series, for their incompetence. But the game was a chance for some of the players who weren't playing and those unhappy with their playing time to get on the ice—Vic Hadfield, Rod Gilbert, Marcel Dionne, Mickey Redmond, Brian Glennie, and Jocelyn Guevremont. Not all were vocal, but they all got to play.

Paul Henderson opened the scoring in the first period, Bobby Clarke made it 2–0 in the second, while Ulf Sterner, who had played briefly with the New York Rangers in the 1960s but returned home because he felt unwelcome in the NHL, made it 2–1 after two. Park and Wayne Cashman closed out the scoring in the third at Johanneshovs Isstadion.

The second game, played the next night, was worse than the first in many ways. The finesse certainly wasn't any better, and there was even more chippy play. Eddie Johnston, who had backed up a few games, was given the start in goal and played very well, potentially giving Sinden an option when they got to Moscow, although the coach already had his goaltending plans mapped out in his head. There was plenty of ugliness in the game. Late in the first period, Cashman and Sterner went hard together into the boards. Sterner brought up his stick and got Cashman in the mouth, the blade slicing through his tongue, though there were Canadian media reports that suggested he bit his tongue. Cashman remained on the bench bleeding for the rest of the period and never returned in the series.

"I just got a stick up in my face, my tongue was sliced up pretty good, and I got a cut on my face," said Cashman, who needed upwards of fifty stitches in and out of the mouth, had a badly swollen tongue, and spent the night in hospital. "One of the reasons I didn't play in the rest of the series in Moscow was I probably went five or six days without eating. When I could eat, the food over there—it was so different I couldn't put the weight back on."

Cashman lost eighteen pounds from his 180-pound frame. Years later, in 2003, hockey writer Jim Kernaghan travelled to Stockholm with the Maple Leafs for their training camp and interviewed Sterner, who claimed Cashman charged at him with his stick up. Sterner said he ducked and caught Cashman with his stick.

"He was trying to kill me," said Sterner. "He wasn't the first. [Phil] Esposito hated us and he told Cashman to go out and kill me. I didn't understand it."

"When we got to Sweden, holy Christ, it was like we were the Mafiosa, and in fact they called us the Mafiosa," said Esposito. "We played really mean in Sweden, we did, not saying that we didn't. But then again, I've never seen any injury like Cash got. It was terrible what Ulf Sterner did, spearing Cash in the mouth."

That wasn't the end of the rough stuff. There was another incident with six minutes remaining in the game. Hadfield broke the nose of defenceman Lars-Erik Sjoberg, earning himself a five-minute major penalty for high-sticking. Sjoberg had his nose splashed all over his face, while the picture of it was splashed all over the front page of the newspapers the next day. Esposito scuffled with Borje Salming, at the time a Maple Leafs prospect, in the hallway on their way to their respective dressing rooms. Even the Canadian ambassador Margaret Meagher weighed in, disgusted by the way the Canadians had played.

"It was a robust game, but it takes two to tango," said defenceman Rod Seiling. "What pulled us together even more, two things—the Swedish people were very, I'm not going to say disrespectful, but they didn't appreciate us, let's put it that way. The coup de grâce was Canada's ambassador to Sweden, she came out after the game, after Cash gets speared, and publicly roasted us in the media about how awful we were, the way we play, and we should be ashamed of ourselves and all those things. It just galvanized things."

And the score? With Esposito's short-hand goal with forty-seven seconds remaining, the game ended in a 4–4 tie.

There was also a bomb threat that night at the Canadian hotel. What else could happen?

It turned out, one more controversy and galvanizing moment before the Canadians departed for Moscow. The Canadians had received word that the wives and girlfriends would not be allowed in Moscow, or they would at least have to stay at a different hotel from the players. That news was not well received.

"There had been some question about whether we could bring their wives over to Moscow," said Sinden. "They were promised they could, but then for some reason it circulated around that they weren't going to let them do that, which wasn't true. We had to straighten that out."

"I remember a meeting at a cafeteria at the rink where we were practising," said Esposito. "Eagleson came in and told us that they didn't want the girlfriends and wives to be coming over to Russia. When Harry and Al and Fergie left the room, we just had it out amongst ourselves. We called Eagleson in and said if they don't agree to what they agreed to, then we want to get out of here. Next thing we knew we were all going to Russia."

Having his wife with him in Moscow was one of the original stipulations Park had made before agreeing to join the team back in July.

"Before we're going to Moscow, we're called into a meeting," said Park. "Harry and Eagleson tell us the Soviets have notified us our wives will not be staying at the same hotel as the team, which wasn't the original plan. They decided to change it. The games were starting. My wife, after having the baby [the day after game 1], decided to come to Moscow. Her mom was a registered nurse, so she was going to look after the baby. I was just twenty-four, so I'm looking around at the older guys for direction. Espo stands up and asks Harry and Alan to leave the room. He says, 'Guys, they don't want to honour the deal. Two options—let them run the show and put the wives in another hotel, or tell them no, honour the deal, or we're not coming.' We had a unanimous vote to tell them we're not coming. That was the first time we had a unanimous vote. We told Harry and Eagle, and they notified them we weren't coming unless they honoured the deal. They backed down and we flew to Moscow."

Despite all the other things that happened on and off the ice, and despite not playing very well in the two games, the Canadians still believed a lot was accomplished in Sweden. In the practices they were able to firm up assorted shortcomings in their game. They improved their conditioning. They spent more time together getting to know each other as people, not just players. They also got used to not only the bigger ice, but the different way the European game is played on that bigger ice, with more of a soccer mentality, in which if the Soviets, for example, didn't like how a rush was unfolding they would circle and try again. And there was a lot of body and stick interference.

Sweden also mattered because they felt deserted by their country, but somehow had pulled themselves together. And they became a much more confident and wiser team than the one that had arrived eight days earlier.

"The week in Sweden was critical," said Bobby Clarke. "We knew we were in a tough series. We knew we had to get better prepared and in better condition. If we started with any arrogance, it was long gone. Now we were just a hockey team battling against a team that was, up to that point, better than us."

"You probably have heard different stories," said Dryden. "I thought Sweden was a bit of a disaster. We played really poorly at a time when we needed to be playing better; we seemed to be regressing, and part of it was that how the Swedes played always set off Canadian teams, and did again.

"What I've heard from other players is that yes, that may be true, but that it was actually the first real time where a team had a chance to be a team. In training camp in Toronto, you're together, but you're going in a number of different directions. It's Toronto, everybody has friends in Toronto. There are things to do. There isn't the immediate urgency of a series that is about to begin; it's still a few weeks away, or just a couple of weeks away, or a week away.

"And then you get into the games in Canada and you're playing every second day and you're travelling in between and you're having to deal with what came out of the previous game. You don't have time to be a team much, either. All of a sudden in Sweden, you're around each other for a week and you're really starting to get to know the other person a little bit more and you're getting to know them in a way that you know the task ahead.

"You at least go from rivals to sharing the same space. And then you have to go from sharing the same space to becoming a team. Those things are steps to take and you usually take them circumstantially. You're put into a different situation and that forces something. Moscow certainly, you know you're up against it every way and you know that you need everybody to deal with being up against it. Even if there are barriers to being a team, you blow down the barriers because the circumstances demand it."

CHAPTER 10

To Russia with Beer

There were actually two historic summits of significance in Moscow in 1972. Both were very political in nature, although one was intended to calm a cold war, while the other was supposed to decide a question of global supremacy.

In late May, United States president Richard M. Nixon met with Soviet leader Leonid Brezhnev, who was quite the hockey fan, although that wasn't the subject of conversation. When the week-long summit was over, it ended in a draw—with the two Cold War enemies signing an anti–ballistic missile treaty, a strategic arms limitation treaty, and a joint space flight agreement. It was hoped it would be the groundwork for détente.

Meanwhile, back on the ice, there definitely was not peace in our time. Far from it. On September 20, Team Canada arrived in Moscow, two weeks after the debacle in Vancouver and following an eventful eight-day stopover in Stockholm.

"It was a war," said Brad Park. "It didn't get political for me in Canada. But it got political when we landed in Moscow. We're taxiing to the gate and there are Red Army uniformed police walking beside our plane with guns protecting the area on the tarmac. You come off the plane and there are Red Army everywhere. These guys are carrying guns. Where we should have been a delegation put right through, we had to wait once we arrived. The longer we were there, it became more political, there were more things done to us to try to throw us off, anger us. It had become more than just hockey, it was our way of life against theirs, our politics against theirs."

Game on. The Canadians had had their eyes opened on the ice, and now they were being opened off the ice, almost all of them for the first time exposed to a different culture, a different mindset, a different way of life. That different country everyone heard about on the news reels. Détente would definitely have to wait for another day.

Moscow, or *Mockba* in Russian, had a population of roughly 7.3 million at the time, and it was a much different city with a much different lifestyle than the Canadians had been exposed to, playing in Montreal, Toronto, and Vancouver in Canada, and big cities in the United States. For all the superpowers the Soviet Union possessed, its everyday existence seemed anything but modern for the times, at least by North American standards. Best put, it felt like they were stuck in the 1950s. The city was gray, the clothing was drab. Under the Communist regime, life was rigidly controlled by the state. Because of a housing shortage in the early 1950s, more than thirteen thousand apartment buildings had been constructed, housing most of the city's population in very similar-looking structures. The vast majority of the cars, and there were many of them, were Ladas—the standard Russian car of the day. Few had windshield wipers, because the drivers would keep them inside the car so they wouldn't be stolen, only installing them when it was raining or snowing.

Yet, for all its apparent dreariness, Moscow also had spectacular architecture, with the stunning and enormous Kremlin and Red Square in the heart of the city, not far from where Team Canada stayed at the Hotel Intourist. Within the Kremlin's walls were churches and palaces, home to both the leader and Lenin's tomb. Moscow was world-renowned for its subway system, which was built during the Stalin regime, each of the original stations featuring breathtaking Soviet art. Subway stops had chandeliers. There was the world-famous Moscow Circus and the Bolshoi Ballet. But amidst all the grandeur and excess and culture, there was also poverty. And there was vodka aplenty, the national drink.

To say Moscow was a culture shock for the Canadians is an understatement. It was the great unknown, preceded by its reputation, and it was right before their eyes, different in so many ways.

"When you think of that roster and ask, how many players on the team, how many Canadians, North Americans, in 1972 had been outside North America?" said Ken Dryden, who had been to Leningrad twice and to Moscow with the national team. "They may have been to the Caribbean. But how many to Europe? What percentage of North Americans had been to Europe in their lives in 1972? A very, very low percentage. Dramatically fewer had been in Eastern Europe and dramatically fewer than that in the Soviet Union.

"It was this *other*. It was a very foreign place in our minds and a threatening place in our minds. The day-to-dayness of the Cold War was over, the kind of day-to-day front pages of newspapers of the fifties. It wasn't the same in the sixties and the early seventies. But there were two powers in the world, and where it came out in a most pronounced way was in the space race and in sports. And in sports it was the Olympics, any kind of sporting confrontation between the West and the East. That's how things got played out most vividly. The rest was stories. The rest was propaganda—theirs and ours. [But there was] something beyond propaganda that couldn't be finessed and orchestrated, like whether your rockets went up or didn't, went into orbit or didn't, landed on the moon or didn't, or what the medal count was at the Olympics."

It was so extreme that in 1972 the world—mostly the Soviets and Americans—were transfixed by, of all things, a chess match, the Match of the Century—American Bobby Fischer and Soviet champion Boris Spassky. But it, too, was mired in politics and the backdrop of the Cold War. The day before the Summit Series began, Fischer became the first American to win the World Chess Championship.

"There was that as well," said Dryden. "What's the percentage of the population, especially in North America, that played chess, that had any interest in chess? This wasn't about Bobby Fischer and Boris Spassky. Up until Bobby Fischer, Americans wouldn't pay any attention to international chess as no American was going to beat the Soviet grand masters. Now there was somebody who might beat a Soviet grand master, so now there was reason to invest all of these feelings into a chess match. But of course it was Bobby Fischer, embodying America and embodying all of what America is about, and that's what was going on across the chessboard."

And then there was a chess match of sorts on the ice, still to be played out with four games in Moscow, feeling much the same.

"You have to ask each person, they may have a different idea of that," said Dryden. "It was team against team, country against country, hockey history against hockey history, way of playing against way of playing—and trying to win out of all of that. That was deep and profound and that's what it felt like to me. The stakes were high and we had to find a way of winning this series."

Because of the time and because the Soviets had a history of subterfuge, because there was a certain degree of naïveté amongst the Canadians and perhaps even because they were feeling this was more than just a hockey series, the Moscow experience was different and bizarre and even scary for them.

"I know some of the guys were paranoid," said Clarke. "But I never got into that. I was just there to play hockey. I actually enjoyed walking around Moscow. It was clean. The people were friendly. I got yelled at more walking around the streets of Toronto than I did there. Let's be honest, the hijinks that happened over there didn't come from the Russian players, and it had zero effect on what was happening on the ice and the outcomes in the games."

When they arrived at the Hotel Intourist, after touching down in the night, they were greeted by their wives and girlfriends, and some fathers and mothers, who ultimately were allowed in the country and to stay in the same hotel. Some of the partners and parents were less than impressed with the accommodations and apparently not pleased with what they had read about the players' nightlife in Stockholm. The team was also greeted by several of the first wave of roughly three thousand Canadian fans who had made the trek.

Mickey Redmond's father, Eddie, had played with head coach Harry Sinden on the Whitby Dunlops when they won the Allan Cup in 1957 and 1959 and represented Canada at the 1958 World Championship in Oslo, Norway, during which Canada defeated the Soviets to clinch the gold. Eddie and Sinden were defence partners until Eddie got hurt in that game against the Soviets. Eddie didn't make the trip, but he urged Mickey to invite his mom, May, to Moscow, which he did. The Mahovlich brothers did the same with their mom, Cecilia.

"They roomed together," said Redmond, who only played in the first game. "They enjoyed their time in Moscow so much."

Even so, the accommodations were at or near the top of the Canadians' complaint list. The hotel was supposed to be amongst the best in the city, new and twenty-two floors tall, though it did have the feeling of a college dorm and the rooms could be somewhat spartan. In some of the rooms, the beds were assembled in an L shape, and nailed to the floor so they couldn't be moved and the couples couldn't sleep together.

"I went back about twenty-five years later on a scouting trip and talk about change," said Peter Mahovlich. "The hotel was so close to Red Square, there was little traffic, it was a very stoic setting. It was brand new, but the Royal York is the Royal York. This was not the Royal York."

"I've always maintained to this day, and I've been back at least three times, it should be mandatory for every Canadian to go to Russia at least once," said defenceman Rod Seiling. "As great a country as we have, people would appreciate how good we all have it. The hotel was supposed to be their best, I doubt it. It was crap. Your bed was a piece of plywood with a mattress about an inch and a half thick. That was it. The streets were cleaned by old grandmothers with sawed-off corn brooms. The GUM store, their big department store, was like the worst Kmart you could possibly imagine. There were lineups to get into any place. That was life in Moscow."

"Our hotel room was very cold," said winger Ron Ellis. "We filled the bathtub with hot water to get a little warmth. I think some of it was just their way of life. Whenever we were waiting for a bus, it would always be a half-hour, forty-five-minute wait. We all said they're just trying to get us upset, but I think part of it is that's the way things happened in Russia at that time. But it felt like there were a lot of things going on."

Indeed, real or imagined, a lot of the players, whose knowledge of the country was limited to what they had read in spy novels, had a sense they were being watched, spied on. And they probably were.

They thought the KGB, the Soviet's secret police, were positioned in the hotel lobby or as floor monitors, which they no doubt were. Some thought their hotel rooms were bugged.

"I wasn't scared because you know the world is watching," said Park. "So, that couldn't take it to a place where people could be phys-ically hurt. Everyone has stories about their rooms. I had an intercom in my room. You could play music, there were four stations on it. At night when I went to bed, I would turn it off, and in the middle of the night it would come back on. I'd turn it off; next thing the phone would ring. It was designed to throw off my rest time. It happened more than once. One day we were going to go to the Bolshoi Ballet. We get on the bus with our wives, they come and tell us the wives have to go on a different bus. We got up and started walking off with our wives. We told them we weren't going, but fifteen minutes later they let us go. Two days later, we're going to the Moscow Circus, same thing, another fifteen minutes before they caved in. Those types of challenges, the ineptness of their society, or it was coming down from a higher level—it stuck in our craw a bit."

Perhaps the most famous, or infamous, tale of a player feeling watched became known over time as the great chandelier story.

"What the Soviets did to us was try to undermine our spirit and throw us off our game," said Seiling. "Of course, the stories about the rooms being bugged, about Frank [Mahovlich] thinking his room was being bugged, pulling up the carpet, seeing some screws and unscrewing them, and a chandelier in the ballroom flying down . . ."

There were other stories about Frank being so psyched out about the Russians that he suggested the team take tents and camp outside the city. As far the chandelier story . . . there are many versions.

"The truth is, that was a made-up story that has been told so much it's evolved into something that 'actually' happened," said Peter.

"Frank said two things back then. First, they're playing us because they think they can beat us. Second, they will be spying on us. There was a lot of nonsense going on. Practice times changed, fire alarms, phone calls in the middle of the night. But that's just fluff. It didn't matter. I didn't need any sleep anyway.

"I came up with the story that my brother was up in room 603, and I was in 503. Frank complained about being bugged. So we make up this story. Frank said, 'Last night I was taking a shower, and I was walking across the carpet, and I feel something underneath the carpet. I peel back the carpet, and finally, there's that bug. So I got my wife's scissors, and I cut the damn bug and cut the wires.'

"I said to Frank, 'What time was that?' He said, 'Around midnight.' I said, 'That's when the chandelier fell on my head.' So that's how that story started. Frank was paranoid about it, though. Our parents were Yugoslavian. They got out before World War II and the country became Communist. We knew the Soviets would do anything to win."

Not all was bad, of course. They did attend the Bolshoi Ballet and the Moscow Circus and museums, though always with some form of inconvenience and eye-opening experience.

"We drove around the city on a tour, there were no single-family homes, it was all apartment buildings," said Park. "We got on the bus after practice one day, there were kids outside the bus clamoring. We were throwing out sticks of gum and the kids were scooping them up. One Red Army guy comes over and steps on one of the kid's hands. Within a few seconds, two or three of us have the Red Army guy up against the bus and J. P. Parise is looking in his face, shaking his head, saying 'NO. You don't step on a kid's hand because he's reaching for gum.'"

"We were totally shocked," said Henderson. "One of the worst memories—the museums were incredible, no question—we went to this museum and there had to be at least five hundred Russians lined up to get in and it was a cold bloody day. We drive up in our bus, we got off, and the guards go up with their rifles and push the people back and let us go in in front of them. I didn't want to go in. I just felt so bad for these people. How can you be treated like that in your own country? If you weren't a Communist you were a piece of crap. I remember we were on the bus, driving into Moscow the first time, and I never saw a house. The apartment buildings, there was a light hanging down, there wasn't even a shade on the light, it was so spartan it was eerie.

"I was thinking, honest to God, if we don't stop these Russians, for God's sake, if this ever came to our country. But I came home from that, and I said to a lot of people, if I owned a company I would take my people over there, I would pay for the trip, spend four or five days and bring them back. They would never complain about Canada again in their life."

"We weren't supposed to go anywhere without a watcher with us," said Seiling. "Now, the wives weren't as closely watched. My wife, Sharon, happened to go with a bunch of them to Lenin's tomb, and she put a "Go Canada Go" sticker on Lenin's tomb and told me afterwards. I'm thinking, 'Ah shit, it looks like we're leaving the country early.' Whatever they had, they said this is the best, this is the best, whether it was the subway system, which was pretty good, the best buses, the best hotels, everything's the best. You just turn it off. On the off nights they took us to the opera, to the circus, we had downtime, but there wasn't much to do in between. There wasn't a lot of downtime, but there was some. You weren't allowed to go anywhere, and what there was, well, it was so third-rate why would you want to go anyway? They were world-renowned for the opera, the circus, and the ballet—they did have a number of world-class attractions, but that was it. You just had to go outside and look at the people. It was pretty sad. If not poverty, then pretty close to it. It's not someplace you'd even want to send your worst enemy."

The other big complaint was with the food. The Canadians had shipped over hundreds of steaks that either started to disappear or were cut in half, leaving them to mostly eat what was not exactly appetizing local fare.

"I was back to Moscow a number of years ago," said Seiling. "I was sitting at a table and we got talking about 1972 and our beer disappearing, our steaks being cut in half, and I'm sitting at the table with this gentleman and he says 'Oh, yeah that's all true—I was selling it on the black market.' I remember [Canadian businessman] Irv Ungerman and his brother, who were big in the poultry business in Toronto, brought two smoked turkeys to Moscow with them. They gave one to the team, and it ended up in Tony Esposito's room and word got around. Before long, all that was left was a pile of bones, the guys were so hungry. The food there was awful to eat. But we persevered. We had been warned these things would happen, but I think it helped to stiffen our resolve that we are going to win."

As for the Soviet players, they were hearing the stories and the complaints and were alternately amused and bemused. And they had no part in any of it—real or imagined.

"We had great respect for them," said Tretiak. "We came to show our hockey. There were no provocations. I know Canadians have said that they had to unscrew chandeliers thinking they were bugged . . ."

"And someone ate their meat and drank their beer," added Yakushev.

"Well . . . the meat part might be true, but not bugging through chandeliers," said Tretiak. "Who would listen? And for what purpose? Someone abroad wanted to exaggerate the situation. I'll say it again, we never mixed sports with politics."

Despite the Canadians' complaints, there were some lighter moments to help break the tension.

"Bill White and Pat Stapleton were quite the characters," said defenceman Dale Tallon. "They told Bill Goldsworthy they had satellite television in their room. Bill was a huge Minnesota Vikings [NFL] fan, and during our time in Moscow the Vikings were going to play a Monday night game. I think [Goldsworthy] stayed up half the night trying to find the channel. But they kept everyone loose."

"One night Whitey Stapleton says, 'Guys, I found a Chinese restaurant and we're all going there, we've gotta go,'" said Phil Esposito. "A bunch of us, I was one of them, he told us where to go, three blocks this way and two blocks that way. We started walking and we didn't find anything. After a while we came back, and Whitey was in the lobby with a bunch of people, including fans, and they all started to laugh at us. They sent us on a wild goose chase. At the time, I went to him, 'Whitey, you son of a bitch, do you know how hungry I am?' But it was funny. Everyone laughed. It was good for team spirit."

"There wasn't a restaurant anywhere near our hotel," said Peter Mahovlich. "The Chicago guys liked to have their fun. Tony Esposito was miserable, but still a good guy. But between Dennis Hull, Pat Stapleton, and Bill White, boy, they liked to have fun."

"Pat and Bill White were not only an excellent defence pairing for us, they were funny buggers," said centre Bobby Clarke. "All the good teams had players like that, who kept things loose and kept you looking around for the next joke or prank."

But there was something that remained no laughing matter. While the players and coaches and management had their steaks either disappear or be sawed in half, the wives and girlfriends and parents were stuck eating the local cuisine and were none too pleased about it.

"Our wives were forced to eat their [Soviet] food because we didn't bring over enough food for them, which was a mistake on our part, and our food was disappearing anyway," said Park. "They were getting the worst food in the world, soup with fish heads, stuff like that. It may be great by somebody's standards, but . . . So the biggest mistake [the Soviets] made as far as antagonizing us was this: the last thing you should do is piss off the wife of a Canadian hockey player, because if you piss off the wife of a Canadian hockey player, *she's* going to make sure that *he's* pissed!"

And you don't take a Canadian hockey player's beer. That's offside.

CHAPTER 11

Deserters

Whatever bonding and team building that Team Canada believed it had achieved in Sweden would soon be challenged yet again the day before game 5 in Moscow. Then again, that bond might only have been further strengthened.

After a few weeks of whispers (and sometimes louder noises) of discontent about playing time—some even went so far as to call it a mutiny—the big skate finally dropped. At practice in Moscow at the Luzhniki Ice Palace, coach Harry Sinden gathered his team at centre ice and announced the lineup for game 5 the next night. Vic Hadfield, who had played in Sweden with his GAG line mates—Jean Ratelle and Rod Gilbert—was not one of the names included on the roster. Frank Mahovlich, who had remained at home during the Swedish excursion, tending to a sore knee, had joined the team in Moscow and would play. That was enough for Hadfield, who was already unhappy during the games in Canada, especially after being scratched for game 2 in Toronto, and had almost left the team back then. He was further annoyed that Sinden hadn't told him privately.

Sinden and Ferguson had finally made the decision they were going to reduce the roster and ride those players through the four games in the Soviet Union. The rest could stay or go. Alan Eagleson and Sinden had delivered that very message a few days earlier in Stockholm when Sinden felt there was an open revolt happening. As many as fifteen players met after that practice to decide whether they would leave the team and return to their NHL training camps. Apparently, most said they would, but the next morning only Hadfield (some say at Sinden's urging), Richard Martin, and Jocelyn Guevremont got on the bus to the airport. Martin and Guevremont had additional reasons for leaving: both were feeling pressure to return to their teams, the Buffalo Sabres and the Vancouver Canucks respectively, and in the case of Guevremont, who insisted he was told at training camp he wouldn't be playing at all in the series, his wife had taken ill back home. After playing well in game 4 and again in the fifth game, Gilbert Perreault later joined the exodus.

"I was very young at the time," Perreault said years later. "My entire career was in front of me. I knew there would be another chance for me to play in a series like this. I talked it over with Harry before I left. I wasn't upset or mad, I just wanted to get ready for the season opener. I was very proud of those guys."

To this day, Perreault refuses to take part in team events, insisting he was not part of the team and the win after leaving.

In his book, *Thunder and Lightning*, assistant coach John Ferguson, who passed away in July 2007, wrote that the blow-up with Sinden was "an innocent oversight," adding "Perreault gave us the same applesauce that the three other quitters did, he wanted to rejoin his NHL team."

So now the team was down to thirty-one players. Others had never made the trip, such as Billy Harris, who was part of the team early on to fill numbers for scrimmages. He instead went to his first NHL training camp with the New York Islanders. The likes of

Stan Mikita, Dennis Hull, Brian Glennie, Don Awrey, Dale Tallon, Mickey Redmond, and Marcel Dionne, amongst others, who had played a little or not at all, opted to stay, including the injured Bobby Orr. Some of them weren't very happy, but they stayed nonetheless.

"They decided to name twenty guys who were going to play in the final four games," said Hadfield. "The guys who weren't going to play weren't even going to be allowed to practise. In the summer, I had signed a five-year contract [with the Rangers], so if I wasn't even going to be allowed to practise or play, I had second thoughts. The guys who weren't going to be playing met with [Alan] Eagleson. They made the arrangements for us to go home to our NHL teams. We were supposed to meet in the lobby the next day and only four of us showed up. Mikita decided to stay because he wanted to visit his homeland after the series. Team Canada was going to play an exhibition game in Czechoslovakia on the way home.

"Eagleson was supposed to call a press conference to explain everything, why we were leaving, how Harry and John decided to go with twenty players the rest of the way, and that we were going to go home. But Eagleson never did follow through on the press conference."

So, when no official explanation was offered, when the players returned to Canada, the media and the fans were not kind. In some ways the veteran Hadfield was caught in the middle—stay and not play, which doesn't look good on the resumé, or leave and, along with the others, be portrayed as a deserter.

"[Eagleson and I] had a little bit of a disagreement right from the start when he was named head of the Players' Association [in 1967] and we were at a golf tournament in Toronto [at Lambton]," said Hadfield. "It was a shotgun tournament, and four or five groups were walking together back up the eighteenth. We were all firing questions at Al about different issues as we walked back to the club-house. The next thing we knew, a few weeks later, every one of us who walked up the eighteenth fairway with Al received an invoice for his knowledge. That just sent me off with him.

"I don't have any regrets, I did what I thought I had to do. I wanted to get back to the Rangers and get ready for the season. I didn't like that we were called deserters in the papers. But Eagleson didn't do his part. He never called that press conference to handle everything, to explain why were leaving."

Though happy they would be playing the remainder of the series themselves, Hadfield's Ranger teammates were sad to see him go, and they knew how he would be perceived by the media and public.

"I felt bad for him," said Ratelle. "I felt bad that it didn't work out for him and that he went home. When Harry called me in the summer to play for Canada, he mentioned that he was going to try and play everybody. We had a lot of good centres. You look at a guy like Perreault. He didn't play much. I figured if I played two or three games, took a trip to Moscow, it would be a nice way to spend some time.

"Harry and John Ferguson decided after we got behind the eight ball to keep going with the same team, win or lose. That way we could play together more. It's not just a [forward] line that has to get used to each other. The forwards and the defence have to get used to each other. It's very important to have good chemistry between the defence and forwards because you have to know what your defence is going to do in your own end. I think the more we played together, the more we stayed out of our end and played more in their end.

"Before he left, the three of us—Rod, Vic, and myself—did sit down to talk. Vic told us that if he wasn't going to play, he was going home. We supported him. It was a tough decision. But we understood."

"I understood why," said Rod Seiling, who sat out some games himself. "Was I disappointed? Of course. But I understood what was going on."

As for the rest of Team Canada, they weren't overly rattled by the turn of events. In fact, it may have been a relief.

"The team stuck together," said centre Bobby Clarke. "The complaints from some of the players about not getting enough ice time weren't unusual in those days. But if you were playing, like I was, I wasn't concerned about the complaints coming from Vic Hadfield because he wasn't playing. He could say whatever he wanted, but it wasn't going to affect how I was playing. I don't blame those guys for leaving. It was good they left. 'Good, get out of here. You're not helping us.'"

"This was the issue," said Peter Mahovlich. "Everyone in camp was promised they would play in at least one game. But after that first game, that seemed to go out the window. I don't think Marcel Dionne, Rick Martin, and Dale Tallon ever played a game. But it was after that first game [in Moscow] that we started to get player dissent. That's when Gilbert Perreault, who only played in a couple of games and was very good, decided to go home with Rick Martin and Jocelyn Guevremont. [Buffalo Sabres GM] Punch Imlach said to them, 'If you're not going to play, you may as well come home and get ready for the season.'

"Vic Hadfield was coming off a fifty-goal season. If you looked back in 1972 and thought, 'Who is going to be a problem, and who is not going to be a problem,' the first person you would think who wouldn't be a problem would be Vic Hadfield. Rod Gilbert, maybe. But Jean Ratelle, absolutely not.

"Jean Ratelle was Jean Ratelle—no problem. Rod Gilbert was the perfect teammate. He worked his ass off. Vic Hadfield was different. But your competitive juices get flowing. You want to get in there. You want to help the team. A lot of people got upset at Vic for leaving, but I wasn't upset with him. I understood.

"But when the players left, that united us more."

David Honsberger, an administrator with the current 1972 alumni group, had a different perspective. He was a close friend of defenceman Pat Stapleton, who died in April 2020. "Pat used to talk a great deal about the significant roles that a few of the players undertook, who remained with the team throughout the series yet never played any games against the Soviets. They were Marcel Dionne, Dale Tallon, and Brian Glennie. They all did play in exhibition games in Stockholm and Prague. The players wanted to get in a game desperately and competed fiercely in practice trying to earn a spot in a game. As a result, it raised the intensity and the compete level in practice so that the players who were already in the lineup had to work that much harder to keep their spots.

"Pat felt that their contributions should not be understated. We also had some great eyes in the sky. We know what a great hockey mind Red Berenson has. Red only dressed for two games [games 1 and 6], but he closely observed and evaluated the series, dissecting the Soviets' play. He would rush to the dressing room after periods to relay his thoughts. He was especially excited after the game five loss, believing that we could win this series."

At thirty-two, Berenson was the fourth oldest player on Team Canada. He had played in three consecutive Stanley Cup finals (1968–70). He was also just one of a handful of Team Canada players with international experience, having played with the Belleville McFarlands, who won the 1959 IIHF World Championship in Prague.

"They had to make changes after losing the first game the way we did," said Berenson. "They made changes and we won in Toronto and tied in Winnipeg. It seemed we were going in the right direction, but, of course, the game in Vancouver was a real downer. So it wasn't about me not playing; it was about us not doing well."

Berenson did return to the lineup for game 6 in Moscow, and his reappearance seemed like something of a surprise. After that game he volunteered to sit out the final two games.

"I think Harry was reaching for guys who could help," he said. "I skated well. I could kill penalties. I could keep up with the pace. I played a decent game. After the game, I talked to Harry and told him he has to go with the guys who were playing, who were starting to round into game shape at that point in the series."

"Stockholm was very important," said Henderson. "We needed those two games to get used to the big ice, but that's also when it was starting to look like who was going to play and who wasn't going to play. Without that, we really would have been in trouble."

Some of the players, including Dionne, decided to stay in part because they were clients of Eagleson. That could have been messy, although Dionne claimed his agent helped explain what was happening. Others simply realized they had a front-row seat for something very special, something historical happening—no matter how the series ended.

"To be included with all that talent and play for your country was quite an honour," said goaltender Eddie Johnston, who dressed for several games but played in just one game in Stockholm, a 4–4 tie. At thirty-six, two months shy of his thirty-seventh birthday, Johnston was the oldest player on Team Canada. The thought of quitting never seriously crossed his mind.

"We all would like to play in every game," said winger Mickey Redmond, who only played in the series opener. "But that's not the way it worked out for me. The number one rule when we arrived at training camp was to check our egos at the door for the team and country. You want to be a good soldier. You know they're going to go with the best players. To be part of this group was an honour."

In fairness to all, the size of the roster, the promise to play, the trip to Sweden that was supposed to be a vacation, not a training camp, even the one-game exhibition in Prague after the tournament, had all been conceived essentially on the basis of one firm belief: the series was not going to be overly challenging for Team Canada. And it was during that bonding time in Sweden that the hard decision was made, and had to be made.

"Thank goodness for that break in Sweden," said Ron Ellis. "I hate to think what would have happened if we went straight from Vancouver to Moscow. Sweden allowed us to become a team, and management made a decision: we're down in this series, we're going to have to go with a set lineup. Team management knew we were an all-star team, we weren't a team in the true sense of the word. That changed in Sweden. The animosities between players and egos all had to be left outside the dressing room, and that's how we proceeded. Unfortunately, when they made the decision to go with a set lineup from that point on, that's when the dissension took hold, because players realized they weren't going to play. It had to be done. We couldn't compete against the Russians without a set group of guys, it just wouldn't work."

"It took a long time for Harry to make that decision and go with a team," said Phil Esposito. "When we got to Russia, he did that. What I respect is that he wanted to make sure that everybody was going to get a chance. I respected that. On the other hand, are we playing to win, or not? That was the question I asked, are we playing to win? We had a lot of conversations with Harry and Fergie. What the fuck were they going to do to me? We won the Stanley Cup, I won the scoring championship, I finished third to Bobby [Orr] for MVP that year [Dryden was second], what the fuck are they going to do to me? Tell me I can't play, fine. They're not paying us.

"So somebody had to talk, speak up. Brad Park started to, Serge Savard I'm sure—can't prove it—talked to Fergie a lot because they were good friends. I told Harry and Fergie many times, I felt bad for the players who weren't playing. People ask me about Hadfield, Guevremont, Martin, and Perreault all leaving, I said I don't blame them one iota. If I wasn't playing, do you think I wanted to stay in Moscow, where you couldn't leave the hotel, can't do anything, can't go anywhere, can't see anyone?"

As disquieting as the departures may have been in the moment, a distraction had been removed. That narrative was gone. It brought some closure for a smaller, closer Team Canada with a mammoth task at hand. And as Sinden said, the loss of those players really wasn't going to hurt the team anyway because they weren't going to play.

Last word to Dennis Hull, who after retirement became an after-dinner speaker, and a hilarious one at that. One night at a Team Canada reunion, which Hadfield attended, Hull couldn't resist a little poke: "We were having [a reunion] dinner, and after the salad, I said, 'Vic left.'"

Pickering land deals costing taxpayers millions

By TOM HAZLITT and PETER MOON
Star staff writers

See PICKERING, page 2

The Toronto Star

• THE CANADIAN • COLOR COMICS • STAR WEEK

Saturday edition

METRO WEATHER

ESTABLISHED 1892   August paid circulation Mon. to Fri. 454,387, Sat. 883,240   ****   Saturday, September 23, 1972—252 pages   Monday-Friday 10c; Saturday 25c; Home delivery 75c

---

Price $6 billion

Arctic pipeline: Nation's future may hinge on it

★ David Crane (left) of The Star's Ottawa bureau today begins a 5-part series on the plan to transport natural gas across half a continent —an undertaking described by some observers as rivalling in importance the building of the Canadian Pacific Railway.

By DAVID CRANE
Star staff writer

OTTAWA —

See ARCTIC, page 4

LITTLE MISS APPEALING

When I grow up I'm going to be beautiful, just like you . . . Little Elizabeth Gilroy, 3, could possibly be a future Miss United Appeal, just like 20-year-old Arlene Ackerman of Dell Park Ave. Arlene, studying social work at McMaster University, Hamilton, won the title last evening at Simpson's Downtown Store out of 12 contestants, each nominated by UA agencies. Afterwards was just shopping with her mom.

Cheered on Prairies

PM predicts $1.1 billion wheat sales

By JACK CAHILL
Star staff writer

SWIFT CURRENT, Sask.

See PRAIRIE, page 8

Sinden analyzes loss: Soviets 'never let up'

By TRENT FRAYNE
Star staff writer

MOSCOW —

See SOVIET, page 2

ALL FRENCH GIRLS OF 21 CAN NOW BE 'MADAME'

Special to The Star

PARIS —

See SOVIET, page 2

Works on animals, scientist says

New cancer treatment claimed

OAK RIDGE, Tenn. (UPI) —

See NEW, page 2

Births, adoptions, deaths and in memoriam notices appear on page 37.

First Ugandan refugees arrive in city

By ANNE MOON
Star staff writer

Ugandan soldiers invade Tanzania

KAMPALA, Uganda (Reuter-UPI) —

See FIRST, page 5

The Toronto Star

The story behind an election slogan

• NDP LEADER David Lewis has coined the phrase "corporate welfare bums" to describe corporations which get tax concessions. Should these corporations be abolished? How do they work? Why do they exist? Insight explores these questions by covering the hottest election slogan of the moment. Page 12.

• A WARNING: The size of the value of your home may mean your home is not insured for its real worth. Torontonians who bought houses 5 years ago may be under-insured by as much as 15,000 because of the increase in house prices. Page 25.

• THE RAPID CHANGE in the price of shares in Rapid Data Systems Equipment Ltd. has the experts puzzled and investors worried. And Rapid Data has become the most talked about small company in Canada. Page 41.

• PENNY-PINCHING: Sara and Pat Cook have evolved what is virtually a post-graduate course in penny-pinching. The Cooks, who have two children, are both attending Toronto universities, And they've had to find a way to live frugally. How they do it is described on page 101.

Ann Landers		Jim Proudfoot	
Apartments to Rent		Jumble Puzzle	
Births and Deaths		Leisure	
Books		Movies	
Bridge		Peter Desbarats	
Classified		Races	
Comics		Radio-TV	
Crossword		Real Estate	
Editorials		Religion	
Entertainment		Star Probe	
Family		Sports	
Financial		Today's Child	
Help Wanted		Travel	
Insight		TV Changes	
Jack McArthur		Want Ads	

Against the backdrop of a federal election, a hockey series gone wrong for Team Canada was becoming political in its own way. (Courtesy of the *Toronto Star*)

CHAPTER 12

Game 5—Ready, Willing, and Unable

"It's very difficult speaking about the fans giving up on us," said coach Harry Sinden. "But in our minds we felt that was the position we were in going into Moscow."

Sinden appreciated the adoration that came when the series was over, of course, but in the moment that was the sentiment of the team. As they prepared for the first game in Moscow, the mentality was less Canada against the Soviet Union, and more just Team Canada versus the Soviet Union. That may sound a bit melodramatic, but the stakes were as high as the emotions when the fifth game of the series arrived on September 22.

When they had left Vancouver fourteen days earlier, some of the players admitted they felt hurt and ashamed of being a Canadian, that the media had turned the fans against them, and they sarcastically suggested they might get a warmer reception in Moscow. Turns out they were right.

That feeling of abandonment and loneliness dissipated when the Canadians arrived at the Luzhniki Ice Palace, which was filled to capacity with roughly fifteen thousand fans—but close to three thousand of them Canadians, noisy Canadians with leather lungs, armed with bells and horns.

In this new setting, the boos that echoed from Vancouver and the bite of the near-empty airport in Toronto when they departed—all of that had suddenly changed to seemingly unwavering support and cheers.

"After they lost in Canada, people knew I was still going, but they were saying 'You're spending all that money to go over, they didn't have good games here,'" said Marie Garraway (née Keenan), who grew up near Whitby, Ontario, a suburb of Toronto. "I just said, we're going to support them, this is a big tournament. Growing up in a hockey family, I never gave it a second thought. People had old plastic horns and they would blow them and wave their flags. The people who went there were true Canadian fans, who wanted to support their team for sure."

"They meant a lot to us," said goaltender Ken Dryden. "They were great. They were amazing. When you're three thousand and you're on the road, you sound like twenty thousand. And they were fantastic. This was just amazing to take in."

It is widely held that the support Team Canada was receiving could be traced back to Vancouver and that emotional post-game speech Phil Esposito had given to the country on national television, during which he reprimanded the fans for turning on the team, telling them how hard the players were trying, how much they had sacrificed and cared, how good the Soviets were, but to not lose faith.

"You look back and Phil giving that incredible speech," said Paul Henderson. "I didn't see the interview until after the series was over and I thought holy crap, we should have seen that back then. That's when the fans woke up. We were over there [in Moscow], we had telegrams and postcards, bags and bags of them. Someone said at one point there were ten thousand of them, the telegrams and postcards. The trainers taped them to the wall in the hallway outside our dressing room. The wall was covered. That had an impact on us. And we wouldn't have won it without those three thousand Canadians."

The groundswell of support may have been inspired by Esposito's words, maybe it was a country-wide fear of losing, but the fans in the stands had booked and paid for their trip long before that. Regardless, it was at this point that the players truly realized they were still playing for Canada. They had been acutely aware of the political underbelly of the series, of pride and bragging rights. But now it really felt like they were playing for themselves as Canadians and for the Canadian fans.

"The fans were fabulous," said defenceman Rod Seiling. "You talk about a sixth man, they were great. Remember, we weren't very popular at home and we all knew it, but to have them come over and be as boisterous and vocal as they were, they were great."

There was even one fan with a trumpet, which the Soviet officials quickly determined was a huge annoyance.

"Do you remember," Seiling continued, "the guy in the Montreal Forum, who played the trumpet before faceoffs? Well, he went to Moscow." (Actually, Pierre Plouffe only filled in for a friend occasionally at the Forum, stirring up the Canadiens faithful, but same idea.) "The Soviets threw him out after the first game. When we went to Montreal to play, I hated when he played that thing because he got the fans going, he got the Canadiens going. Well, he's playing in Moscow and we can hear it. When he plays it, the Soviet army are in the building, running up and down trying to get it, and the fans would pass it around and hide it. When there was a stoppage in play, we would hear him on the trumpet playing 'Charge!' This went on the whole game, him playing the trumpet and the army trying to get their hands on it."

The behaviour and enthusiasm of the Canadian fans was, to say the least, new to the Soviet fans, who dressed in dark suits, almost sombre tones. There was very little cheering from them during the play and no booing. They expressed their displeasure, usually with what they perceived as roughhouse play by the Canadians, with a chorus of whistles. Part of the subdued nature of the crowd was because most of them were political officials on their best behaviour, or as one Soviet player put it, they didn't know much about the game. Some Canadian fans could relate to that these days with the lower bowl corporate seats in NHL arenas.

"We never expected that," said Sinden of the fans. "They were all around and about Moscow, too. A couple got into trouble in the bars and we heard about those. But it was great to know we had people there to cheer for us, especially in the position we were in at that time."

"Having those fans there, it was huge," said Phil Esposito. "I can't explain how huge it was. Those people made more noise than all the Russians combined. It was unbelievable."

The Luzhniki arena was different than any of the NHL arenas for a variety of reasons. Obviously, the ice size was different, the rink a dozen feet wider, though the length was roughly the same. There was more space behind the goal and the corners were squarer than traditional rinks back home. There was netting behind each goal, no glass. And there wasn't any glass along the side boards. Behind the boards was what could best be described as a moat: a wide space from the ice surface to the first row of seats, which were actually benches. In an odd twist, the Soviets had sold ads on the boards to Canadian companies, while in the games in Canada the boards remained empty and white.

"The netting behind the goal was unpredictable," said Brad Park. "The puck would spring off it. You wouldn't get a true bounce off it. You wouldn't try to rim the puck because there was no guarantee where it would go. And the stands set back twelve to fifteen feet from the boards, all the way around the rink, lined by the Red Army, that was interesting. And no glass on the sides of the rink, we had to adjust how we moved the puck up and out."

And then there was the presidential box, in which Leonid Brezhnev, the general secretary of the Communist Party (the most powerful man in the country) sat grim-faced—even when the game was going well—with Alexei Kosygin, the premier of the Soviet Union, and President Nikolai Podgorny. Perhaps it was a sign of just how important this series was to the Soviets, especially for their propaganda machine. Then again, there had been no shortage of politicians in the seats at the Forum on opening night. It mattered to both countries.

Lineup-wise, Sinden had taken Don Awrey out on defence and replaced him with Guy Lapointe, who was again heathy and a new dad. Up front, Bill Goldsworthy, Dennis Hull, and Vic Hadfield (who had now left the team) were scratched, replaced by Jean Ratelle, Peter Mahovlich, and J. P. Parise. Tony Esposito started in goal.

The Soviets made two lineup changes, adding Alexander Gusev and Yuri Liapkin to the blue line, both of them good offensively. Many years later, the book *1972: The Summit Series*, by Richard J. Bendell et al., revealed that the Soviets might have taken their foot off the pedal a little bit upon their return home. While Team Canada spent eight days in Sweden, several of the Soviet players were returned to their club teams to play in the *Sovetzky Sport* playoff round. Those whose teams had already been eliminated were given a week off. After an intense six-week training camp leading up to the tournament, time away during the two-week break was quite unexpected. The Soviets didn't resume practising as a team until three days before game 5.

"Our coaches let us go a bit too much," said goaltender Tretiak. "They should have been a bit tougher with us. We figured that, if we could play such good hockey on the small rinks and beat such a strong team, then on the bigger surface in Moscow we were 100 percent certain that we would win."

If there was a difference in the series from when it began three weeks earlier, until where it was now for Team Canada, it was that they were much better prepared than on opening night in Montreal. No overconfidence by this time, there was a well-earned respect. No more surprises, either. Now they knew what they were facing, how good the Soviets were. They knew how they cycled the puck, what their forecheck was like, their special teams, and just how good the twenty-year-old Tretiak was in net.

Despite trailing 2-1-1 in the series, despite being behind the Iron Curtain, and all the attendant distractions and emotions that might add to the task at hand, strangely enough Team Canada had a quiet confidence going into the fifth game.

"We had a good practice week in Sweden, where we really trained pretty hard on the big surface, which was important for the games in Moscow," said Sinden. "That's why we did it, to spend some time on the big surface. We were [now] relatively equal to them in the conditioning process, maybe not quite, but close. I talked to a lot of the players to get their thoughts and ideas and they weren't worried, either. Especially after the games in Canada, they knew there was an awful lot on the line in the remaining games, which included their reputations. They weren't talking about it, but there's no doubt when you're playing in the best league in the world and you're one of the best players in that league and then you find some other team that can beat you, that's quite a blow to everybody's ego and I think they came to grips with that. That helped us."

Prior to each game there was a ceremonial exchanging of gifts between the teams. At the start of game 5, Team Canada was presented with a gift of a loaf of bread, which was a welcoming gesture of hospitality. All the players lined up across the blue line and each was presented with a bouquet of flowers by a group of school-age figure skaters. When Phil Esposito was introduced, he took a stride forward, stepped on a fallen flower petal, promptly slipped, and fell on his butt. Thud. An omen, perhaps?

"We all laughed," said Sinden. "Knowing Phil, we had to take ten seconds to evaluate whether it was intentional or not. We had to think about it, but we all came up with the answer that it wasn't intentional."

"Or, did he have a heart attack!" joked Esposito. "I did slip, no doubt about it. But when I did—it was a split-second reaction—I looked up and I made perfect eye contact with Brezhnev. I waved my arm and blew him a kiss. I put my glove to my lips and waved. The guy beside him started to laugh. Brezhnev looked at him and he stopped laughing. The guys said they were going to send him to Siberia! Then I started to screw around, hold on to the boards, stuff like that when I was being introduced."

"It loosened the mood a little bit, broke the tension, but once the puck dropped it was all business," said defenceman Brad Park, who was standing close to the fallen Esposito and reached out to help him up. It was a seemingly innocent gesture, but it was also an important sign of the times. Park and Esposito were NHL rivals and hadn't particularly liked each other in the beginning, but in this moment they were teammates, one helping up the other.

In many ways, Esposito may have taken a great fall, but in Moscow he continued the business of picking up the team. He had become the heart and soul of the club. No player had officially been designated as captain, but it was quite apparent who the leader was on Team Canada, and he was intent on willing his team to victory.

"Espo brought that team together and played the best hockey he could possibly play," said Bobby Clarke.

Feeling better about their game and their conditioning, Team Canada started well, putting pressure on the Soviets and forcing mistakes, and they led 1–0 after the first period. Perreault used his speed to barge into the Soviets' zone, drew a couple defenders, and made a nifty backhand pass into the slot to Parise, who beat Vladislav Tretiak at 15:30. They had a few more good chances in that period, but couldn't convert. But the start certainly added to the confidence with which they entered the game.

"We were on the bigger surface and we had made adjustments," said Park. "When you're killing a penalty, don't go to the corner, because you can't get back to the front of the net in time. We changed some of our systems, how we were going to do things in special situations. The bigger ice surface was good for their criss-crossing system. They can play more of an east-west game than we could in the NHL. We had a very experienced defence. We knew eventually when they hit our blue line they'd be coming down a lane. We were experienced and patient enough to wait for them and be there. I think it surprised them. It didn't matter how many times they went east-west, when they got to our blue line we stood up."

"Their defencemen were very good and very strong," said Alexander Yakushev. "It was difficult to play our game against such a defence. All the more because of the physical nature of it. Canadian defencemen loved to check, particularly into the boards. It's not that it was the first time that we experienced a lot of hitting. But there was so much of it and so much of it was really hard. So it's not surprising that we had so many skirmishes. We had hitting in the Soviet league and in the European games, but not so often and not so hard. Because of that it was, of course, difficult to play against such a physical defence. Having said that, our team did score goals and played very admirably against such a strong opponent."

Team Canada continued to dominate, essentially for the first time in the series, in the second period. Just a couple minutes in, Clarke won a faceoff in the Soviet zone, Henderson got the puck back to him, and Clarke drove hard to the front of the net and tucked a backhand shot between Tretiak's legs. Later in the period, Clarke won another faceoff in the Soviet zone and the puck eventually deflected to Henderson, who scored at 11:58. That line, with Ellis doing a terrific job of checking Kharlamov, had another strong game. Team Canada played a very physical game against Kharlamov, even took a couple penalties, but they were leading 3–0 after two periods. And the fans were chanting: "Nyet, nyet Soviet, Da Da Canada."

"Clarkie was a young man at the time [just twenty-three years old]," said Phil Esposito. "But you could tell he was going to be a great leader."

There was a mighty scare for Canada late in the period, when Henderson, on a partial breakaway, tripped and fell. At high speed, he slid backwards in a sitting position into the boards, slamming his back and neck and hitting his head. He remained down for a long time before finally being helped to the dressing room.

"I was so fortunate to come back because I got a concussion in that game," said Henderson. "The guy knocked me down, I went into the boards, I was knocked out. Jim Murray, the doctor, came in and he said, 'Paul, you've got a concussion, you've got to take your equipment off.' Harry came in after the period was over and [told me the same thing]. I said, 'Harry, don't do this to me, please. Don't do this to me. I'll take care of myself. I want to play so bad.' He looked at me and this is exactly what he said: 'Paul, we sure as hell need you and if you want to play I'm not going to stop you.'"

Despite a pounding headache and a little bit of dizziness, Henderson took a couple packets of smelling salts and returned for the third period, something that likely wouldn't be allowed to happen today. But whatever headache Henderson was experiencing would be shared with his teammates before the game was over.

After Frank Mahovlich had missed a chance to make it 4–0 and all but seal the win, the Soviets scored early in the third period. Defenceman Pat Stapleton got caught out of position, then Yuri Blinov tucked the puck around a lunging Tony Esposito to make it 3–1. But just 1:22 later, Henderson, on a great pass from Clarke, broke in alone and beat Tretiak between the pads. And it seemed order had been restored, with Canada leading 4–1.

But the Russians, known for scoring in bunches, kept coming, and Team Canada seemed to relax its forecheck at times, falling back into a dangerous defensive shell. At other times, it felt like they were trying too hard to add to their lead. Try as they did to convince themselves not to stray from the game plan, sometimes it's almost instinctive and unavoidable. The Soviets scored two goals— Vyacheslav Anisin and Vladimir Shadrin—just eight seconds apart midway through the period, and suddenly it was a one-goal game. A little over two minutes after that, at 11:41, Gusev beat Esposito with a high screened shot to the short side and the game was tied. Gusev was one of the defenceman added to the lineup for this game because of his offensive skills. He had earned an assist earlier. Liapkin, the other defenceman added, also had an assist.

At 14:46, Vladimir Vikulov scored the game-winning goal on a breakaway. Five goals in a span of eleven minutes and twelve seconds on just eleven shots. The final four goals were bunched into just five minutes and forty-one seconds.

Final score: Soviet Union 5, Team Canada 4.

Before it was over, Ratelle, Frank Mahovlich, and Yvan Cournoyer all had great scoring chances: Ratelle hit the post, the Big M stopped on a breakaway, and the Soviets held on for the stunning victory. Tony Esposito blamed himself afterwards, but make no mistake, this was a team collapse. Another shocking Soviet win. They had come back from being down 2–0 in the series opener to win handily, then battled back from 3–1 and 4–2 deficits to earn a tie in game 3 in Winnipeg. And now this with the stakes even higher.

"The first half of the game, two-thirds of it, we came out of the chute and we were playing extremely well, we got that lead," said Ellis. "We just had that let down for a few minutes, and all of a sudden we lose the game. We all knew the Russians scored in bunches."

"After we lost that game," said Peter Mahovlich, "Harry came into the dressing room afterwards, closed the door, and said, 'Guys, that was the best game we have played.' And then he walked out. He was right, but we were stunned."

Sinden was far more in control in the dressing room than he was in the coach's room. After the game, in frustration and rage, he threw a cup of coffee against the wall, most of it spraying on his suit. But as stunned and demoralized as the Canadians were afterwards, there was also a sense of confidence that really hadn't existed before. Yes, with three losses now in an eight-game series, the margin for error was gone, but that didn't seem to weaken their resolve.

"We were pissed off," said Park, "but there was a quiet confidence in the room. Why? For large portions of each period we controlled the play. We were in control. Our conditioning was kicking in. As disappointed as we were, everyone's chin was starting to stick out a little bigger because we knew that now we can skate and play with them. And we were down to our main roster, there wasn't going to be a lot of changes."

Not overlooked, of course, was that Team Canada was facing three must-win games on Moscow ice.

"It was one of our best games even though we lost it," said Sinden. "We felt we were the better team that night, which happens to teams when they lose sometimes. But it's nonsense to try to convince anybody of that after you've lost. So you have to live with it. But I think that's how the players felt that night, that we've caught up—we were behind when the tournament started, but we've basically caught up. We played a good game. You win most of the nights you play like that. You can't dwell on it, because you win or lose as far as everyone else is concerned. But I do think we felt we were capable—I don't know if we felt we could win the next three games, but we were capable of doing it."

"That was the game that turned our heads," said centre Red Berenson. "We realized this was doable."

Post-game, Phil Esposito told anyone who would listen that Team Canada would not lose another game. What else could he say? But he believed it, and a lot of the other players did, too. They were confident, their conditioning was much improved, and they were emotionally invested in the best way possible.

"Even though we lost, we came out of that game confident we could play with these guys if we played the right way, staying out of the penalty box, getting the puck in behind their defencemen," added Berenson. "I think we thought we had to play differently because they were the Russians. But we started to see that if we control the puck in their end, go to the net, it frustrated them not having the puck."

After they stood on the blue line, listening to the Soviet national anthem, heads down, dejected and pissed off, the Canadians skated off the ice at the far end of the Luzhniki arena, but not to a chorus of boos. Instead, they were given a standing ovation by those three thousand Canadian fans.

"We gave them the standing ovation for their effort," said Garraway, who was on her feet cheering. "We were 100 percent supportive and we cheered them on no matter what. For them as players, they had to look and think, 'Here are these fans, who have travelled all this way, let's step up our game.'"

"I just couldn't believe it," said the late Howie Meeker, who was a TV analyst for the series, in his book *Golly Gee It's Me: The Howie Meeker Story*. "There were a lot of things about that series that I will never forget, but those fans are at the top. They were telling the players, 'We're Canadians, we're proud of you, you're going to win,' and the message got through to the players. Next day at practice you could see that confidence."

"We were very disappointed," said Henderson. "But what I remember most after the game is as we're going off the ice the three thousand Canadians gave us a standing ovation. It was unbelievable. And it was a miserable night weather-wise in Moscow. We got back to the hotel an hour or so later and there were at least a thousand of them lined up outside, and when we got off the bus they were cheering like crazy. The fact most of them were hammered had nothing to do with it. When we got back to the room, I said to my wife, Eleanor, if we don't win these last three games, we're going to be known as the biggest losers in the history of the sport of hockey. I'll tell you what, fear is a great motivator because every one of us knew it."

CHAPTER 13

Fans

Pierre Plouffe wasn't the best-known Canadian hanging around the Luzhniki Ice Palace and the hotel bars and streets of Moscow in September 1972. Far from it. But as Phil Esposito was to Team Canada, Plouffe was to several Canadian hockey fans who had landed behind the Iron Curtain and were intent on having a good time. Esposito was the players' unofficial leader, while Plouffe was the ringleader of the rowdies. And quite the character.

According to historians, perhaps with tongue in cheek (and perhaps not), the arrival of the Canadians was the largest invasion of tourists since before the 1917 Russian Revolution, which led to the creation of the world's first communist country and for a time the slamming shut of the tourist doors.

An estimated three thousand Canadian hockey fans landed in Moscow in and around September 20, 1972, to take in the sights and sounds of the city as an aside to watching hockey history being made—one way or the other. Truth be told, after the first four games in Canada, it seemed they might be having more of a wake than a party during their visit. But their presence was noticed and felt—by Team Canada and by the Soviet authorities. And especially that of

Plouffe, who was just twenty-two years old and enjoying himself immensely.

A year earlier, Plouffe was both a World Cup and Canadian water-ski champion. He would go on to become a water-skiing legend in his home province and was inducted into the Quebec Sports Hall of Fame in 2000 after winning multiple Canadian championships. In the fall of 1972, he competed at the Summer Olympics in Munich on September 1 and 2. Water skiing was a demonstration sport, and Plouffe competed in three events, doing quite well on the international stage. The water-skiing events were held in Kiel, West Germany, about an eight-hour drive north of Munich. So that meant Plouffe missed the first game of the Summit Series. He did manage to watch the second game from the CBC broadcast centre near the Athletes' Village in the small hours of the morning. It was September 5 in Munich, the day that eight Palestinian terrorists broke into the Olympic Village, killing two members of the Israeli team and taking nine hostages, who eventually were all killed, as were the five terrorists and a police officer.

That same early morning, Plouffe and his group decided to jump the fence of the Athletes' Village upon their return from watching the hockey game. It was about the same time the eight members of the Palestine Liberation Organization had done the same to begin Black September.

"To get there, you had to go all the way around to the other side of the village," said Plouffe. "On the way back, we decided to climb the fence. We heard a bang-bang. But I didn't know what a gun sounded like back then. The next morning, we found out what happened."

Plouffe returned to Canada shortly after he was done with his competition. But before going to the Olympics, his stepfather, who owned a potato chip company, had wanted to buy six travel packages for the games in Moscow. Plouffe promised to help out his stepfather if he would buy him a package to go to Russia. Depending on the storyteller and the tour operator, each package cost roughly $600 Canadian, which would be worth about $3,750 in 2021. But that covered flight, hotel, most meals, and game tickets.

Plouffe arranged to buy seven packages through Montreal Canadiens defenceman Pierre Bouchard, who was a friend from high school.

"I wanted to go directly to Moscow from Munich," said Plouffe, who lived in Montreal. "But I was told that wouldn't be possible. I had to return to Canada and go with the group from Montreal. We arrived in Moscow, at our hotel, in the late afternoon. It was quite a ways away, a ten- or fifteen-minute drive from where Team Canada was staying at the Hotel Intourist. When we were in the hotel room, my friend hung on to my belt, and I leaned out the window playing 'O Canada' on my bugle. Then I waved the Canadian flag. An hour later, there was a knock on the door. I was in trouble. Some Russian officials weren't happy with us. Don't forget, this was the Iron Curtain in 1972. They weren't used to having three thousand Canadians around. But it wasn't the most intelligent thing to do on my part. I was a party guy, though. I didn't learn my lesson."

That was just the beginning of the fun and games for Plouffe in Moscow, in and out of the rink.

Marie Garraway was another one of the group of three thousand.

"At the time, I was working at the Westbury Hotel in Toronto, just down the street from Maple Leaf Gardens," she said. "I was assistant to the director of sales. One day a flyer came into the office about the trip. I thought it would be an awesome trip, so I phoned the travel agency and I got one of the last tickets and booked it. I think, all in, it cost me six hundred dollars.

"I asked some friends if they wanted to go with me, but no one was interested. They all thought I was nuts. Who wants to go to Russia? I come from a hockey family, and I thought it was the opportunity of a lifetime that I'd probably never do again. It wasn't on my bucket list until that flyer came in. I figured, opportunity only knocks on your door once, I've got to go. And I never thought I would go back."

Little did Garraway know she would return forty-one years later, again to watch hockey, but the country would look significantly different. Marie's maiden name is Keenan, and her brother is Mike Keenan, the legendary coach, who won championships at all levels, including a Stanley Cup with the New York Rangers in 1994 and a Gagarin Cup, in the Russian league, with Metallurg Magnitogorsk in 2014. He is one of only two professional head coaches (Bob Hartley being the other, in 2021) to win a championship in both the NHL and the KHL.

Mike Keenan was also the coach of Team Canada in 1987, a team that featured Wayne Gretzky and Mario Lemieux and beat the Russians in a thrilling three-game final, each game finishing with a 6–5 score—the identical score as the final game in 1972. That 1987 team also required an amazing comeback, in their case from being down 3–0 early in the final game. It is widely agreed that 1987 was to a new generation of hockey fans what 1972 was to an older generation. Phil Esposito and Paul Henderson in one series, Gretzky and Lemieux in the other. Great hockey both times. And 1987 would never have happened without the Summit Series. For another generation still, it was Canada winning gold for the first time in fifty years at the Salt Lake City Games in 2002, or Sidney Crosby scoring the Golden Goal in the 2010 Winter Olympics in Vancouver. Again, the events of 1972 ultimately had a profound influence on what transpired years later.

"When I checked in at the airport, I didn't know a soul," said Garraway, who turned twenty-one midway through the Summit Series. "It was a chartered flight on Aeroflot. We flew from Toronto to Paris, refuelled there, and then flew from Paris to Moscow. There was lots of singing on the plane, we were singing the anthem. Being on Aeroflot [the Soviets' national airline], they were not happy with us at all. Drinks were included on the flights, big drinks. They weren't the typical airline stewardesses we were used to. They weren't happy with us, we were too noisy and too undisciplined.

"We were the largest group allowed in the country at the time. All we needed was a passport, no visa because we were part of the group. Most of us stayed at the Hotel Intourist, which is now a Ritz-Carlton. It was brand new, or just a couple of years old, but it was pretty plain, pretty basic. We had a banquet room where we had our meals. When I went back in 2013 to visit Mike [Keenan], it was like we had gone from one end of the spectrum to the other."

Although Team Canada also stayed at the Intourist, most of the fans didn't see a lot of the players.

"In the evenings, sometimes the players would come down to the bar, but there wasn't a whole lot of exposure to them until the very end," said Garraway. "They were there to do a job. You might see them on the elevator, but they weren't hanging around the lobby. They ate in the banquet room beside us, and I remember a few of them were sick."

Seems the Soviet Union had its own version of "Montezuma's Revenge," a diarrhea that often tortured tourists in Mexico.

"Yes, there was that, and the food was a new experience," said Garraway. "I know the team had some of its own food, but the food over there was very different from what we were used to, for sure. It was the first time I had borscht. They did a lot of chicken, potatoes, lots of root vegetables. And dessert. They loved their dessert. Everything was saturated in grease. I lost ten pounds because I just wasn't eating very much."

Overall, though, the experience was different, but good. Not unlike a lot of the players, the fans were somewhat naïve and really didn't know what to expect when they arrived. The Soviet Union and its people, after all, were still very much a mystery to those in the West back in 1972. Most thought they were venturing to the dark side.

"Was it the dark side? Very much so," continued Garraway. "I never felt threatened. You knew you were in their country, so you abide by their rules. And we were always in groups of people. I had a roommate, but her boyfriend was one of the reporters, so we didn't really hang out much. There was a group from Timmins, Ontario, and we all ended up doing the same tours, chumming around.

"The first day there was an orientation. They told us if we weren't on a tour, when we went out on the street, we had to have our passport. We couldn't go beyond the perimeter of the city centre. We were told don't give the police a hard time because there would be consequences. One day we were waiting in line to go into a museum, there was a school next door, and the kids were on their recess. We went to the fence to give the kids some gum and candy, and we got reamed out like you couldn't believe by some soldiers. We only did that once. What bothered me most over there was to see the young people on the streets, the expressions on their faces. There was no gleam in their eyes, no smiles. Their clothing was drab, nothing bright. They would come up to us and look at our clothes and ask, 'Do you want to sell them?'

"We did tours, but they only showed us what they wanted you to see in the city. We had a couple of really good evenings planned between games. We went to the opera, which I don't like, but it was still an experience. We had a big dinner banquet with entertainment. We went to the Moscow Circus, we saw some of the museums and the university, we saw Red Square. You weren't allowed to travel on your own too much. And no matter where you went, there were lots of police and soldiers. You always had to have your passport.

"The stores were only open for a few hours each day, and there were always long lineups. Their big [department] store was the GUM store, but it was pretty ordinary. One day, I remember a group of us went to church, to mass. We put money in the collection plate, and the guy taking the collection, his eyes were wide, he couldn't believe the rubles we were putting in. Overall, the trip was very well organized. It was a good trip, a good experience. I'm glad that I did go."

Pierre Plouffe also had a good experience, but a slightly different trip.

"As I said, I was a party guy," said Plouffe. "When the rest of the group was touring around during the day, visiting places like Lenin's tomb, I slept on the bus."

Prior to game 5, the Canadian fans were given some rules of behaviour in the arena. They were told to stay in their seating sections, follow orders, and there was to be no flag waving. And no bugle playing, as it turned out.

"The first game, when we walked in, we're all hyped up," said Garraway. "We bussed from the hotel and went in as a group and took our seats. Well, there weren't seats, there were benches, the old wooden ones like we had as kids. The rink was pretty ancient. They had guards stationed in the stairways in each of our sections. We took up a few sections and we all sat on the one side, the Russians on the other. There was no mingling with them; we all came in and out the same doors, and there were guards along the hallway. One thing I noticed was there were no women on the Russian side. By the end of the series there were actually Russian women in the crowd, but not the first game. It was an old boys' club."

One of the oldest boys in that club was Soviet Communist Party General Secretary Leonid Brezhnev, who had a private box and was surrounded by other top party officials.

"He was at every game," said Bill Watters, who attended the games with his pregnant wife, Naddy. Watters, who went on to become a prominent player agent and hockey executive, was also close with Bobby Orr, running his sports camp in Orillia. "He [Brezhnev] had that big box. It was almost surreal."

The Canadian fans were easy to hear from the minute they walked into the arena, singing the national anthem loud and proud, cheering on their team, which was in a deep, deep hole but playing significantly better than they had in the first four games back home. In fact, Team Canada dominated for long stretches, leading 1–0 after the first period on a late goal from J. P. Parise, and goals from Bobby Clarke and line mate Paul Henderson gave them a 3–0 lead after two periods.

"The first time Canada scored, we jumped up and cheered like crazy," said Garraway. "We were waving flags, they didn't like that at all. The soldiers walked up the aisle pointing their guns, basically telling us to shut up and be quiet. That happened a few times. They said we were too rowdy, that we shouldn't cheer like that. We cheered, their fans whistled. But how do you stop a group of Canadians cheering on their team? We were something they had never seen before."

It didn't take long for Plouffe alone to draw the attention of the army guards. He played his bugle during stoppages in play, which always drew a crowd. Plouffe occasionally filled in for his friend Michel Blanchard, playing the trumpet at the Montreal Forum, charging up the fans. But there they were welcome.

"We waved the Canadian flag, we cheered," said Plouffe. "I took the bugle to the first game over there. The Russian army surrounded the rink. They didn't like it that I was playing the bugle. They would come to our section to try and get it. We would pass it through legs, behind backs. They never did get the bugle from us.

"It was quite the feeling to be part of this group. There was no talk about language or religion. We were Canadians, cheering for Canada. We were the best at hockey, and we cheered our hearts out in the hopes this still would be the case when the series was over. It was an expensive trip, and it was expensive over there, but this was a historical series and worth the cost."

Team Canada, of course, ended up blowing that seemingly cushy lead, the Soviets mounting yet another comeback, scoring five times in the third period to win, putting a stranglehold on the series. But there were no boos from these Canadian fans. Instead, as the players left the ice after the heartbreaking loss, they were given a standing ovation.

"You have to support our team," said Garraway. "We were there to cheer them on. We had to let them know how we felt."

And the players noticed and appreciated it.

"I always say thank you to the people who came to Russia to see us, to cheer for us," said winger Yvan Cournoyer. "I think they were like the sixth player on the ice. They really helped us to be in the game and to ultimately win. Any time I see one of them, I thank them because they were a big part of what we were able to do. It wasn't easy for them being over there, either. It was quite something for them. But three thousand was a lot of people. We really felt that support."

40,000 launch drive for United Appeal's $14,120,000 goal

By SAMUEL CAMPBELL
Star staff writer

At dawn today, a United Appeal army of more than 40,000 volunteer citizens set out on a blanket canvass of Metro to raise $14,120,000—the 1972 needs of 78 health, welfare and character-building agencies.

Side by side, and knocking on doors from now until Nov. 2 for the largest amount of money in the fund's 17-year history, are laborers, executives, bus drivers, bankers, doctors, housewives and university and high school students.

When they approach you at home or at work, they will appeal on behalf of deserted children, handicapped and blind workers, teenagers caught up in crime and drugs, ex-convicts who never had a chance and old people who need another son.

Norman Paton, campaign chairman, says this year's drive is starting on an optimistic note with a head-start subscription of slightly more than $2 million... That's $250,000 ahead of last year's opening figure.

But Paton warned today that the appeal could collapse by 1975 if it fails to meet its goal this year.

In a speech prepared for the opening of the campaign today, Paton said this is "a crucial year" which could make or break the fund.

Nothing that the fund has fallen short of its goal for the past two years, Paton said "if we take a business as usual approach to this year's campaign, we can expect to be 12 per cent short. Then 18 per cent and so on."

"I predict we will not have a United Community Fund unless we close the gap this year," he warned.

The 1971 drive fell short of its $12,850,000 goal by $50,000. The difference had to be drawn from the United Appeal's dwindling reserves.

Paton points out that an increase of $1,770,000, or 14.3 per cent over last year, is needed in the next six weeks. Since the fund began it has never increased its yearly contributions by more than 6.6 per cent.

A colorful torch-lighting kick-off rally was held at noon today in Nathan Phillips Square. The drive was officially launched by Mayor William Dennison with Bobby Gimby and his band and friends. Miss United Appeal, campaign chairman Paton and other dignitaries.

The Mackenzie pipeline

METRO WEATHER
Fog Tuesday morning. Low 60, high 70. Pollution Index 4 at 11 a.m. Details page 2.

The Toronto Star
four star ★★★★ edition

ESTABLISHED 1892

August paid circulation Mon. to Fri. 494,257, Sat. 653,240

Monday, September 25, 1972—80 pages

Monday-Friday 10c; Saturday 25c; Home delivery 75c

Raising $6 billion could threaten nation's economy

★ David Crane of The Star's Ottawa bureau today continues a 3-part series on the plan to transport natural gas across half a continent—an undertaking described by some observers as rivalling in importance the building of the Canadian Pacific Railway. This is the second instalment.

By DAVID CRANE
Star staff writer

OTTAWA — The immense financing problems of Canada's proposed northern gas pipeline, the cost of which could run as high as $6 billion, will clearly overshadow all the other complex difficulties this huge frontier project is bound to face.

The money is needed to build one of the longest pipelines in the world, tapping natural gas deposits in Alaska and the Canadian Arctic and transmitting the fuel 1,500 to 2,500 miles—depending on what route is finally approved—down the Mackenzie Valley, across the Prairies and into the markets of central Canada and the United States.

The amount is unprecedented in Canadian history. And all the financial ingenuity that can be mustered in Canada and the United States will be needed.

Some financial analysts doubt the money can be raised without government help.

"The financing may be too large for private capital and that could require government assistance in the form of loans or guarantees," says a study by Wood Gundy Ltd.

But even more critical, perhaps, is the broader impact such financing could have on the Canadian economy.

The financing could push up the value of the Canadian dollar to that manufacturing and agriculture suffer, raise the level of interest rates, cause severe inflation, deprive other Canadian projects of growth financing and, in sum, tie the future direction of the Canadian economy to U.S. energy needs instead of domestic priorities.

Wage, price controls

Concern over the implications for Canada of the pipeline and other big energy projects in the 1970s is now appearing in Canada's financial community.

Wayne Clendinning, economist for Richardson Securities of Canada, says it is "a major economic issue for Canadian policymakers."

Clendinning fears that the government and the Bank of Canada will no longer be able to manage the country's economy and suggested that, in any event, both wage and price controls and foreign exchange controls might be required for several years during the height of financing activity.

Harris and Partners Ltd., a Toronto investment house, says "Because of its fundamental importance to the development of the Canadian economy, energy has become the central economic issue of the 1970s."

In fact, the investment company says: "It becomes more and more clear that to many of the separate issues which have been examined in this war recently are peripheral to a solution of the policy questions involved in the development of Canadian energy resources in this decade."

Yet the Trudeau government, while spending millions of dollars on environmental and social research in the north and promising more than $100 million to build an Arctic highway to facilitate the pipeline, has hardly begun to look at some of the major implications of the pipeline and other energy prospects.

Northern vision

But this has not stopped the government from saying it wants the pipeline built. And Prime Minister Trudeau himself has spoken of plans for a $10 billion northern vision over the next decade that includes the Arctic highway, the gas pipeline and an oil pipeline.

An energy policy statement is to be published today by the government for everyone at early next year.

But indications are that it will be simply that, a policy statement with most of the real research concentrated for a year or more in the years to come of the government.

In particular, much of the financial and economic research appears destined to be published from public advisory.

The financial problems of the pipeline emerge on two levels—the raising of money, especially if there is to be $1 per cent Canadian ownership of future states, and the broader economic impact of the project on the Canadian economy.

Guidelines issued by the Canadian government

See FINANCING, page 1

TRUDEAU BLOWS HIS COOL

Prime Minister Pierre Trudeau shows his exasperation after a persistent heckler taunted him as he walked across a Vancouver street Saturday on his way to a radio hot-line show. The PM twice told the heckler to "shut up." Later, when the man continued his taunts, the PM grabbed the man and uttered an obscenity.

Trudeau defends admission of Uganda's expelled Asians

Special to The Star

VANCOUVER — Prime Minister Pierre Trudeau strongly defended his government's decision to admit Asians expelled from Uganda in a campaign speech here on Saturday.

"We would have been false in ourselves, false to our ideals, false to our history, had we ignored their plight," he said. "We would not have been Canadians if we had turned our backs on them."

Trudeau's statement came on a day of campaigning during which he had continuous contact with several groups of demonstrators during each campaign stop.

During an encounter with one persistent demonstrator, Trudeau became red in the face and said up and swore at him when the man did not do so.

With the last large group of Ugandan refugees expected to arrive this week, Trudeau repeated in a speech to about 2,500 specially invited Liberals that Canada is a warm society that cares for other peoples.

"When human need has appeared," he said, "Canadians have opened their arms. Refugees from Hungary, Czechoslovakia and Tibet have come to Canada in their tens of thousands.

"We welcomed the Ugandan Asians because they were in need. They brought with them skills which added value to our economy and cultural traditions which have enriched us as a people."

At that time Canadian didn't pause to ask about the cost of immigration to the country or the availability of housing," he said. It pushed on simply, immediately, as because it was right to do so.

Trudeau has faced repeated questioning on radio hotline shows about the future of all newcomers to at least 6,000 a month.

See PM DEFENDS, page 2

Canada-bound Asians to leave Wednesday

NAIROBI, Kenya (Reuters)— The first group of Uganda Asians going to Canada about 165—will leave Entebbe on Wednesday, the Canadian high Commission said today.

The Asians will fly in a Canadian chartered DC-8 to Longue-Pointe, Montreal, Ottawa, a spokesman the immigration department said the Asians would be housed for several days at Longue-Pointe, where they will be classified.

Not until the classification procedure is complete would their eventual destination in Canada be known, he said.

● Uganda's last premier president Milton Obote must leave Tanzania, page 41.

Lewis would take old-age pensions from Canada's 'rich'

New Democratic Party Leader David Lewis suggested yesterday that he would adjust taxation to cut off "the rich" from old-age security pensions if he wins the Oct. 30 federal election.

Interviewed on radio station CFRB's Let's Discuss It program, Lewis refused to define what he meant by rich.

But he said "anyone who has a taxable income of $20,000, $30,000, $40,000, $50,000 a year ought not to get an old-age pension out of the public treasury."

Lewis' party is committed to increasing the present pension from $82.88 to $150 a month on a universal basis, and he indicated an NDP government would recover the money from the rich through taxation.

He told commentator Gordon Sinclair, 72, he'd deprive him of his pension if he didn't need it "without batting an eyelash."

'TAX IT BACK'

"The way to make sure those who don't need it don't take money out of the public treasury is to tax it back," he said.

He said hundreds of thousands of Canada's pensioners are living in poverty and squalor.

He pointed out that about half of the 1,800,000 receiving the old-age pension are so poor they qualify for the federal government's guaranteed income supplement. To qualify for the supplement, he said, "they have to have practically nothing more than the $82.88 they get a month."

$150 MONTHLY

The supplement increases pensions up to $150 monthly for a single person and $283 for a married couple where both are pensioners.

At present, the old age pension and payments from private pension plans are provided in a person's earnings and taxed accordingly. Old age supplements are generally not taxable.

British Columbia Premier David Barrett has promised his new NDP government will raise the income of all pensioners to at least $200 a month.

Lewis, 63, noted that he

See LEWIS, page 2

'Simply a farce' Eagleson says of refereeing

By JIM PROUDFOOT
Star sports editor

MOSCOW —Being Alan Eagleson is fiercely proud of the little empire he made of international hockey but even he, in moments of frankness, admits to see serious fault.

"Our refereeing hasn't developed at the same rate as the rest of our game," says the controversial chieftain of the International Ice Hockey Federation.

Team Canada is prepared to agree, without knowing what the officiating was like at the joint part on the basis of last night's game here against the Soviet Union. The Canadian pros won 3-1 a 2-2-1 right, but they are express of today that the biggest obstacle they had to overcome was the work of the West German referees. Josef Kompalla and Franz Bader, and on the victims from the Streets

Kompalla and Bader imposed 33 penalty minutes and 31 of those were served by Canadians, including a five minute major for Phil Esposito. The was it marked out, the Soviets were shorthanded only twice, while the Canadians had to stand off the enemy power play a total of 21 minutes.

That war bad enough, even though most of the infractions called against Team Canada were genuine. What was most galling were the incorrect officiate calls and the abrupt end of approval which seemed to have been applied to the Russians' subtle use of interference an no offensive weapon.

Both Harry from Czechoslovakia and Sweden's Gu Duhltenz are scheduled to work tomorrow night's match and that breaks up an intriguing possibility. If Team Canada should happen to win and seven their series against the Soviets at three wins each and one draw then, Kompalla and Bader should be on the podium for the deciding game Thursday evening.

That won't happen, of officials of the Canadian hockey delegation have been in the most way. And they usually do, remember.

"I would think, if to be prepared to be adamant about the selection of referees, after the experience right up to a point of speaking the spirit of this series," said coach Harry Sinden.

Al Eagleson, who is so recognized here as the leader of Team Canada, went further.

"I have told the Russians that if these men are assigned to the eighth game, there may not be one or that's quite clear. What won't be taught up his mind. I couldn't sell the players to go through the same thing again."

What the whole meant and that's precisely what it want—points up is that a better system of refereeing must be worked out if these trans-Atlantic hockey championships are to continue. Bad and Kompalla certainly were bad by major league standards, but the real problem is that very officiate the sport from a fundamentally different point of view and inore conditions that would severely test a John Ashley or a Bill Friday.

That is to hang up which must be resolved.

If you don't now the Team

See EAGLESON, page 4

A praise critic in penalty box

PHIL ESPOSITO

'I'm sorry, I'm sorry,' pilot mumbles

Jet crashes into U.S. ice cream parlor, 22 killed

SACRAMENTO, Calif. (AP-Reuters-UPI) — Twenty-two persons—including at least 10 children—were killed yesterday when a privately owned jet warplane crashed into an ice cream parlor packed with parents and children celebrating birthday parties.

At least 20 persons were treated at three hospitals for injuries.

Witnesses said the plane, an F-86 Sabre jet fighter of Korean War vintage, lost power about 200 feet in the air after takeoff from Executive Airport, crashed into the ground, bounced once, hit a culvert and skidded across a road into the ice cream parlor's front window.

The plane had been on exhibit at a local air show.

The pilot, Richard Bingham, 36, of Richmond, Calif. was pulled from the wreckage of his aircraft with a broken arm. He mumbled to rescuers: "I'm sorry, I'm sorry, get the people out."

Police said the heat created by flames from the sliding fireball was so intense it burned the paint and tires off cars more than 50 feet away and the shopping centre stores nearby with smoke and debris.

Dick Kostac, manager of Parrell's Ice Cream Parlor, said: "We had a full-house about 100 people, laughing like that. There were birthday parties, that sort of thing."

Alan King of Sacramento said he had been in the air show when the jet came in for a crash landing.

Kurz said: "I saw the nose drop and it hit. A wing tank exploded. The plane skidded across the road, and when it hit the ice cream parlor it just exploded."

● Sixty-two persons died accidentally in Canada during the weekend, 36 of them on the roads. Page 41.

See JET, page 2

Crossing crash kills 2 in truck

NAPANEE (CP)— Two unidentified persons in a truck were killed early today when a CN passenger train on its way to Toronto collided with it at a level crossing.

CHAPTER 14

Game 6—Win, or Else

One shift at a time...

"After game five, Harry came in the dressing room and he said maybe the most profound thing he might have said the entire series," recalled Brad Park. "He said, 'Don't even think about the next game. Don't even think about game seven, or game eight. The only thing you're going to concentrate on is your next shift. You're not going to think about a period, or a game. All you're going to think about is your next shift.' It was profound because you didn't think about how big the hole was that you were in. Which means, you're looking ahead, you're not looking behind."

"I had so many different experiences with so many different coaches during my career," said Peter Mahovlich. "Some were quiet, some were screamers and yellers. Harry wasn't a screamer or a yeller. He liked to talk and explain. But he was even-keeled. It suited that series. Other than Kenny [Dryden], we were a bunch of truck drivers. For us, the best motivation was just to give us the right information on what to focus on and tweak on what we weren't doing well. That's what Harry was about."

"It was one of the greatest coaching jobs ever," said Dennis Hull.

Whatever the strategy, or the mind games, the challenge facing Team Canada heading into the sixth game was as obvious as it was daunting: win, or else. Technically they could have tied the game, but then they still would have needed to win the final two games and hope the tiebreaker worked in their favour. Deep down, with the cagey and manipulative Soviets, they knew it would not. So the secret to success was to win the final three games to win the series—but do it one shift at a time. Remember, too, at this point they had won just one of the first five games, so the ask was huge.

"A tie could have allowed us to both end up with three wins and two ties and we could win on goal differential," said Dryden. "But even a tie is likely not going to be enough because the goal differential was not in our favour. I think Canadians would have been quite happy to say we won the series even though we won it on goal differential. I don't think it would have been completely unsatisfying at that particular stage. But the point being really is that, yes, you had to go into that game feeling it had to be won."

This was not the first time Team Canada had faced a must-win scenario. It felt that way in game 2, after being shockingly blown out in the series opener. But this was different. Now they were trailing in the series 3-1-1 with virtually no margin for error, and they were coming off a game in which they played their best, but somehow managed to blow 3–0 and 4–1 leads. As much as part of that might have inspired some confidence, it also would have added some doubt.

"After the fifth game, you're mostly feeling crushed because you played so well and then lost in the end," said Dryden. "You snap out of feeling that way probably a little faster because we had played as well as we did. As the hours pass and the morning comes, you've got a little more energy than you might have otherwise. You had started to be what you had imagined yourself being.

"And there were great competitors on that team, players that have been in situations where you're down far enough that it makes no sense that you come back. Well, you make your own sense and you come back. Even with us in Montreal, in the '71 Stanley Cup, we fell behind Chicago in the final, two games to nothing [and again three games to two] and came back and won. There were enough moments [in Moscow] to decide that things were over, if you make that decision. But competitors don't make that decision."

Dryden, who had been beaten seven times in the first game and five times in the fourth, was given the start for the crucial sixth game. He hadn't played a game in two weeks and had only backed up in Sweden. Deep down, he didn't think he would start again. Tony Esposito, of course, had played game 5 and had largely played well, but he was also beaten for five goals in the third period—not that it was entirely a goalie loss. But that might have made it easier for Sinden and Ferguson to contemplate making a change. They had insisted all along they would need two goalies to win the series, that the workload and pressure were too big. The goaltenders were told after game 5 that Dryden would play game 6, Esposito would start game 7, and Dryden would play game 8.

"Tony is as cool as a cucumber and you'd think nothing would rattle him, but it's not true with goalies," said Sinden. "It's like a pitcher preparing for his next start, he's on his own. Fergie and I agreed it might be too much to expect them to be on top of their game two games in a row when it's such a pressure-packed situation. We could've been wrong. Tony might have been great, but we made that call and that's why we put Kenny back in. We were a little disappointed in his play up to that point. We certainly knew what a great goalie he was. That was our thinking. I'm sure if we had asked the goalies, they would have said, oh no, I'm good to go, I can play two in a row. But it was a different series and it was a different kind of pressure being put on the players. I don't think they even knew what effect it might have on them, especially the goaltenders."

Dryden, of course, had been an overnight sensation when, in March 1971, he made his NHL debut with the Canadiens. He wound up playing six of the final regular-season games, and played quite well. Despite having experienced goaltenders Rogie Vachon and Phil Myre, Canadiens coach Al MacNeil decided to give Dryden the start in their opening-round playoff series against the powerhouse Boston Bruins, featuring Bobby Orr and Phil Esposito. No one gave the Canadiens much of a chance in the series, so perhaps MacNeil believed he had nothing to lose.

The Bruins won the series opener and were ahead 5–1 in the second game, but the Canadiens staged an amazing comeback to win 7–5. Dryden continued to get better even though the Canadiens eventually fell behind 3–2 in the series. But with stellar goaltending from the six-foot-four Dryden—whom Phil Esposito later called "the Thieving Giraffe," they won the final two games, including a 4–2 victory in Boston in game 7, to complete the upset. They went on to defeat the Minnesota North Stars in six games and the Chicago Blackhawks in seven to capture the Stanley Cup. Dryden won the Conn Smythe Trophy as the playoffs' most valuable player. What a story. The following season he was named the rookie of the year in the NHL and then he was named to Team Canada.

Dryden went on to win the Stanley Cup five more times and the Vezina Trophy for five straight seasons before retiring at age thirty-one. He was inducted into the Hockey Hall of Fame in 1983. When he was named one of the top 100 NHL players of all time, Dryden was quoted as saying: "A goalie's job is to stop pucks . . . Well, yeah, that's part of it, but you know what else is? You're trying to deliver a message to your team that things are okay back here. This end of the ice is pretty well cared for. You take it now and go."

Going into game 6 of the Summit Series, Team Canada was in desperate need of the type of performances Dryden had assembled that magical spring of '71, but they also needed that feeling from him: "things are okay back here." That feeling hadn't previously existed in the series.

Dryden, who turned just twenty-five a few days before the opening of training camp, had realized early in the series, particularly prior to the start in Vancouver, that he needed to adjust his playing style if he was going to have success against the Soviets. He was used to moving out of his net on top of his goal crease and further to cut down the shooting angles. That worked well in the NHL, but the Soviets liked to pass the puck in close, and that made for a longer distance to travel side to side to make a save. So Dryden had to get used to playing deeper in his net. The problem wasn't the adjustment itself, but that he didn't have a lot of time to get used to it. And he still had the bad memories of games 1 and 4 fresh in his mind.

"I get nervous, but essentially when I go out onto the ice, it's gone," said Dryden. "Then you're into the game. The nervousness pretty much comes from having a number of things to think about and worry about and you are unsure about. Once you're on the ice, you're immersed in what you're doing, so all of those other things are gone. You don't have the luxury of feeling."

Despite the gut-wrenching loss in the fifth game, the Canadians were surprisingly upbeat. Yes, they were pissed off after the game, but they were buoyed by the fact they had played so well, save for that wicked stretch in the third period when they surrendered the lead. They were determined to do better.

"We felt good about the way we played and we took that as a

positive," said Ron Ellis. "Now we're down to three games. It seemed like a large task, it was a large task, but no one lost hope or faith."

Just as important as how Team Canada was feeling is how were the Soviets feeling? Where were their heads after another amazing comeback and leading the series 3-1-1 at home? Revealingly, according to various accounts, the Soviets allowed their players to go home between games, the first time that had happened for most of them since before the series had begun. They also made five lineup changes, resting some of their better players and even resting some early in the game.

"After the game five victory, practically speaking, we just didn't think that we would lose three games in a row at home," said Tretiak. "Therefore, I think that the coaching staff should have been tougher with us to get us up for those games. Unfortunately, that didn't happen."

"They couldn't motivate us psychologically after that fifth game," said Yakushev. "The win in game five had a negative impact on the coaches and the players alike. That's because the players were sure that we would win at least one of the last three games and, therefore, win the series. And the same sentiment coming out of the coach, kind of, was 'You've done extremely well, now you need to push just a little more after game five.' Well, psychologically we just couldn't play well after that."

"After winning the first game at home, game five, we were all very certain we would win the series then," agreed Mikhailov. "Maybe the team had become overconfident."

The Canadians sensed there had been a mood swing.

"That's why I said, in 1967 when Toronto beat us [Montreal] in the Stanley Cup final, we didn't respect them," said winger Yvan Cournoyer. "We thought we were going to win easy. It showed us, no matter if you have a good team or a better team, if you don't respect the other team you have a chance to lose. That's exactly what happened in the series. We didn't respect them at first because we thought we were going to win easy, and I think they did the same thing, they didn't respect us at the end. They never thought we were going to win three games in a row to finish the series. What they didn't know is we had to win—we couldn't lose, because if we lost the series, we would have had to stay in Russia!"

Joking aside, even with that added motivation, game 6 still was not easy. While the Soviets made significant roster moves, one they couldn't make was to spell off twenty-year-old Vladislav Tretiak in goal. Their plan originally had been to give him a rest in either the Winnipeg or the Vancouver game, but his understudy took ill. It got worse for backup goaltender Viktor Zinger, who wound up breaking a finger a few days before the fifth game after he stopped a shot by Valeri Kharlamov. Speculation was, the Soviets didn't want to dig too deep into the goaltending pool, so they kept playing Tretiak, whether there were subtle signs of fatigue or not.

As for Sinden, he had whittled down the numbers of his playing roster and it continued to make a difference.

"Fergie and I realized we weren't going to be able to play everyone and beat this team," said Sinden. "We had to figure out who our best seventeen players were."

"At a certain point," said Dryden, "you've got to go with the people you think are the right ones for that next game. That's what a team is. That's how a team functions."

For the sixth game, on September 24, Sinden did make a few lineup changes. In addition to Dryden replacing Esposito, winger Frank Mahovlich and defenceman Rod Seiling were taken out. Centre Gilbert Perreault had returned home after the fifth game. In their place, winger Dennis Hull, defenceman Serge Savard, and centre Red Berenson were added—all played key roles.

"I think Harry was reaching for different guys who could help," said Berenson. "I skated well. I could kill penalties. I could keep up with the pace."

In the case of Hull, he was put on left wing with Jean Ratelle and Rod Gilbert, replacing Mahovlich, who was suffering with a knee injury and had played poorly the previous game. Hull ended up playing very well with his new line mates, all three instantly finding chemistry.

"It was a funny thing," said Hull. "With Vic [Hadfield], they were one of the best lines in hockey. But I played on a pretty good line, too, with Pit Martin and Jimmy Pappin. I think that had something to do with it. I was disappointed our line didn't get a chance to play in the series. I think we could have done well. They were not only my line mates in Chicago, but my best friends. Jean and Rod were easy to play with. Jean was like a mini Jean Béliveau. He was the nicest guy you could meet. Rod Gilbert was the same. We clicked. When I got back to Chicago afterwards, my coach, Billy Reay, and manager Tommy Ivan pulled me aside and told me that I had made quite an impression on the Rangers. They had called about a possible trade for Vic Hadfield. It never happened, but that's a true story."

It was Hull who opened the scoring for Canada, tying the game early in the second period. Berenson was also a nice addition, checking well, taking faceoffs, and especially killing penalties, which became a huge factor in the game as the West German officiating crew of Josef Kompalla and Franz Baader, whom Team Canada had been exposed to in Sweden, worked this game and were at their inept worst, missing calls that needed to be made and finding others that didn't exist.

The other key move was the return of Savard on the blue line. He had suffered a fractured ankle in practice after the Winnipeg game when he blocked a Berenson shot, and was believed to be done for the series. Savard handled the puck well and was a strong defensive presence, especially on the penalty kill, paired with his Montreal teammate Guy Lapointe. Savard, who wound up playing in five games in the series, none of them losses, admits he wasn't 100 percent healthy, but his mobility, however limited, was still very important against the quick Soviet forwards, and he could eat up big chunks of ice time. Sinden liked his defence pairings of Savard and Lapointe, Brad Park and Gary Bergman, Pat Stapleton and Bill White. Indeed, they would play all three of the final games.

Despite the offensive skill Team Canada had on defence, they didn't get a lot of production from the back end, though that group did chip in with some key assists in the final couple games.

"The Soviets played a different game, their puck possession game," explained Scotty Bowman, the winningest coach in NHL history, who took over as head coach of the Montreal Canadiens during the 1971–72 season and watched the series. "One of the things they did is their wingers would take off out of their end. Our defencemen didn't have to worry about that in the NHL. We didn't do that. We stayed in our own end. But they would spring a guy up in the neutral zone. It took your defencemen out of the offence. The Canadian defencemen didn't score a lot of points because they had to worry about the Russians leaving the zone so quickly. Our offensive defencemen like Brad Park and Serge Savard didn't get many points compared to what they did in the NHL. And remember, the games in the series were high-scoring."

Indeed, the Team Canada defence combined for just two goals and eleven assists in the eight games, with Park leading the way with one of those goals and four assists—half of all Team Canada's defencemen points.

Canada had adjusted not only its lines, but its game as well, to deal with the Soviets criss-crossing on their rushes, how they broke out of their zone, passing from areas the Canadians would normally shoot from, and various other subtleties. The Soviets, meanwhile, didn't veer far from what had been working for them.

"When you become predictable, sometimes you also become beatable," said winger Ron Ellis. "The Soviets were very rigid in their play."

Indeed, they often lacked creativity; in fact, the coaches frowned upon it. They had set plays and sometimes set units and they stuck to their game plan. Or else.

And those three thousand fans continued to cheer, during the player introductions and the emotional singing of the national anthem prior to the game. Roughly one thousand of them were originally denied their tickets to the sixth game, a supposed hiccup in the Soviet system. After considerable squawking, the tickets magically appeared. Just another annoyance . . .

"I would suggest the Canadian anthem was never sung with more fervor than those last three games," said Henderson. "I can remember, there were goose bumps on my arm, just hearing them sing."

The story of the opening period was the officiating of Kompalla and Baader (or Baader and Worse, as they were nicknamed by Alan Eagleson), who started to butcher the game, either intentionally or through incompetence. Truth is, the two officials' system was not appropriate for a series of this magnitude. The officials acted as both the referees and linesmen, and in this case they were not good at being either.

"It wasn't up to the standards that were needed," said Sinden. "It was bad. It was as expected. We had the feeling they were very intimidated in Moscow. I don't know whether they were or not, but the officiating was amateurish and all the players were top professionals."

"It wasn't the calibre that was needed for that talent," said Yvan Cournoyer.

In the first period, which ended goal-less, the Canadians were called for two penalties, though one was a double minor for charging to Phil Esposito, who on his way to the penalty box made a throat slashing gesture at the Soviet player Yuri Shatalov. The other penalty was a tripping call against defenceman Gary Bergman, who threw his arms into the air in disgust.

"The other frustration throughout the series was the refereeing," said Seiling, who watched game 6 from the stands. "It's like [the Soviets] got a sixth man out there all the time. He just happened to be wearing stripes. We had to learn how to channel our emotions and not lose our cool because of the refereeing. We got better at it; we weren't perfect, but we got better. We had to or we would never have won."

Whatever concerns there might have been about Dryden and how well he would play were silenced in the first period, when he turned aside a dozen shots, including a few nice saves during the six minutes of penalty kill time.

The Soviets took the lead just 1:12 into the second period, when defenceman Yuri Liapkin beat Dryden with a low, screened shot from the blue line that hit a skate on its way through. Hull tied the game at 5:13, putting in a Gilbert rebound over Tretiak. Just sixty-eight seconds later, Berenson set up Cournoyer in the slot to make it 2–1. Just fifteen seconds after that, Henderson intercepted a pass near centre ice and surprised Tretiak with a shot from the high slot, the eventual game-winning goal. Three goals in just eighty-three seconds, 3–1 Canada. But then the Canadians got nasty, essentially just playing their game, and the referees got creative. They made a couple offside calls against Canada on plays that might have led to scoring chances. Replays showed both plays were onside.

A controversial play occurred midway through the period when Clarke, on a backcheck, slashed star winger Valeri Kharlamov on an already sore ankle, earning a two-minute slashing penalty, a ten-minute misconduct, the applause of some, and the contempt of many.

Although Kharlamov, who had been a major pain for the Canadians, was able to finish the game, he did miss the seventh game and was largely ineffective in the final game. It was believed he had a fractured ankle.

At the time, Kharlamov had scored or assisted on all three game-winning goals for the Soviets and had six points in the series. Canada had assigned Ron Ellis to shadow him, which was a difficult assignment, although he did a good job. Several Canadians had tried to rough up Kharlamov. According to several players, after the first period Sinden allowed Ferguson to address the team and he essentially said, "Somebody's got to get that guy, he's killing us." Clarke apparently thought Ferguson was talking to him.

"My view on this: I don't care how we win, as long as we win," said Ferguson.

"Fergie might have said that, I don't know what he meant by it," said Sinden. "He might have said that. When you're getting hurt by a player on the other team, then you try, especially in days gone by, 'You got so-and-so tonight and I want you to take care of him.' That was a very big part of coaching. Clarke was a rough player. He wasn't big enough to bodycheck, but he could check. It was a Bobby Clarke check. Because it was on such a star player it got a lot more play than it normally would get."

"There was so much emotion in that game," said Clarke. "We were cranked up. I cracked that guy's ankle. We had just reached the end of it. The refereeing was one side of it. We had just had enough. I'm not sure how to describe it, but it was almost like, 'Fuck it, let's just go play our hearts out.'"

As for the slash, "it was in the course of the game. I know I whacked him pretty hard. No one said anything about it at the time. I got a penalty. There was nothing until much later."

Indeed, there were several members of Team Canada who insisted they were unaware of the slash, or at least the severity of it. Most, not all, weren't sad to have seen or heard that it happened.

"At that point in time, it's anything we can do to get an advantage—again this was war," said Seiling. "I know Canadian purists derided it and derided him. It's not something that didn't happen in the NHL. We couldn't lose; you lose the game and we're done. They did a lot of dirty things during the series, too. Nobody was a white knight. Nobody had their hands clean. They kicked. Back in those days when you played the Soviets and the Czechs, you were going to get spit on, you were going to get kicked, speared. Clarkie gives him a two-hander, they did things, so be it. It's war. I'm certainly not going to apologize for it, that's for sure."

"Hockey was rough," said Cournoyer. "He played like he did for Philadelphia, things happen. Hockey is like that; you don't think, you just do it. It could have happened to us, too, because they weren't clean, either. They were not angels."

Park had a clear view of the play, as Kharlamov was rushing into the Canadian zone and Park and his partner Gary Bergman were defending.

"He was coming up on us and I'm looking at him, it's a two on two," said Park. "I'm looking at the two guys. I don't even see the slash and it's right in front of me. Because my focus is on the angle I might have on Kharlamov, I don't even see the slash and it can't be more than eight to ten feet from me. Was it an intentional slash? Absolutely. I know that of all the guys on the Soviet team, who would go toe to toe with you after a hit, it was Kharlamov. He could be belligerent, too, which was great, it's what made him such a great player. And you know what Clarkie is like. We were doing a tour a few years ago and somebody asked the same question—hell, I've been slashed by Clarkie like that. He did pretty good damage. I would have probably slashed the guy, too. I don't think any slash is intended to break an ankle, or break a bone. It's meant to do damage. Do I think Clarkie slashed him to break his ankle? No, he slashed him to give him a bruise. He came back for game eight, but he was laboring for sure."

Clarke said he never did talk with Kharlamov afterwards, nor did their paths cross again as Kharlamov died tragically in a car accident in 1981.

"I am convinced that Bobby Clarke was given the job of taking me out of the game," Kharlamov was quoted as saying years later. "Sometimes, I thought it was his only goal. I looked into his angry eyes, saw his stick, which he wielded like a sword, and didn't understand what he was doing. It had nothing to do with hockey."

Clarke was quoted after the game by columnist Dick Beddoes as saying, "If I hadn't learned to lay on what you call a wicked two-hander, I would never have left Flin Flon, Manitoba. It was necessary."

"He couldn't keep up with him using the rules, so he had to take him out," said Mikhailov. "The coach gave him the assignment to cover Kharlamov within the rules. But he couldn't, so he had to neutralize him and that's what he did. Was it deliberate or accidental? Let God be his judge, that's all."

"Even Bobby Clarke admitted that he became a kind of anti-hero not just among our fans, but even among Canadians," said Tretiak. "It's wrong to knock a player out of the game like that. He said, 'My coach gave me this assignment and I did it.' Perhaps we should blame the coach for such an assignment. But I guess, in such battle, everything is allowed—just as long as you win."

"Kharlamov's injury didn't really affect us emotionally," said Yakushev. "It affected us on the ice. One of our leading forwards practically missed two games. He missed one and played on one leg in the other. So, from a hockey perspective this was a huge loss."

Clarke was an amazing story. When he was twelve years old, he was diagnosed with type 1 diabetes. He was a good junior, but a lot of NHL teams were concerned he wouldn't be able to play pro hockey as a result of the disease and passed on him in the draft. Clarke proved them wrong. One of the final players added to the original thirty-five-man Team Canada roster, essentially because Walt Tkaczuk couldn't leave his hockey school, Clarke proved any doubters wrong again and clicked immediately with Henderson and Ellis. He took key faceoffs, helped set up goals, had a few himself, and was a pest. And he played with poise beyond his years.

"It's like I told him after the series was over, 'Bobby, I had a problem with you doing that,'" said Phil Esposito. "He said, 'What do you mean?' I said, 'You should have done it in the first game!' I had no problem with it. They were doing things to us that I had never felt before. Bobby was one of those guys who would do whatever it took to win."

Although Savard and Clarke became good friends over the years, in his book *Forever Canadien* Savard was critical of his teammate. "Nobody can approve of Bobby Clarke's slash. The problem was, the National Hockey League let him play like that. He wasn't doing anything different." Savard added that what happened in Stockholm, then in Moscow, with the Canadians, "darkens the whole picture a bit—it's a stain on the canvas."

"I didn't like [the slash] at all," said Henderson, adding that there was no sportsmanship in it. "Hockey's a tough game, you can hit guys, but just to go out—you might as well just do it in the hallway, what's the difference? Clarkie, that's just who he was. I don't think that's a part of hockey. I think the Philadelphia Flyers [known as the Broad Street Bullies in the 1970s] ruined hockey for a while there. There's a line there, you've got to respect your opponents. That didn't sit well with me. But today, that's who he is. Everybody has a style of play.

Hockey's a tough game *not* when you try to hurt people purposely. I can't think of one other guy on the team that would do that. But that's who Clarkie was . . . he played that way his whole life."

"[Paul Henderson's] a guy who scored the winning goal in the last three games," said Peter Mahovlich. "But I'm at odds with Paul about some things I don't want to get into. He was a great teammate at the time. What Bobby did was part of the game back then. Are you trying to tell me Bobby never slashed or stuck somebody in the NHL? It's just like if you knew somebody had a sore shoulder, you tried to hurt his shoulder. It wasn't Mr. Nice Guy playing Mr. Nice Guy over there. Trust me."

The difference in opinion between Clarke and Henderson boiled over in September 2002, on the eve of the thirtieth anniversary reunion. Henderson was asked what he thought of the Clarke slash. While he was full of praise for Clarke's overall play, Henderson called the slash "the lowest point of the series," to which Clarke replied, "This doesn't show any courage . . . Why rip someone for what happened thirty years ago? We were teammates, line mates, it's foolish. He's a hypocrite. If it bothers him so much now, why didn't he say anything then?"

In a separate interview, Clarke said, "Paul has got this huge head, a huge ego because he scored three goals and now Paul thinks that he's the only guy who played on that team. All of a sudden he has an opinion on everything. There were things that happened in that whole series that were not done in the NHL. The Russians did lots of dirty things, like kicking out our legs from behind us, and they used their sticks more because they didn't have fighting in Russia. I didn't sit back and decide to [slash Kharlamov]. One of the coaches said something. Paul is way out of line."

Henderson apologized to Clarke "for causing him aggravation" but stood by his opinion in terms of sportsmanship. Clarke told TSN, "To me, it was phony."

Looking back on that incident in 2002, Clarke said, "It never bothered me. I didn't give a shit whether or not Paul liked it. I did it. I never hide. It wasn't like I pretended I did it by accident. I did it and I'll live with it."

After the Clarke slash, officiating became the story of game 6. Later in the second period, Hull was called for a soft slashing penalty at 17:02—just nine seconds later Yakushev scored on the power play to cut the lead to one. Just thirty-five seconds after that, the Canadians got into more penalty trouble when Esposito was given a five-minute major for high-sticking defenceman Alexander Ragulin. Ferguson was then given a two-minute bench penalty for complaining. At that point, the Canadians had been given twenty-nine minutes in penalties, the Soviets just four.

"I remember Ragulin, he was a massive human being," said Esposito. "He was big and he was strong. He was coming at me. In our day, when a guy is coming at you like that you put your stick up to protect yourself. We're head to head and he's saying something in Russian—I said to him, 'Geezus your breath stinks!' He was full of garlic. I don't know how true this is, but apparently they ate raw garlic. Who the hell knows, but he stunk, I can tell you that. I was happy they didn't know how to fight. I thought if this guy grabbed me, it would be worse than when Timmy Horton grabbed me. It was my first year in the league, we're in Chicago, I'm behind the Maple Leafs net, and we start pushing and shoving, and Timmy grabbed me and bear-hugged me. I swear to God I went from six-one to six-two. He was strong. That's what Ragulin reminded me of."

"The coaches gave me the unenviable task of covering Phil Esposito," said Ragulin. "He was a different kind of centre for me—very big, strong, always in the slot. Ours was a battle of two huge bears."

Before the period was over, Kharlamov was involved in another controversial play. It seemed like he had scored a goal in the dying seconds, but the officials either didn't see it or didn't think it went in. On that two-man power play, Kharlamov, wonky ankle and all, set up on the corner of Dryden's crease. Yakushev passed the puck through the goal crease and Kharlamov shot. The puck ended up hitting Dryden's pad, deflecting up towards the open net. Dryden said he didn't know after that what exactly happened, and video of the play breaks up during the replay. It's believed the puck might have hit a mesh hanging down in the goal by the post, which was designed to keep pucks in the net, but instead might have fired it back into Dryden's glove. The referees stopped the play, the Soviets complained, but no goal. Did it hit the post or the mesh?

"I don't know [if it was a goal]," said Dryden. "I couldn't figure out afterwards how it could be in, only in that pucks that hit the mesh just inside of a post don't come back out, especially like the mesh in their nets. It's one of those things that happens. I deal with it, they deal with it, and that's what you do. I don't think it was a terribly significant moment. There was lots of time to go, for the game to go one way or another."

"Ken Dryden actually retrieved the puck from that netting and it was a goal," said Tretiak. "One hundred percent. But the referee didn't count it. If he had, it would have been a tie and the series would have been clinched."

"I think we played well," said Mikhailov. "We scored a goal which the referees disallowed. That had a negative effect on us psychologically."

Team Canada managed to kill the penalties, Savard and Lapointe, Park and Bergman, Peter Mahovlich and Phil Esposito, Berenson, J. P. Parise, and Ratelle ultimately killing all but one of eight penalties, including the major. After some harsh words from Sinden between periods and a reminder they had to stay composed and play a smart, close-checking third period, Team Canada did just that and Dryden was excellent. The only real scare came with just 2:21 remaining, when Ellis, of all players, was called for holding.

"When you say game six, it wakes me up," said Ellis. "When you look at the stats, the game is 3–2, but with a couple of minutes left in the game I took a penalty, or at least I was assessed a penalty. Boy, that was a difficult two minutes of my life. The call was ridiculous. You know the way I played. I don't take penalties with two minutes left in the game. But that's what happened. My feeling is the referees wanted to give them one more chance and I was the guy. I was pretty down sitting in the penalty box. One of the best memories I have is Phil Esposito and Pete Mahovlich, they were out there to kill the penalty, and they skated by, gave me a nod and a wink, basically saying, 'Ron, don't worry, we've got this.' That's my memory of game six. We hang on to win and we're starting to play better shift by shift."

The Soviets had a couple chances on the power play, but Dryden came up big. What was also important is that they were able to hold a lead.

Final score: Team Canada 3, Soviet Union 2.

"I can only remember, after the fifth game, how I was feeling," said Clarke. "And again, I was angry with myself. I was down. But that loss, even though we played much better, put us in a situation in which we had nothing to lose. So many times over the years, we've seen the Canadian teams in that situation play their best hockey. You think, 'We're not going to lose. We're going to somehow figure this out.' There was pride and determination that we weren't going to lose that game and the series."

And so, Team Canada lived to play another must-win game . . . one shift at a time.

By PETER DESBARATS
Star Ottawa editor

OTTAWA — Documents prepared for Manpower Minister Bryce Mackasey claim that, because of stricter enforcement of the law, 742,000 claimants were declared ineligible for unemployment benefits in the 12 month period up to last Aug. 1—30 per cent more than in the previous 12-month period.

The report tends to disprove campaign charges that Mackasey's new unemployment insurance program is as generous and loosely administered that it is contributing to unemployment by permitting large numbers of idlers to freeload on the backs of working Canadians.

The document claims that 60 per cent increase in rejections was the result of "more rigorous examination of eligibility" by unemployment insurance officials.

7,000 INELIGIBLE

It reveals that a "recent concentration" on the 16-25 age group in the files of the Unemployment Insurance Commission resulted in 7,000 claimants being interviewed and found ineligible for benefits because they were not "available, capable and willing to work."

The dossier states that, since mid-July, the commission has started to enforce a new regulation adopted last July 17 which requires that a claimant for unemployment insurance "must provide positive evidence of his interest in being employed." Before that time, a claimant merely had to state that he was available for work.

"SUSPECT" RETURNS

In one region, 1,400 questionnaires were sent to unemployment insurance recipients brought in on "suspect" returns. Fourteen of these returns resulted in 200 claimants having their benefits reduced, suspended or cut entirely.

According to the documentation now in Mackasey's hands, the commission's "abuse-detection program" has produced better results in the past than a similar program in the United States. Current upgrading of the program will

See OTTAWA, page 4

METRO WEATHER
Thursday sunny, cloudy periods. Low -3, high 60-65. Pollution Index 8 at 11 a.m. Details page 2.

The Toronto Star

ESTABLISHED 1892

August paid circulation Mon. to Fri. 494,257, Sat. 483,349

Wednesday, September 27, 1972—120 pages

Monday-Friday 10¢; Saturday 25¢; Home delivery 75¢

four star
★★★★
edition

Team Canada, Soviets threaten boycott in new referee dispute

Special to The Star

MOSCOW — The great refereeing dispute has broken out again with both Team Canada and Soviet Union hockey officials threatening to boycott the deciding eighth game of their international series unless they get their way.

The game is scheduled to begin at 12.30 p.m. EDT tomorrow.

The Soviets are insisting they have the choice of naming the referees for the game and have nominated West Germany's Josef Kompalla and Franz Bader.

These two were the object of vehement criticism and charges of incompetence by the Canadians following the sixth game, won by Canada, 3-2.

Team Canada spokesman Alan Eagleson announced Monday night that an agreement had been reached with the Soviet federation in use Sweden's Uve Dahlberg and Rudi Batja of Czechoslovakia for the two remaining games. The Russians insist that deal covered only the seventh game yesterday, won by Team Canada 4-3.

Paul Henderson of Toronto Maple Leafs scored what he called "the greatest goal of my life," to give Team Canada the win. It came at 12.56 of the final period and tied the series, three wins each with one game tied.

A summit meeting of Canadian and Soviet officials adjourned this afternoon with no resolution of the refereeing dispute in sight.

"We may get together again later tonight," said Joe Kryczka, president of the Canadian Amateur Hockey Association

"We're quite prepared to

See TEAM, page 17

★ Team Canada unbeaten with Montreal Canadiens' Serge Savard on defence. Page 21.

WITH 126 SECONDS LEFT TO PLAY, Team Canada's Paul Henderson lies sprawled in front of the Russian net with a Soviet defenceman wrapped around his legs after scoring the winning puck in yesterday's game to even the hockey series between Canada and Russia at three wins apiece and one draw. The puck hits the net high behind Soviet goalie Vladislav Tretiak (right). It was "the best goal of my life," he said later. It gives Canada a chance tomorrow to win the first world series of hockey. The Toronto Maple Leaf's series leading shooter with six goals.

— Star photo by Frank Lennon

Henderson's girls are 'too popular' after Dad's goal

By ROBERT SUTTON
Star staff writer

It was quite an exciting TV show that 9-year-old Heather Henderson saw at the library at Mississauga's Runningbrook school yesterday.

Heather's dad is Paul Henderson, and it was her dad who scored Team Canada's winning goal when the Canada national team 4-3 and tied the international series at three wins and a tie apiece

"They were slapping and slapping," Heather said after a lot of congratulatory hands came down on her shoulders. "I've got a sore back."

Henderson was trapped as he moved past the tied Soviet defender, but too late to prevent the goal, which he made while he was slamming past the net on his final moment.

He later called it "the biggest goal of my life."

"If the puck hadn't gone in," Heather told The Star, "there would have been a penalty shot. But that wouldn't have been no good because it might not have scored."

Why wasn't Heather in class? A sympathetic teacher had smuggled the Grade 4 pupil—and 10-year-old sister on the girls' floor hockey team at Runningbrook—into the library.

It wasn't an isolated incident of which schools around Metro, many teachers brought radios to class instead of trying to compete with Team Canada.

A few doors from the Runningbrook library, another Henderson 7-year-old Jennifer—had not asked to see the game but was not contrasting on her protests and her sentiment and trying to forget her radiated popularity with the boss because she wanted the Soviet Canada series.

But word got out when school was out. It was an awful "Jennifer isn't "The boys chased her all the way home."

A third Henderson daughter.

See HEATHER, page 17

PROUD DAUGHTERS of Paul Henderson show their delight at father's winning goal. Heather (left), 9, and Jill, 2, saw game on television. Jennifer, 7, missed it.

— Star photo by Reg Innell

Game replay tonight at 7

There will be a repeat of the broadcast of yesterday's Team Canada victory at the Toronto's CBC network at 7 p.m. tonight on the Soviet series at 7-2 p.m. Toronto time.

Tomorrow's deciding game — the final game in Canada's series — starts at 12.30 will be seen on Channel 6.

No 1972 peace prize Nobel committee says

OSLO (AP) — The Norwegian Nobel Peace committee announced today that it has decided not to award any Peace Prize this year.

This is the 19th successive year the prize started in 1901.

The 1971 Peace Prize went to Willy Brandt, chancellor of West Germany.

The committee gave no reason for its decision.

Trudeau is splitting the nation: Wagner

By VINCENT DEVITT
Star staff writer

Claude Wagner, chief of the Quebec Progressive Conservatives, accused Prime Minister Pierre Trudeau last night of developing Canadians by telling them the problem of national unity has been solved.

"The problem is graver than ever, and he himself must be held chiefly responsible," said Wagner, speaking at a dinner sponsored by the Toronto Junior Board of Trade.

"Let there be no mistake about this in English-speaking Canada," said Wagner, Trudeau's intransigent, arrogant attitude could lead Canada straight to disaster."

He said the separatist Parti Quebecois received 23 per cent of the vote in the 1970 Quebec election, and has continued to grow since then.

In his speech to the dinner, one of the Board of Trade holding an Adelaide St. W. Wagner described the personality of Trudeau as an issue capable of uniting such divergent forces as true-blue separatists and English-speaking Canadians of the polls Oct. 30.

Wagner was given six rounds of applause, including one standing ovation for speech which pleased separatists as frustrated Canadians as eloquently as a denounced Trudeau.

Asked after the dinner if he was attempting to make Trudeau an emotional symbol to unite the anti-establishment, Wagner said:

"I think Trudeau is the target of this campaign. He offered great expectations in 1968 and I am setting out in relation that he failed miserably."

He indicated that it was his toughest attack on Trudeau and added, "to me, but the campaign has just started."

"The question is growing that every, but I would venture into English-speaking Canada by the former judge and Quebec Liberal cabinet minister since Trudeau have three weeks ago and

accepted the party's Quebec leadership last weekend.

"I believe the Tories have Canada's greatest benefactor," he said. "Every time Trudeau smears a separatist, he creates another because..."

At the same time, Wagner

See TRUDEAU, page 4

★ NDP, Conservatives are hardly visible in Quebec poll, page 6.

Business, labor agree

Imposed settlements are no substitute for right to strike

By ROSEMARY SPEIRS
Star staff writer

Rene vice-president of Xerox Mines Ltd., Larry Alvarez, director of personnel at Riverdale Hospital, and Claire Edwards, president of the Public Service Employees, all agree that a strike of working people is a small price to pay for free labor.

As an employment vice chairman and Alderman Basil Rotenberg, he was proposing that much nobler piece of legislation before the next major event of public service negotiations.

Rotenberg was one of five panelists speaking at a Star Forum, held in the St. Lawrence Centre's Town Hall, on the topic "Should government strikes be banned?" Other panelists were Stanley Little, president of the Canadian Union of Public Employees, Peter

See BUSINESS, page 15

Pimp deported eight times got unemployment benefits

By PETER MOON
Star staff writer

A man who has been deported eight times from Canada to the United States, and who is currently appealing a deportation order, was jailed yesterday for living off the avails of prostitution.

Crown Attorney Robert McGee, reading John Lee Sheeley's immigration record, told Judge J. Lloyd Graham: "This is a ridiculous situation ... a penitentiary term may discourage him from coming back again."

But Graham didn't send Sheeley to penitentiary; he sent him to reformatory for 18 months.

The court was told that Sheeley, while living off the avails of prostitution collected unemployment insurance for almost a year.

Sheeley, 30, of Niles, Ave. is cited by Metro police as an enabling example of the ease with which Canada can take advantage of two holes in Canada's immigration laws.

Visitors who apply for landed immigrant status have an automatic right to

appeal to the Immigration Appeal Board if their application is refused. But they apply from their own country, they have no right of appeal.

The catch is that marginally qualified immigrants can come to Canada as visitors and apply here, even if they are rejected by specifically trained immigration officers they appeal to the appeal board's process that can involve a wait of penalty any. But that wouldn't have been no good because it might not have scored.

Sheeley first came to Canada in 1962 to light as a professional boxer. He applied for landed immigrant

See DEPORTED, page 19

Huge gas pipeline threatens the Arctic's fragile environment

★ David Crane of The Star's Ottawa bureau today continues a five-part series on the plan to transport natural gas across a five thousand mile northern Canada — an undertaking described by some observers as rivalling in importance the building of the Canadian Pacific Railway. This is the fourth instalment.

By DAVID CRANE
Star staff writer

OTTAWA — The huge northern gas pipeline, which will carry the rich reserves of Arctic natural gas to energy-short United States utilities, in certain to damage the precarious Arctic environment and disrupt the lives and culture of northern Indians and Eskimos.

Although the environmental and social consequences of the planned pipeline are widely screened at less central than its economic impact, these questions will have to have a thorough public airing if the pipeline project is to go ahead.

The pipeline itself will run 1,200 miles through some of the last remaining great wilderness areas in the world. It will stretch hundreds of miles over permafrost, cross several hundred rivers and streams, run through treacherous muskeg, and progress work sites along the banks of Canada's greatest waterway, the Mackenzie River.

In the process, it could cause serious disruption to plant and animal life, create problems with landslides and erosion, and upset the North's fragile ecological balance.

The presence of thousands of construction workers will open earth-moving machines digging a wide trench through the unbroken country, building up air strips and service roads, setting up huge work camps, and shipping in thousands of tons of pipe, steel, oil and other supplies, is bound to create severe problems.

I recommended caution will have to be exercised in carrying out one of the biggest construction projects in history.

In the process the northern native peoples—about 30,000 Indians, 20,000 Eskimos and several thousand Metis —the northern pipeline project could bring some benefits. But it also would bring social and cultural problems.

Northern natives are gradually moving away from their historic hunting and fishing based on a nomadic way of life.

They are increasingly settling in small communities across the North, giving up a way community while their children are being educated in new schools.

This change in lifestyle coincides with a new awareness and militancy. More than ever before, northern natives are concerned about protecting their traditions, languages, culture, and their hunting

See PIPELINE, page 1

The prime minister had been accused of splitting the nation, while Team Canada was continuing to bring it together. (Courtesy of the *Toronto Star*)

CHAPTER 15

Game 7—Nothing Short of a Win

Heading into the seventh game, a few important assets were missing in action. The Soviets were without star winger Valeri Kharlamov, the victim of that slash from an unrepentant Bobby Clarke the previous game. And the Canadians had a stash of their beer and steaks disappear, victims of more off-ice gamesmanship and an apparently vibrant black market. Neither side was terribly happy.

"There were some mind games being played, no question," said coach Harry Sinden. "They did things like that, screw around with our practice times, they even did it in Toronto. They practised and wouldn't get off the ice when it was our time to get on. They're notorious for that kind of stuff. They had been doing it for years. The day before this game, we went to practice and there were two hundred school kids on the ice."

To solve that particular problem, a few of the Canadians took to the ice with pucks. The children exited—unharmed, but mindful of the power of the slap shot. But the late-night phone calls, the intercoms mysteriously switching on, the KGB lurking in the shadows—it all continued. Somehow, it became more motivating than annoying after a while.

"They did it in Oslo [Norway] at the World Championship," continued Sinden. "You're always screaming at them. I remember, I wanted to meet the coach of the Russian team in 1958—[Anatoly] Tarasov—so we had breakfast, Wren Blair and I, Tarasov, somebody else, and an interpreter. Tarasov said something and the interpreter interpreted it and Blair shouted back, 'Oh, bullshit.' Tarasov jumped out of his chair and yelled in Russian, 'Don't call me a Bolshevik!' He was very, very upset. At the time, I'm saying 'No, no, it's bullshit not Bolshevik.' But they were sensitive politically. I didn't notice that as much in '72, but it was there. We found it strange when our food started to disappear. That was the first indication there might be something going on, but that didn't have anything to do with their hockey team. The hotel workers were hungry."

Meanwhile, Team Canada was faced with an identical challenge in game 7—win or else.

"When we won that sixth game, I really believed 'We've got them now, we can beat these guys,'" said Paul Henderson. "I remember, Tarasov once said of the Russians, 'We can do everything as well as the Canadians, but we just can't match their heart.' He was the architect of Soviet hockey. And that's the difference between communism and democracy, I think."

There was a belief, amongst the Canadian players and even some fans and scouts, that the Soviets were robotic when they played. The Canadians were more emotional, and sometimes that made a positive difference. The thinking was the Canadians were allowed to express themselves, the Soviets weren't, the difference in systems and ways of life.

It was back when Team Canada had arrived in Moscow that Henderson and assistant coach John Ferguson had a talk. Ferguson, a heart-and-soul type in his playing days, brought a lot of energy and emotion to the team. He was, after all, the driving force behind Clarke taking down Kharlamov. Amongst his many duties, Ferguson was in charge of pep talks—unless you were a referee. He could motivate with fear, or the fear that he would motivate with fear. He was a menacing individual with a heart of gold. That day, he had some inspirational words for Henderson.

"I remember the first practice in Moscow and Fergie skated up beside me and he said, 'If we're going to win this series, we really need you to play well, we need you to score some goals. I want to let you know we are really counting on you,'" said Henderson. "I don't care who you are, you need a little encouragement. But he said they were really depending on us [Henderson, Clarke, and Ron Ellis] as a line. I never forgot that. We had one of the reunions years later and I sat down with Fergie and we had a beer or two and I told him that really solidified my confidence. Geez, these guys are counting on me."

And they delivered.

Henderson, remember, had scored two goals in the fifth game, and had they not blown the big lead in the third period he would have been credited with the game-winning goal. Clarke had a goal and two assists. Henderson scored an unassisted goal in the sixth game, which turned out to be the game-winner. But the best was still to come.

"That line really meshed," said Phil Esposito. "The big ice worked well for Paul and Ronny especially. And Clarkie was just such a determined guy."

"Phil was a leader," said Peter Mahovlich. "He was the main voice. Most of the guys were quiet. Bobby Clarke would only say something if somebody said something stupid. He would tell them to 'shut up.' Both Phil and Bobby were fabulous teammates. They were guys I didn't like, who became good teammates and friends for life."

Of all the gamesmanship and hijinks away from the ice, perhaps the most significant happened the day before the seventh game, when the glow from the victory on Ferguson's face turned red with rage. Ferguson and Sinden met with the Soviet officials prior to Team Canada's practice to talk about officiating, in particular the work of West German referees Josef Kompalla and Franz Baader. They'd worked the night before and were stunningly awful—the most incompetent Sinden had ever seen, he insisted.

The seventh game was to be worked by the Swede Uwe Dahlberg and Rudolf Bata of Czechoslovakia, who had both officiated the fifth game. They were competent enough and far better than the other two. The meeting had been called by Sinden and Alan Eagleson to determine which officials would work the eighth game. Remember, earlier in the series, the Soviets had gone nuts during and after the second game in Toronto over the work of Americans Steve Dowling and Frank Larsen and insisted they not be allowed to work their next scheduled game, which was the fourth game, in Vancouver. The Soviets wanted Americans Gordon Lee and Len Gagnon, who had worked the first game, in Montreal, and the third game, in Winnipeg. Not knowing a Soviet official had stormed the officials' dressing room between periods and the overall contempt they had for Dowling and Larsen, in good faith Sinden agreed to the change. Now he was hoping for a little good faith in return from the Soviets. Good luck with that, Harry.

"I had done them a favour in Winnipeg," said Sinden. "We had a meeting about it and they announced they were going to bring in someone else. They had a Swedish official [Dahlberg] assigned to the [eighth] game, then changed it at the last minute. Eagleson said we wouldn't play if Kompalla and Baader were the officials. I remember Fergie got so upset, he said we're not going to show and he walked out of the meeting. He told us to come with him, we're not going to play. That's how much we thought the officials could influence the game."

Just prior to the seventh game there was still another twist to the plot in the officiating story. The Soviets had said they would not assign the two West Germans to the eighth game if, incredibly, defenceman Gary Bergman stopped chirping the Soviet bench during the game, in particular coach Vsevolod Bobrov.

"I didn't realize he was doing that," said Sinden. "He certainly wasn't doing it in Russian. Bergy was a very good player in that tournament."

Bergman was a thirty-three-year-old defenceman from Kenora, Ontario, who had played eight seasons with the Detroit Red Wings at the time. He wasn't flashy, though he had a couple seasons in which he put up pretty good offensive numbers. But he was very reliable. Balding, and playing without a helmet as most of the Canadians did, Bergman was almost an unassuming, but very effective, presence paired with Brad Park.

"That son of a gun came to play," said Bergman's teammate with the Red Wings, winger Mickey Redmond. "He knew how to compete. He was ready to go right from the start of training camp. Every team like this one has its stars, but you also need your soldiers. He was a reliable soldier, an unsung hero, who raised his compete level to quite a level in this series."

"Everyone was looking for a role to play on that team in training camp," said Red Berenson, also a teammate in Detroit, who had played against Bergman for years. "We had thirty-five players and just more than half of that number would dress for games. Bergy ended up pairing with Brad Park and they just connected. They really clicked. Bergy ended up playing some of the best hockey that, he would admit, he ever played. He was good with the puck, without the puck. Everything seemed to come together for him. Part of it may have been the big rink for the final four games in Moscow. He was such a good skater.

"He didn't let anyone off the hook in that tournament. He was such a competitor, and he was really caught up in the emotions of this North American way of life versus communism. A lot of us were, but it showed up in Bergy's strong play, his effort and his mindset."

Later in the game that emotion came to the fore in a vicious tussle with Boris Mikhailov. As for the chirping, Park didn't seem to notice.

"I know the Russians would talk to each other, not necessarily us," said Park. "They'd shrug their shoulders at us and look at us like we were crazy. We'd try to get in their face between whistles. I was never a yapper. I was from the Gordie Howe school of hockey: never yap when you're emotional because you're probably liable to say something stupid and everyone will remember that."

Sinden only made a couple lineup changes for the seventh game on a snowy September 26. Tony Esposito, of course, was in goal as planned, with Ed Johnston the backup. Dryden, who was scheduled to start the eighth game, watched from the stands. Sinden stuck to his goalie plan, something not a lot of coaches would have done— removing a hot hand after a victory. But it worked. Up front, winger Bill Goldsworthy replaced Berenson, who had suggested Sinden make a change.

"I played a decent [sixth] game," said Berenson. "After the game I talked to Harry and I told him to go with the guys who were playing, who were starting to round into game shape at that point in the series."

Berenson watched the final two games in the stands with his wife. With Berenson out, Sinden decided to dress just three centres and four wingers on each side. His plan was to double shift his centres, especially Esposito, to get him some more favourable line matchups. The Soviets, meantime, made several changes, including dressing seven defencemen. Kharlamov, of course, was out, a big loss, while forwards Alexander Bodunov and Yuri Lebedev were dropped, replaced by Yuri Blinov and Evgeny Mishakov. On defence, Yuri Shatalov was scratched, with Alexander Gusev and Viktor Kuzkin dressed.

The start was somewhat cautious for both teams, but of course the stakes were again incredibly high. Esposito opened the scoring from the slot at 4:09, just nine seconds after the Soviets had killed a tripping penalty to Mikhailov. Esposito took a centring pass from Ellis after he and Park had won a puck battle along the boards. Yakushev, who stepped up his game with Kharlamov out, beat Tony Esposito with a long slap shot through the legs midway through the period.

Esposito was showing that Canadian heart to which Tarasov had referred, along with a lot of rage, in what was another very physical, nasty game. Later in the period, Esposito applied a crosscheck to Mikhailov, who was a noted pest.

"On the ice, he was a fighter," said Mikhailov. "And I didn't want to concede anything. So we had good, verbal fights. Very functional back-and-forth swearing. Other than that, everything was great. We had a saying in Russian: 'Don't just go by.' So we would skate by someone and he would inevitably do something—push or trip. We tried to be patient, so the Canadian players got penalized and we were on the power play."

Vladimir Petrov, who also had been a royal pain for Esposito playing head-to-head, gave the Soviets a 2–1 lead on the power play at 16:27, with Bill White in the penalty box for interference. After Tony Esposito had tried a poke check and found himself out of position, Petrov tucked the puck past him. But before the period was over, Esposito scored his second of the game on a nifty setup from Serge Savard, who performed what became known as the "Savardian spin-o-rama" at the blue line. Savard basically had the puck on his stick, circled around with it to avoid Soviet forward Alexander Maltsev, who was going to be called for a penalty, and then set up Esposito for the goal.

"It was a crucial game, and that goal sent us back to the dressing room with it all tied up," Savard wrote in his book *Forever Canadien*. I was already performing that move when I was still very young. I soon realized how effective it was. Doug Harvey was doing it long before me, but I never tried to imitate him. It just came naturally to me."

Both teams were given three minor penalties in the first period, but the parade to the penalty box picked up in the second, during which the Soviets held a 13–7 edge in shots, but the score remained 2–2. Just 2:13 into the final period, Rod Gilbert, playing well on that newly formed line with Jean Ratelle and Dennis Hull, intercepted a Mikhailov pass, swung in front of the goal, and put a backhand shot between the pads of Vladislav Tretiak. The Canadians never really thought they had found a weakness in Tretiak, but they did think he was beatable in close, especially if they shot quickly. That lead lasted just over three minutes before Yakushev tied it on a power play, with Bergman in the box for holding.

The Soviets pushed hard to get the go-ahead goal, as the Canadians at times seemed weary, but Tony Esposito was brilliant. He had complained of feeling under the weather earlier in the day, a little rundown from the long haul of the series, but it didn't show in his performance. As the third period wore on and the two teams changed ends midway through (as was the custom for the series and in international hockey), it seemed like the Soviets were almost content with playing for a tie, which effectively would have won them the series.

The game turned ugly with 3:34 remaining. Mikhailov and Bergman started mixing it up behind the Canadians' goal in a battle over the puck. Each had a glove in the other's face. Bergman was banging the Soviet's head against the wire mesh, while Mikhailov was kicking Bergman in the shins. Punches were soon thrown and the benches emptied. The usually mild-mannered Yvan Cournoyer even jumped into the melee, throwing punches at Mikhailov. Earlier in the game, Phil Esposito had threatened Mikhailov with a throat-cutting gesture (not the first time he'd made such a gesture in the series), and Bergman did the same later.

Comparing it to the Clarke slash on Kharlamov, "the Mikhailov kick on Gary Bergman was in the same boat," said Ellis. But it did lack the same outrage. "Mikhailov's tip of his skate went right through Gary's shin pad, it cut his leg. After the game, I saw Gary pour blood out of his skate. Mikhailov probably hadn't done that before or after, either. It's hard to describe the emotions that we were all going through at the time. I even had to admit I did some things that I wasn't proud of. They weren't terrible-terrible. I just took that extra jab I wouldn't do in the NHL, but it was strictly because I was caught up in the moment. That's where the word 'war' comes from that Phil had mentioned."

War. None of them thankfully had been to war in the traditional sense, but it felt like the perfect metaphor for what they were experiencing in this series, the perfect description to give perspective to what had become much more than just a hockey series.

"I said I would kill to win, I did say that," said Phil Esposito. "I said I often wondered, even in a war, how somebody could shoot somebody else, but in my mind there was no doubt I would have killed those bastards to win. That scared me. That's how emotional I got."

"It was political, their systems versus ours, that was the subtext," said Park. "You don't skate up to a Soviet guy and say, 'I think your culture sucks.' You don't know if he would understand it number one, and number two it's irrelevant. Its about who's going to score the most goals and who's going to walk out winners."

"I would never have killed anyone, it would never have gotten to that point," said Henderson. "But it had gotten so political, all the crap that was going on, it took on another dimension."

"The Russians had the same emotions as us at this point in the series, but they didn't show it that much," said Clarke. "They were stoic. But their competitiveness on the ice was just as much as us. We just had an emotional aspect that could help us rise to the occasion."

Whatever the emotions at the moment, the Canadians had to focus on scoring in order to keep their hopes of winning the series alive. With just 2:20 remaining, the teams playing four-on-four after the melee, Clarke won a faceoff in his own zone. Guy Lapointe picked up the puck and passed it behind his net to Savard, who eluded the chase of Soviet forward Vladimir Vikulov and threw a perfect backhand pass to Henderson, who was cruising towards the centre line.

Henderson had two forwards in chase and two defenders—Valeri Vasiliev and Gennady Tsygankov—ahead of him. He faked to his right, pushed the puck through the two defencemen, then cut to his left and darted around them, scooped the puck, and rushed in on Tretiak. As he was being hip-checked by Vasiliev and falling to the ice, Henderson shot the puck up and over Tretiak's blocker. It was Tsygankov who drew the public wrath of coach Bobrov.

With just 2:06 remaining, the Canadians emptied their bench again, but this time for entirely different reasons. According to Conacher, the goal light didn't immediately switch on, something that would become an issue in the next game.

"When we went out on the ice, I looked up at the clock and I thought, 'This will probably be my last shift,'" said Henderson. "'I've got to do something here.' I remember saying to myself, 'We've got to get a goal on this shift.' Then, of course, I score the best goal I ever scored in my whole life, a one on four. It was the only time in my whole life—one on four—and I put it in the top corner. The big ice was perfect for me. When you play with the best players in the world and your assets are your speed and shot, they're going to get you the puck and they did.

"That was the most satisfying goal I ever scored in my life, no question. I said to my wife after the game, 'I will probably never score a bigger goal in my life unless we win the Stanley Cup in overtime and I score that goal. But I can die a happy man.' And then, of course, two days later I score the only garbage goal I got the whole series, and you've got to be a good hockey fan to remember the one I scored in the seventh game."

One thing is for certain: it may have been the best goal Henderson ever scored, but time would indeed soon prove it wasn't the biggest.

"When he deked the two defencemen and scored the winner," said Phil Esposito, "that was one of the greatest plays of all time. I remember I was on the bench and I jumped three feet in the air."

Final score: Team Canada 4, Soviet Union 3.

Two other Canadians were also excited by the latest round of Henderson heroics. Alan Eagleson and Toronto Maple Leafs owner Harold Ballard, two of the more outspoken characters in the game, who were also business partners in the series, held court in the buoyant dressing room afterwards. According to Dan Proudfoot of the *Globe and Mail*, Eagleson, who was Henderson's lawyer, approached Ballard and said, "Harold, that goal has to be worth $25,000."

Both Henderson and Ellis played for Ballard with the Maple Leafs. Henderson had just signed a new two-year contract that summer.

"Why not make it $50,000?" said Ballard.

Eagleson insisted a $25,000 gift was more than generous, and he brought Ballard to Henderson to tell his star winger the good news. Ballard quickly changed lanes and made everything out to be a big joke.

"Eagleson was in one of his foolish moods," said Ballard. "He was joking and yelling like he does when he's all excited. He did all the talking. But he's not spending my money. It's a lot of crap."

"I have a long memory," said Eagleson at the time. "And if he doesn't give them [Henderson and Ellis] something for this, they'll both go to the World Hockey Association when their contracts expire, if the WHA is still going."

Ironically, Henderson played out those two years on his contract with the Leafs, and in the summer of 1974 he signed with the Toronto Toros and played for Team Canada WHA in their Summit Series, which the Soviets won, 4-1-3, still much closer than many had expected since the upstart league didn't have the same depth of stars. On that 1974 team along with Henderson were '72 teammates Frank Mahovlich and Pat Stapleton, while the team also featured Bobby Hull, Gerry Cheevers, and J. C. Tremblay, who were not allowed to play in the 1972 series because they had signed with the WHA.

To his credit, Henderson refused to talk about Ballard and money after the seventh game. The goal and the win were reward enough. And he and his teammates were focussed on the big prize at hand.

After all, the series with so many improbable twists and turns was now tied, 3-3-1, with the historic eighth game two days away.

"I don't think we could say we were taking over," said Park. "But shift by shift, period by period, we were starting to shut them down, we were controlling large portions of the game. We're attacking, we're getting back in time, everyone's on board with the program. But there's one thing the Russians had never faced when they would go to the World Championships or Olympics. Back then, they played each team once. They never had to play the same team back to back to back . . .

"In the NHL, we're used to seven-game playoff series. We're used to playing the same guys night after night, trying to wear them down and lean on them, punish guys now and it pays off later—that's part of a seven-game series. They had never had to do that. Remember the old line from *Butch Cassidy and the Sundance Kid* when the guys are coming? 'Who are these fucking guys?' To a certain extent I think that's what the Russians were feeling because we weren't going away."

Henderson has scored for Canada. And a country celebrates. (Courtesy of the *Toronto Star*)

CHAPTER 16

Game 8—Fight Until the Last Second

He can't remember exactly what day it happened, but it was late in the series and Phil Esposito was experiencing mild chest pains. Nothing severe, but just enough that he talked with the team doctors, and interpreter Aggie Kukulowicz accompanied him to hospital for an examination. The doctors there gave Esposito a fluoroscope, he believes, which allows them to see the pumping action of the heart, amongst other functions.

"The Russian guy said something, I had no idea what he said of course, so I said to Aggie, 'What did he say?'" recalled Esposito. "Aggie said, 'The doctor can't believe the size of your heart. He says no wonder you can stay on the ice so long.' The size of my heart? No one's ever said that before. I always had great cardiovascular, but no one ever talked about the size of my heart. Okay, so what does that mean? 'Am I having a heart attack or not?' 'No, you're not having any problems.'"

But the extra big heart did give the Soviets problems throughout the series, and especially in the eighth game and the final period.

213

"Those four games that Phil played in Moscow were the best four games he ever played in his life," said centre Bobby Clarke. "He was the guy who in a lot of ways played differently over there than he played in the NHL, but he still scored. I thought he was the most impressive player."

"We all knew that Phil was our leader, our best player," said Henderson. "I really believe the best period of hockey ever played by a Canadian hockey player at that time was the third period of game eight that Phil Esposito played."

Before there were any heroics, however, from Esposito or Henderson or any of the other Canadians and the Soviets, there were more hijinks to be played out off the ice, once again involving the game officials: the first act in a real-life twisted comedy-drama. Otherwise known as: just another day in the Summit Series.

Team Canada thought it had an agreement in place long before the eighth game as to the officials who would be working that night. In their minds, it would be the Swede Uwe Dahlberg and the Czech Rudolf Bata, who had together worked game 5 and game 7. The Canadians could have settled for anyone but the two West Germans, Josef Kompalla and Franz Baader, whom they had encountered in Sweden and who had worked game 6 and given the Canadians thirty-one minutes in penalties.

Having done the Soviets an officiating favour earlier in the series, the Canadians expected the favour returned and believed it had all been decided and agreed upon. Concerned perhaps that the series might be slipping away, and claiming the officials didn't want to see their associates "discriminated" against, the Soviets decided the West Germans should work the final game.

Team Canada—coach Harry Sinden, assistant John Ferguson, and Alan Eagleson—threatened to not play the game. There were meetings and debates and standoffs, and eventually it was proposed by Gary Smith, who worked in the Canadian Embassy, that each team select one official each. The Soviets predictably selected Kompalla, while the Canadians asked for Dahlberg. But just when it seemed the problem was solved, at least in the best way possible, Canada was told that Dahlberg was sick and couldn't work. Eagleson insisted he had spoken with Dahlberg earlier and called him later and he was fine. But Dahlberg was told by Andrei Starovoitov, the big shot in the Soviet Ice Hockey Federation, who had stormed the officials' room in Toronto, that he would never work again if he didn't say he was sick, and the official played along.

"Just before midday, I got the information that I would be officiating with Kompalla," Bata told the *Globe and Mail* at the fortieth anniversary. "Very honestly, I wasn't happy with this arrangement because Dahlberg and I worked well together. We were really a team."

"We had to put up with it," said Sinden.

"We were told the day before that the Russians wanted to change the referees," said defenceman Brad Park. "They wanted guys they controlled. And it had showed with their preponderance for giving us penalties. One of the games we had thirty-one minutes in penalties, that's more than half the game we had someone in the penalty box. And nobody died! It was bad. It was tainted."

"All these years have passed, and you are still trying to push politics into these wonderful games," said Boris Mikhailov. "Why all this politics stuff, what politics? We were simply defending the honour of our country and Team Canada theirs. We wanted to prove to each other who was better hockey-wise. What politics?"

And so the scene was set for what would alternately be one of the greatest and strangest and most controversial hockey games ever played, on September 28, 1972—in what would truly become a "where were you" moment.

"Tonight, we're making hockey history," broadcaster Foster Hewitt told roughly 16 million Canadian television viewers. "I wouldn't miss this game for all the tea in China."

Indeed, twenty-six days after it all began, when Team Canada was supposed to sweep the eight games but instead the hockey world was turned upside down, the final chapter of either the greatest upset in hockey or the greatest comeback was about to be penned—the series tied 3-3-1, with the pressure-packed game 8 at the Luzhniki Ice Palace in Moscow. Hockey supremacy and all the real-life and political bragging rights that were attached to it came down to one amazing hockey game.

"We'd brought the series back to even, we were ecstatic," said Park. "A few guys had called home by this time, and we realized what was going on, that the entire nation was shutting down to watch the series."

Canadian fans, who had all but abandoned their hockey heroes after the first four games at home, in which the Soviets won twice and tied another, were suddenly back on the bandwagon with both feet, flags waving, hearts beating. On game days, the country stood still watching, but especially on the day of the eighth game. Schools ground to a halt, with kids ushered into gymnasiums or doubling up in classrooms to watch on TVs. Offices emptied out. People took days off work. Others stood in front of appliance store windows to watch. This was "our" game still, and what would happen in the eighth game mattered greatly to the Canadian psyche.

For the final game, Sinden made two lineup changes, putting in, with hope he could help the offence, winger Frank Mahovlich, who had sat out the previous two games because of a sore knee. He replaced belligerent winger Bill Goldsworthy, who wouldn't have stood a chance with Kompalla officiating. Sinden admitted he did give some thought to perhaps dressing Bobby Orr, who hadn't played a game in the series. Orr had travelled with the team and had practised, but his injured left knee still wasn't fully recovered enough to play. If Orr dressed, Sinden said, he would have used him on the point of the power play, but then, he thought, the Canadians didn't get enough power plays to justify playing a body short the rest of the game.

And the Canadians already had several wounded on the blue line: Bill White (sore heel), Gary Bergman (back), and Pat Stapleton (knee) were banged up, though all three were able to play. Sinden had rookie Dale Tallon, who hadn't played a game other than in Sweden, take the warm-up just in case. Sinden, by the way, didn't watch the warm-up, instead remaining in his coach's office, drinking six cups of coffee. He had skipped watching warm-ups before game 6 and made that his new pre-game superstition, along with wearing his alligator-skin shoes. There were also the two glasses of scotch whiskey with Ferguson back at the hotel a couple hours before the game. As if they needed to be any more annoyed, Sinden reported that steaks had magically disappeared again, these ones reserved for the pre-game meal. In fact, most of their game-day schedule had been in flux, because of the officiating controversy.

"Harry told me that I was going to have to play that night," said Tallon. "I was pretty nervous about that. I skated around in warm-up, but Bill and Pat found a way to get themselves healthy enough to play the game. I had an option to either sit on the bench or in the dressing room. I was too pent up with emotion to sit on the bench. So I stayed and moved around the locker room. I could tell by the fans' reaction what was happening. The Russian fans whistled and the Canadian fans cheered. I finally found myself a comfortable spot in front of Bobby Clarke's spot in the dressing room. He had this rabbit's foot hanging there."

The Soviets only made a couple lineup changes, with winger Valeri Kharlamov returning after missing a game. He, of course, had been wounded by a Clarke slash in the sixth game. While Kharlamov was back on the ice, he was also seen hobbling into the arena before the game. Veteran defenceman Alexander Ragulin was taken out because of his lack of speed and a supposed leg injury.

The next round of mischief occurred just prior to the pre-game exchanging of gifts. The Canadian players were giving the Soviets white Stetsons, but Team Canada also had brought a totem pole to present to the Soviet ice hockey federation. But they were told for television reasons there was no time for that to happen.

"We had a totem pole that we brought over from Canada to bring out on the ice as a gift, and they told us it wasn't in the program," Canadian emissary Gary Smith told the *Globe*. "I told their guy, 'look, you got to present your Petrushka dolls in Canada; this is our gift and we're going to bring it on the ice.' He said, if we did that, all TV coverage would be cut. So, before the faceoff, we snuck on the ice with this thing, made our presentation and nothing happened."

During the introductions, Phil Esposito hung on the boards as he skated forward, something he had done since the pratfall prior to game 5, but it was all done in jest. Bergman waved "V" for victory and did it with purpose.

After all that, history—one way or another—was about to be made, and the players knew it and felt it all too well.

"Yes, very much," said goaltender Ken Dryden, the other lineup change. "It does [weigh on you], you know that this has been and will be a big event."

"Absolutely, we were going to make history one way or another," said defenceman Rod Seiling, who did not dress for the game. "We all knew the significance. You just want to keep playing the way you've been playing. It doesn't always work that way. You tell yourself, don't change a thing, but subconsciously you do. We didn't want to change a thing, we had a winning formula, we were on a roll, just keep riding the wave."

"Going into the eighth game, we knew we had to win," said Mikhailov. "There was much pressure to succeed on both teams."

Sinden had mapped out his goaltending plans after the fifth game, and he stuck to his word, despite Tony Esposito playing well in the seventh game. Of course, Dryden had played well in the sixth game, and that was enough to overlook that he was beaten 7–3 in the series opener, then 5–3 in the fourth game in Vancouver, and hadn't played particularly well in either game. But he rebounded to win that sixth game 3–2 and was given the start in goal. Sinden made sure to remind Dryden that he would not only start, but he would finish.

"For me, Ken Dryden was the best goalie I ever played with," said Canadiens teammate Yvan Cournoyer. "The Russians had a different game, that's why we lost 7–3 in the first game. We had to protect the middle of the ice. The angles on the big ice were different. He had to adjust, too. Ken, for me, I would have played him there for all the games. We won so many Stanley Cups with him. He saved us so many times. He was the best I played with."

"We had Dryden in net," said Phil Esposito. "I remember, before game eight, the morning of that game, both Tony and Kenny were going to dress. I said to Harry, with no offence to Ken, Harry you've got to play Tony. He said, we're not sure yet who we're going to play. I said, you've got to play Tony. He's won these games. He said, we'll see. So, Kenny went in."

Dryden remembers Phil Esposito walking by him between games and saying "You'd better be hot tomorrow night."

"I knew he meant it good-naturedly—I knew that—but it was there nonetheless," said Dryden. "No one ever seems to go to a defenceman, or a forward, and say: 'You have to win it for us.' They come to the goaltender. If the goaltender doesn't contribute, his team usually loses."

Which may not be fair, but it is often reality. As such, Dryden admitted that he was feeling nervous from just about the time the seventh game ended until arriving at the rink and eventually puck drop for the eighth game.

"I was more nervous than I've ever been," he said. "The physical manifestation of nerves for me was always my stomach; it never quite felt like butterflies to me, it was more like an echoing emptiness. But from the moment I woke up the morning after the seventh game, right up until getting to the rink and about to play, it was my legs. It was jelly. I had never been nervous in my legs before, and that surprised me. I had never had that before."

Dryden did what he could to distract himself from the feeling in his legs, even touring a Soviet sports facility, which helped, but then the strange new feeling came back. How unnerving is that?

"It gets your attention," he laughed. "Again, it's just something you have to have an answer for. If you know that you don't have to find an answer for a day and a half, it would be nice if you could find that answer the day before, but if not, that's all right, then it's the next day. Then it's noon, well then it's afternoon. The game's going to be played, you've got to be ready—it doesn't matter whether your legs are feeling that way, you have to have an answer for that."

The lead up to this final game seemingly had everything, from the squabble over the officials to the future president of Russia, nineteen-year-old Vladimir Putin, sitting in the stands with his father. In subsequent years, Putin, an avid hockey fan who has often used on-ice appearances to bolster his political image, has hosted both teams for reunion festivities.

But it was also a game that on the ice had everything good and bad.

"I would say that's right and if it didn't have everything, I'm not quite sure what it didn't have," said Dryden. "And because it's amazing, you don't know what it's going to be."

The first amazing thing wasn't entirely unpredictable.

Every worst Canadian fear about the officiating came to pass in the first few minutes when White, at 2:25, and then Peter Mahovlich, less than a minute after, at 3:01, were both penalized for holding, putting Team Canada two men short. To say they disagreed with the calls is an understatement.

Just twenty-three seconds into the two-man advantage, Alexander Yakushev opened the scoring, tapping a rebound past Dryden. The Soviets were called for a penalty at 3:44, Vladimir Petrov for hooking, but then J. P. Parise was called for interference, for bumping into Alexander Maltsev at 4:10, and he became entirely unglued.

"Somehow the game starts, in the first couple of minutes we're two men short," said Brad Park. "They score and just after that, that's when J. P. Parise goes ballistic because they call him for interference."

Maltsev had the puck at the Soviet blue line, pushed it past Parise, who then shoved him and watched as he fell to the ice a second later. The call was made, although it appeared that Bata, who was closest to the play, waved his arms to suggest the play was okay. Parise was incensed. He swore at Kompalla, earning himself a misconduct, then left the penalty box, took a circle around centre ice and the Canadian bench, then charged with his stick raised at Kompalla, who was standing against the boards. Parise threatened to club him, but wisely decided otherwise, instead shouting more obscenities at the official. That immediately earned him a game misconduct. Team Canada was irate, with chairs, stools, towels, and (more) obscenities hurled from the bench.

"J.P. said he [Maltsev] had the puck. How was that interference?" asked Park. "I knew he wasn't going to hit the referee, but he sure made the referee think he was."

"That's not in his character to act like that," said Sinden. "He played for me in the minors and in Boston before he went to Minnesota. He turned pro with me. I knew him very well. I'd never seen him act up like that. I got blamed for throwing the chair, but it wasn't me. That's why you have an assistant coach, who wasn't allowed on the bench, but he was right beside it."

Sinden's fingerprints no doubt were on something that hit the ice and he admitted he was trying to get the officials' attention and exploded on purpose, knowing it would have an impact, perhaps intimidating them.

"It was crazy. Parise was crazy, crazy," Bata told the *Globe*. "[Parise] didn't like the call. Kompalla called a misconduct and Parise then skated at us with his stick up and cried, 'I'll kill you.'

"I skated to the penalty box and told the off-ice official, who was the second chief of Russian hockey, 'The game is over. We can play no more.' The Soviet official said, 'Rudy, be so kind and finish the game, we have to play and we have to finish in regular time. Please try.' I decided to listen to him. God helped me in that moment."

"That game, the refereeing was the most dreadful I've ever experienced," said Parise. "During the game, the frustration just built up to such a high level. That incident, I did it for a couple of reasons. I wanted to let them know that we had had enough. If they're not going to play fair, we won't. It was war. It was bullshit that Kompalla was the referee in the first place and not Dahlberg. It was just more of their bullshit. The first call just before that was questionable. Then we get the second penalty while we're still killing a penalty. Then he calls me. It was a good check. It was an honest check. It's not interference when the guy has the puck. So I say, 'What the fuck! Are you kidding me?' Then he gives me ten minutes and now I'm saying, 'You son of a bitch!' I was going to hit him right over the head, but between starting and reaching where he was standing, I thought about what would happen, and I would probably have been banned for life. I had enough sense to pull back. When I got kicked out of the game, I felt like such a shit. You know, you're part of a team and you have a certain responsibility to the team. But no one said anything to me. I think they were happy I had done it."

It was just another extreme example of the politics of the game and the series, but also the pressure under which the players were performing.

"The start of the game was a disaster," said Ron Ellis. "It didn't look like it was going to be a fair shake. I'm sure J. P. scared him. I remember his reaction, he put his arms up to protect himself. He didn't have to worry about Parise. This is the thing that was so amazing about the series. J. P. was such a solid, consistent player, he gave his 100 percent every game he played. I never saw him do anything like that before or after, it was just emotions. It was such an emotional time. I don't believe in my heart he would have gone through with it. But that was just the toll it was taking on the players."

While the Soviet fans whistled in derision, the three thousand Canadian fans chanted "Let's Go Home." Meantime, more Red Army troops swept into the building and a police guard was put around the Canadian bench. There were already soldiers in the moat around the rink. There was a fear among many that matters could get worse—on and off the ice. It took a while for everything to quiet down, or as close as it would get, and the key for Canada was to maintain its composure, to not allow the Soviets another goal in the heat of the moment.

Once everything calmed slightly, Team Canada felt more determined than ever—determination fueled by more rage. Just a few minutes after the Parise explosion, Soviet defenceman Gennady Tsygankov—who coach Vsevolod Bobrov had said "cost us" game 7 on the Henderson goal—was called for interference. On the ensuing power play, Esposito put a Park rebound past Vladislav Tretiak to tie the game. But the penalties would continue—Ellis for interference, then Petrov for interference—and finally Yvan Cournoyer was called for interference at 12:51. Defenceman Vladimir Lutchenko put the Soviets ahead again, beating Dryden with a screen shot from the point. Less than four minutes later, Park tied it again (at even strength), finishing a nice give-and-go passing play with Jean Ratelle.

"Between you and me, I got the first two goals," said Park. "Lutchenko put it in, not Phil, off the rebound. I didn't find out until years later, I watched it on a DVD. But it didn't matter, it was in."

There were more antics after the first period, when the soldiers blocked the walkway to the Canadian dressing room, forcing Sinden to "lower my shoulder" and barge through.

In the second period the penalty calls slowed—"Kompalla was out for the rest of the game," said Bata, "he didn't blow his whistle after [Parise]."

The Soviets, however, did take the lead just twenty-one seconds in on a bizarre play. Henderson lost the puck at the Canadian blue line, and Yakushev's shot sailed over the net and hit the mesh behind (remember, there was no Plexiglas), then sprung back in front, where Vladimir Shadrin put it past a surprised Dryden. From the amazing to the bizarre, the sublime and the ridiculous were awaiting.

"That was different," said Dryden. "It's not that I was unaware of it. We knew that's what the netting was. We knew the puck would come off differently. I think what happened with this one was the shot came pretty much from right in front and hit, then slingshotted back right over the net and that was a surprise. The problem is that when [the puck] comes back at you that way and you're that shocked by it, you're not quite ready to do anything with it. It landed on one of their sticks and then it was in the back of the net."

Dryden managed to maintain his composure and played well, keeping the difference at one until Canada could even it up again. They got their chance midway through the period when White, sliding down the right side from the point, tapped in a beautiful pass from Rod Gilbert. But for whatever reason, as they had done in previous games, the Canadians stopped skating in the second half of the period. Less than two minutes after the White goal, Dryden made another big save, but Yakushev—a huge presence in the game—scored again to make it 4–3. Not long after that, Esposito, of all people, swept away a puck that was just inches from the goal line, after Yuri Blinov had deked around Dryden and was about to tuck it in the goal.

"I remember that play, I'd never done it before, never done it after," said Esposito. "I was back in the one corner, [Blinov] came out and got around Kenny. The guy was coming from the left and I was somehow in the goal crease, and I stopped it from going in. It was right on the goal line. When I got back to Boston after the series, Gerry Cheevers said to me, 'What the fuck were you doing backchecking?' I said, 'I'm telling you, Cheesy, I was doing things over there I've never done before.'"

"I'm not even sure he had ever been in our zone," laughed Dryden. "Not only that, but he took great pride in it. It was part of his identity to never go back in our zone."

But it was a huge play. A short while later, Stapleton was called for crosschecking, and on the power play—with a delayed penalty being called—defenceman Valeri Vasiliev fired a shot in off a leg to make it 5–3. It was the Soviet's third power-play goal of the game, with Yakushev again involved although not officially credited with an assist.

Despite trailing by two goals after seven games and two periods, the Canadians insisted they were not panicked. For the most part, they had played well, and Sinden had mapped out a strategy for the third period.

"In the dressing room there was some talk," said Esposito. "I know I said, 'Guys, let's get the next one and we'll beat them.'"

"We were calm," said Ellis. "Quiet. There was no frustration. You would think after everything we've gone through and we've got ourselves in this position now being down 5–3 going into the final period, that there would be some frustration. None of that. It was almost like we were preparing. We felt—it's hard to describe, but sometimes you do get these feelings—we felt we could win. We felt we could come back and win. You look across the room and catch eyes with a teammate like Cournoyer, you're almost saying to each other, let's play our role, let's just go out and do what we're supposed to do and we'll be fine. It was a very positive room. It stands out to me and my memory of the series."

"Being down 5–3 obviously wasn't what we wanted, but you're playing a good team with a good goaltender, you've got to be lucky, you've got to be good to be lucky," said Seiling. "There was no Knute Rockne speech. We knew what was there. You know collectively what has to be done. You just hope and pray that you can do it. You've come this far, you don't want to see it slip away now. Call it the gods, call it the Big Fella was on our side in the third period, but we staged a comeback."

Not unlike his strategy going into the sixth game, when Team Canada trailed in the series 3-1-1 and were in a must-win situation, Sinden essentially dusted off his "next shift" plan.

"You almost had to have that kind of philosophy," said Sinden. "You hear it a lot, but in that final game, it showed up pretty good. We were down two goals. I said to the team, 'Listen, you don't have to tie it up in the first thirty seconds, because if you do try that and you fail, they'll probably score and we're dead in the water. So,' I said, 'we can all cut it loose for the last five minutes of the game.'"

"I don't know this, every player will have a different response," said Dryden, "but I doubt there's anybody who would say it was when 'Fred' said this, that was the galvanizing moment. I think really what it was is we knew the circumstance. We're down 5–3. There are twenty minutes to go. That's it. There's not overtime. There's not a shootout. There's not a ninth game. It doesn't matter what is said, it doesn't matter the eloquence of the words, it doesn't matter the standing of the person who says it. We have extremely eloquent words echoing inside us and that's that—we have twenty minutes to go and we are down two goals and we have to find a way."

As much as they couldn't press too hard, too quickly to try and tie the game, it was obvious the Canadians couldn't give up the next goal and fall behind by three right away. In fact, giving up a goal at all was going to be disastrous.

"You just know it, in a situation where there are twenty minutes to go and you're down two goals, you know what you have to do," said Dryden.

In other words, don't give up the next goal. Or any more goals, period.

"I thought in the first two periods, Ken wasn't as sharp as he should have been," said Phil Esposito. "But in the third period, Holy Christ, was he good."

Seven games and two periods. One period left. History in the making—one way or another.

The plot thickened one more time prior to the third period, when Eagleson was informed there was a tie-breaking procedure in place, one that he and Team Canada were not aware of.

"We go in the dressing room, we say all right, boys, let's tie it up and get the fuck out of Dodge," said Park. "That's all we've got to do. Get one in the first ten minutes, one in the second ten. About two minutes before we're to go on the ice, Eagleson and Harry come in and say the Russians have notified us if the game ends in a tie, they win the series because they've scored more goals (32–28 after two periods). Well, like, where the fuck is that written? We know it's going to be propaganda. That's bullshit. So, tie it up and get the fuck out of Dodge? Well, that goes out the window in a hurry."

"I had seen [Alexander] Gresko [second in command of Soviet hockey] earlier and I said to him, 'Wouldn't it be nice if we come back and it ended in a tie?'" said Eagleson. "But he says to me if there was a tie we would lose on goal differential. Going into that game, they had scored twenty-seven goals and we had scored twenty-five. I went into the dressing room going nuts, screaming. I was yelling, 'If we get a goal early, they'll fall apart.' I went absolutely berserk for about twenty seconds."

"None of us had ever thought of that," said Sinden. "I should have known better because it was in play in the World Championships for years. I don't recall talking about it in July [during the pre-series meetings]. I was shocked when I heard that they were ready to claim victory if there was a tie."

And so, trailing by two goals, now informed a tie was as good as a loss, the third period began. The Canadians followed the coach's orders, playing smart and not trying to do too much, too soon. It paid off better than hoped. They were led by Esposito, who was determined they would not lose and produced one of the greatest performances ever in that third period. Just 2:27 in, Esposito scored to cut the lead to one, his fourth goal in the past two games. Peter Mahovlich did all the legwork, winning a battle to get the puck in the corner and feed Esposito in the slot, and Esposito then knocked the puck down with his glove. He missed on the first attempt, but not the second. Ironically, Mahovlich had moved onto the left wing with Esposito and Cournoyer because Parise had been ejected earlier.

A minute or so later, the game that had everything made room for one more amazing thing when Gilbert got into a fight—the first real fight of the series—with winger Evgeny Mishakov. Both were given major penalties for dropping their gloves and throwing punches, but no ejections. No doubt the officials didn't want to deal with the fallout of making that call, which is normally the standard. But normal had left this series long before.

"My emotions were so high, I lost total control," said Gilbert. "One of the few fights I ever had was with Mishakov. He raised me in the air and body-slammed me to the ice. I was not a fighter."

"Soviet coaches prohibit fighting, they asked us not to fight in the series," said Mishakov. "Because Gilbert was quick to use his fists, I had no choice. Fortunately, Bobrov was not upset."

The Canadians continued to play a controlled, now more disciplined game, while in the last ten minutes the Soviets seemed to sit back a little, playing more defensively, not putting as much pressure on the Canadians as they had typically done. In other words, they tried to protect their one-goal lead. It didn't work. At 12:56, Team Canada scored the tying goal. Again, it was another great effort by Esposito, who won a faceoff in the Canadian zone, working the puck back to Park.

"I ended up with the puck in my zone and I skated up and fired it across to Phil in full stride," said Park. "He goes in, tries to split the defence, shoots, Tretiak stops it, Phil whacks it, comes in front, and Cournoyer puts in his own rebound and it's tied."

Interestingly, after Esposito took the initial shot, the rebound floated through the air and he appeared to knock it down, towards the side of the Soviet goal. He retrieved it and fought his way in front, where Cournoyer ultimately scored. But years later there was talk that Esposito might have touched the puck with a high stick and the play should have been whistled dead. But there was no call and it was an incredible effort by Esposito.

Team Canada 5, Soviet Union 5.

But the celebration was short-lived.

The goal light was not switched on. Manning the light was a Soviet referee by the name of Viktor Dombrowski, who would later become the Kompalla for a next wave of Canadian players. He insisted the light switch didn't work, although it did work earlier—and later. Regardless, Bata had signalled goal, but Eagleson still tried to get to the scorer's box at rink side to make sure the goal counted and was announced. In the process of doing that, soldiers intervened and were applying a beating.

"I don't blame Al for that," said Phil Esposito. "The guy didn't put the light on, they weren't sure, there was confusion, and I think the Russian soldiers were shocked."

The Canadians on the ice stormed the penalty box area, sticks raised high, poised to do something. Eventually the bench emptied, including Sinden and Ferguson, the extra players in suits, and the support staff. Peter Mahovlich leapt over the boards, brandishing his stick to defend Eagleson, and grabbed him. The players pulled him across the ice to the bench, Eagleson and trainer John "Frosty" Forristall saluting the crowd in an unfriendly manner.

"We see Peter hop the boards, holy shit," said Park. "Now we all skate over and we see why he's there. They're hauling Eagleson out, the Red Army. Peter's grabbing them, we're swinging our sticks, jabbing at them to let him go. The Russian players are standing at centre ice looking at us, going, what the fuck is going on? We're fighting with the Red Army."

"With skates, Pete was six-foot-five, maybe six-foot-six, and he was coming with a hockey stick, but these guys had guns and we had fucking hockey sticks," said Esposito.

"If I was to do that today, everybody would be all over me for challenging authority," said Peter Mahovlich. "But time out here. We had scored a goal. We were down 5–3, but now we scored and the light doesn't come on. Al is sitting across from the benches. He sees the light didn't go on, so he runs down, and you can't do that in Russia. The guards didn't like it. I skated over and jumped right over the boards. It wasn't too smart because all there was was cement there. I slipped on my ass. I was going to swing my stick at the guards, who had guns. That wasn't too smart, either."

After the rescue, the Canadians retreated to their bench, including Dryden, who left his goal until some degree of calm and order was restored.

"This wasn't about details at that particular point," said Dryden, "it was the frenzy of the moment, the frenzy of the arena, and the energy and noise of the crowd of everything that's going on."

"Alan's always close to losing it," said Sinden. "I don't know what he was doing that was so bad. There were so many crazy incidents in those eight games, especially that one."

"It was Eagle being Eagle," said Seiling.

It appears Eagleson's indignation wasn't necessary, though at the time he couldn't have known that.

"I was very near the goal and saw the puck in it," said Bata. "So there was no matter for me whether the light was on or off."

The scene could have been worse, as more troops marched into the arena, the Canadian fans chanting again "Let's Go Home."

"I turned to Cashman and said, 'Well, how do you feel about spending the rest of your life in Siberia?'" said Bill Goldsworthy, but no one was laughing at the time. The reaction on both sides was severe, but think of the emotion, think of everything that had happened, people doing things they never otherwise would do. It wasn't just another game.

"I think both teams wanted to win equally, which is why the games were so interesting," said Mikhailov. "It was unusual for us to see a player showing that he would cut someone's throat, or that the head of the delegation [Eagleson] would run out on the ice and gesture something. This was a first for us and just crazy! We were wondering how the leader of the Canadian delegation could jump on the ice and argue with the referees, the fans, and the other team."

"And the police," said Yakushev.

"Yes, and the police," continued Mikhailov. "They should have arrested him [Eagleson] and thrown him in the slammer for fifteen days. I mean, if you're the head of a sport delegation, you just can't do that."

Making matters worse for the Canadians, and more interesting, apparently, some of them didn't hear about the tiebreaker formula until later, on the bench, when the score was tied 5–5.

"The minister of propaganda tells Fergie, 'If it's a tie, we're claiming victory because we've got one more goal than you,'" said Phil. "Fergie said, 'It's not over yet.'"

As Sinden had scoped out earlier, once tied, the Canadians didn't sit back, they played to win.

"At that point, you're just playing," said Dryden. "You don't have the luxury of writing a scenario of the next, you're just playing to deliver the next."

With all that had transpired—the two goals, the fight, the Eagleson ruckus, and seven minutes to go in a rowdy arena that felt like a ticking time bomb—the Soviets seemed either shocked, or bewildered, or perhaps they were just thinking that a tie was fine with them.

"Our opponents were stronger," said Mikhailov. "We just weren't doing enough on defence. The Canadians were very strong. We had to play sixty minutes and we didn't play well towards the end of games. It's what happened in game seven and this game."

There were seven minutes to go . . . The Canadians, meanwhile, were fired up.

"It was good for our team at that point," said Clarke. "The incident brought us together."

"We've got a tie game, we've got Eagleson back, now we have to get our composure back with seven minutes to go," said Park. "It keeps hitting us in the face: if this ends up in a tie . . . With about three and a half minutes to go, we have a two-man rush, but the two are myself and Gary Bergman. Up in their zone, two defencemen going in. But that's because of what they told us. We just kept a full-court press on until Henderson calls Peter off and jumps on and history is history."

Indeed, there would be another chance to test the goal light.

With just 1:42 left in the game there was a faceoff in the Team Canada zone. Esposito huddled the players—Peter Mahovlich, Cournoyer, Savard, and Lapointe. It would be the last stoppage until history was made. As the play evolved, Stapleton ended up replacing Lapointe on the fly on left defence. With less than a minute remaining, Savard had the puck on the right side at the Canadian blue line. He moved it across to Stapleton, who fired a pass to the right wing and Cournoyer alone at centre ice. He shot the puck into the Soviet zone, wide right of the net, and that is when everything started to unravel for the Soviets.

Vasiliev retrieved the puck, but, with only modest pressure from Esposito on the forecheck, uncharacteristically for the Soviets, he fired the puck around the boards, where it was intercepted by Cournoyer on the right wing by the faceoff circle.

"The defenceman shot the puck around the boards, and that was unusual for them," said Seiling. "They didn't give it away and they didn't throw it around the boards very much."

Cournoyer fired the puck into the slot towards a streaking Henderson, who made a try for a one-timer shot and fell, sliding into the boards. Vasiliev wound up with the puck again, with partner Yuri Liapkin alongside, but lost it to Esposito, who made a fadeaway shot from the faceoff circle on goal. Tretiak made the save, but kicked the puck out to Henderson. Tretiak made another save, but then Henderson flipped his rebound past a sprawled Tretiak with thirty-four seconds remaining.

"Henderson has scored for Canada!"

"I wasn't coming off the ice, no way," said Esposito of that final minute. "I'm sorry. I trusted the other guys, but I trusted myself more. I just knew I had to be on the ice, I had to be, and Harry knew it, too. That's what I respected about Harry. And quite frankly, the best coach I had in pro hockey was Harry Sinden. I just wasn't going to come off the ice. As I looked at it, I see the play in my mind. Henderson goes behind the net and is slow getting up. Liapkin was coming across, and he and Vasiliev fumbled the puck a bit by the faceoff dot to the right of Tretiak. While I'm skating backwards, I got enough on it to get it on the net like I always did. That was my forte. Henderson got up, and for some inexplicable reason Tretiak kicked the rebound straight out, which I'll never understand. I never asked him. I don't care, but I never understood that. Paul got the rebound and beat Tretiak with it. And boy oh boy, I know there's a famous picture of Henderson jumping into Cournoyer's arms, and I was like two seconds late to be in that picture. But it's always in the memory. I remember jumping on him two or three seconds after. I told Paul, 'This is as close as I'm going to get to kissing another man.' I was in love with the man, right there."

"I was exhausted," said Cournoyer. "I was at the end of my shift. I was on the other side of the rink from the bench. I think if we had been ahead in the game, I would have gone to the bench. The puck was behind their net—when the puck is behind their net and you're tired, you want a change—but I was so far away I didn't think I could make it. I don't know why the defenceman threw the puck around to clear the zone, but that is where I got the puck. I didn't know Pete had changed with Paul, but I see Paul trying to go to the net and I tried to get him the puck. But it was just a bit ahead of him. Somebody tripped him, he went into the boards behind the net. When the puck went in the corner, Phil got it and passed it in front of the net. I was just behind Paul when he scored. If I would have had a camera, I would have had the best shot that someone could take. That's why Paul jumped in my arms, I was right there. I said, 'Yeah! We did it! We did it!'"

"I can't even explain it to this day—I had never done it before and I never did it again," said Henderson, who had tweaked his groin earlier in the game. "I was sitting there on the bench and I had to get on the ice. What happened was Yvan, Peter, and Espo went on [with 1:42 remaining]. Harry came down and said to the three of us, if there's any time left you guys take it. So, we knew we were up. I'm sitting there, and all of a sudden, I just started yelling at Peter Mahovlich to come off the ice. Maybe it's because I had scored the goals in the other two games, but I just have to get out there. Thank God, Peter thought it was the coach yelling at him. I jumped on."

"I didn't hear him," said Peter Mahovlich. "I was tired. We had less than a minute to go, and I knew if I went into the offensive zone, I wasn't coming out. So I went to the bench."

"Henderson went on because the wing came off and we were waiting for the other two," said Sinden. "Cournoyer stayed out, too. I expected Phil to say out there. The game was running down, we were pretty desperate. If it was tough to get Phil off under normal circumstances, it was really tough to get him off under that situation."

"Paul stood up and called Pete off the ice," said Ellis. "It was very bizarre. You do not call another professional off the ice. That's just a no-no. I'm trying to think of Pete, why did he come off? The only thing we could come up with is maybe he thought Harry was calling him. I was ready for Yvan if he had come off, but I do remember Paul standing up beside me calling Peter to come off."

Henderson was confident he could make something happen.

"Yvan had it at the far side; I yelled at him and he saw me," said Henderson. "I'm a right-hand shot, so I was hoping to one-time it, but it was a little too far out in front of me and the defenceman came out at me, I was going so fast I crashed into the boards. I remember thinking, I've still got some time—because I went through the whole bloody team [in game seven] the only time I ever did it my whole life—I've still got time, I can do it again. I moved out in front, the guy tried to clear it, and Phil just whacked it at Tretiak, and of course, he should have covered the puck, he should never have given the rebound. But oh my God, there's the puck. I absolutely panicked.

I tried to put it along the ice, he got his pad on it, but the rebound came back to me, and I scored on the second shot. I almost broke Yvan's back when I jumped into his arms. I was bear-hugging him. The first reaction, the first emotion was total elation."

Henderson confided years later that after scoring, during the celebration, for a moment he thought of his father, Garnet, who had died in 1968. He wished his father could have been there to see him score. In all that excitement, there was still a bit of sadness for the Canadian hero. Just one more twist for the game and the series that had a bit of everything.

"It turned out to be my worst nightmare," Liapkin said years later. "Everyone knew that Paul Henderson scored when Yuri Liapkin gave up the puck."

When the goal was scored, the celebration was incredible. The three thousand Canadian fans went crazy, the twelve thousand Soviet fans went quiet. The Team Canada bench emptied, and even players not dressed to play ran onto the ice. Dryden, who had saved his best for the final game and especially the final period, skated the length of the ice to join the mob scene.

"[The goal] was a scramble," said Dryden, "you could see the puck going out in front of the net and you could see—and that moment I wasn't identifying that it was Henderson. You could just see the stick whacking at it, and then at some point it was either the arms in the air, the red light going on, or both, that made me know what had happened for sure.

"There was the celebration in their zone and I joined it. And I do remember in the midst of the celebration, as if I was sort of slapping myself in the face, saying, 'There are thirty-four seconds to go. I've got to get hold of myself. I have got to get back and get ready for this.' I suppose for a moment there was anxiety and nervousness, but then it was instantly gone because you're going back into your net and back into the game again."

"We had nothing left," Yakushev told the *Globe* forty years later. "It was done."

"We were still afraid," said Cournoyer. "We were just hoping they're not going to come back."

"In that moment, you may not realize it, but you look up at the clock," said Sinden. "And you hope there's only two seconds to go, not thirty-four. We were ecstatic. It looked like they were going to get the puck out of their end, but as soon as I saw Paul score, as happy as I was, that Soviet team was absolutely dynamic on odd-man rushes, they'd either score or they'd make the goalie make a fantastic save, or they'd hit the post, or something. They seldom messed up as they approached your end. I said to the players, 'Don't get caught and give them an odd-man rush.' We were up to the task."

"Losing that game was the worst moment of my career, I had a sick feeling for a long time," said Mikhailov, in the *Globe*'s oral history.

"We lost the game and that play will be remembered forever," Liapkin told the *Toronto Star* during the forty-year reunion. "It was not a nice feeling. I wish it didn't happen, but that's the game."

"The psychological turning point was after game five," said Yakushev. "We were losing and came back to win 5–4. There were three games left, and we figured that surely we'd win at least one and everything would be fine. Team Canada showed something that made it even stronger, that you have to fight until the last second, never relax, and fully give of yourself—something that is so inherent to how Canadians play hockey. All these great Canadians showed great character and battled until the very end in each of those last three games. Team Canada gave us a lesson for life."

"This is what happens when two great teams meet," Soviet assistant coach Boris Kulagin said afterwards. "We were not weaker than the Canadian team in this game. We lacked a little supporting luck."

Later that night, at a post-series reception, Tretiak complained that his defence didn't help him, and he told Henderson he was lucky to have scored. Years later, in 2013, after they had become friends, while introducing Henderson for his induction into the International Ice Hockey Hall of Fame, Tretiak said he had the real reason why Henderson scored—bad goaltending! That same year, Henderson received the Order of Canada and the Order of Hockey in Canada.

"I think I paid more attention to Phil Esposito, Yvan Cournoyer, and other players because they seemed to be more dangerous for me [than Henderson], especially Esposito, who would camp himself near the crease," said Tretiak. "Henderson has said himself that God gave him that last goal, and it's really true that this simply was his series. I wouldn't say that he stood out among other players, but he scored the right goals—those that brought him fame. That's praiseworthy, and he is a great guy, but I think that was God's work!"

Henderson ended up scoring five goals in the four games in Moscow, including all three game-winners. Had they not blown the first game in the Soviet Union, he would have had four. Just as Ferguson had said during that first practice in Moscow, the team was relying on Henderson and his line, with Ellis and Clarke, to come through big. And they did.

"I don't think anybody expected Paul to do what he did in that series, that's for sure," said Esposito. "The big ice worked well for Paul with his skating. I think he played the greatest hockey of his life."

As much as Henderson was the hero, and a great player throughout, it was ultimately Esposito who was the leader and the best player from start to finish.

"If there was a hero on the team, it was Phil Esposito," said Henderson.

Yes, the guy who wanted no part of the series in the beginning; who scored the first goal of the series thirty seconds in; who gave the verbal, emotional spanking to Canadians after the loss in Vancouver; who assisted on the series-winning goal—he was the driving force behind the improbable yet remarkable comeback and Team Canada ultimately prevailing, 4-3-1. They declared world hockey supremacy, but without the same vigor they envisioned twenty-six days earlier.

And it was Esposito who said the night of September 28, 1972, that he was "not going to let us lose."

"Espo scored the first goal, then again in the third, and set up the last two, he had four points, the Roadrunner was plus three in the third period," said Henderson. "Yvan scored the great backhand goal to tie the game, then [unofficially] assisted on mine. The cream came to the top, they were two of the best players we had and that's what best players do. Yvan and Phil were just incredible. We went out and followed their leads."

"We didn't have a captain, but Phil was our captain," said Cournoyer. "He was our leader."

"It was Phil's finest hour," said Sinden. "I saw him play an awful lot of good hockey, but that was as fine as he ever played. He was the leader of the team, no question about that. That was as fine a tournament as anyone could play. He led the team, he scored, he set up plays, he killed penalties, and with the big ice surface for a guy who didn't skate quite as well as some of the other players, especially the Russian players, he really handled himself well. He was terrific."

"I knew how difficult Phil was to play against, you appreciated the skill set," said Seiling. "I never got to appreciate Phil like I did playing with him. You see it happen. You see the game a bit differently not being on the opposite side. Phil was excellent the whole series. But that final game, the third period, might have been as good as I've seen him play. Without Phil being Phil, we don't win the series."

Esposito, at thirty years old, finished the eight games with seven goals and six assists and a team-high fifty-two shots on goal. And he was the only player on either team to have a four-point game—the final game.

"I don't think it was my finest hour," said Phil. "Being the first [NHL] player to score one hundred fifty points, being the first player to score over seventy goals, those are moments that are personal. And winning the Stanley Cup in 1970. This was different. People have said that's the greatest period of hockey they ever saw me play, I'm not going to deny that. I was so into it. I felt like I was in the open air back at King Edward School in the Sault, playing with all the guys. You just keep going, you don't stop. For an hour, maybe more, you play, you just keep going. There wasn't changing of lines. We had four or five guys per team. I don't know where all the energy came from."

From a big heart, apparently. The Soviet doctors proved that. All of Canada witnessed it.

CHAPTER 17

Celebrations and One More Game in Prague

When it was over on September 28, 1972—when Team Canada had miraculously won "the Borscht Cup," as defenceman Gary Bergman back then liked to call the historic Summit Series—there really were no printable words to describe it all other than these three:

"We did it."

The front-page headline in the *Globe* the next day was "From Russia With Glory," but it was those three words—We Did It—that resonated most with Team Canada.

"That's what we kept saying," recalled winger Yvan Cournoyer. "We did it. We did it."

Indeed, the Canadians did do it. They accomplished the near impossible. Someone once said: "Impossible only means that you haven't found the solution yet." And so it was with Team Canada, somehow at the very last moment finding a way to overcome a horrible start to the series at home, conditioning issues, an opponent they had severely underestimated, a feeling of abandonment from their fans, and then a deficit that seemed insurmountable, which is really just another word for impossible.

The task at hand, to win the final three games of the series on Moscow ice, seemingly against all odds, was a journey from impossible to improbable to "the greatest hockey comeback ever," said Brad Park, voted the top defenceman in the series.

And the greatest hockey series ever.

Trailing 3-1-1 in games, after blowing a huge lead in game 5 in Moscow, in a must-win situation, the Canadians battled back and made the eighth and final game not just meaningful, but dramatic and unforgettable.

"We have the one thing the Russians haven't got—heart," Bergman was quoted as saying after the game. "They take it as a game, not as an episode in life."

When it was over, when the buzzer went, the celebration was crazy. Three thousand Canadian fans in the stands at the Luzhniki arena cheered and hugged and cried and cheered some more, singing the anthem and giving anyone who cared shivers. On the ice, there was an enormous mass of humanity in front of the Canadian goal. And there were tears and hugs and eventually sighs of relief, but not for a while.

"As we skated off the ice, I stopped for one more look around that old barn," said Bergman. "I realized that never in my life would I be prouder or have more respect for a group of men than I did at that moment."

The celebration soon spilled into the Canadian dressing room, which quickly filled with team management and support staff and family.

"The dressing room was wild," said Esposito. "But there were also a lot of guys just sitting there soaked with sweat, drinking beers. Yeah, we celebrated, but it was like, thank God it's over. At least

It was an angry fan base that greeted Team Canada in Winnipeg for game 3, not so much angry at the players for the early results, but at the organizers and the NHL for not allowing star Bobby Hull to play because he had signed with the upstart World Hockey Association. Many fans passed this billboard opposite Maple Leaf Gardens (top) aimed at NHL president Clarence Campbell, petitioning him to allow Hull to play. On the ice, Team Canada knew it had to be physical, led by Phil Esposito (centre) and Bill White (bottom) to compete with the slick Soviets.

The Canadians lost game 4 in Vancouver 5–3, the performance worse than the score indicated and a low point in the series. They were greeted with a cascade of boos from the fans throughout, especially when a frustrated Frank Mahovlich pinned Tretiak well out of his goal crease (top). While many fans had given up hope, some still loved their heroes and were greeted by the players roadside on their way to the Toronto airport (centre). It was during the stopover in Sweden that the team truly came together, though it was a rough stop for Wayne Cashman (bottom), who took a stick to the mouth and had to miss the final four games in Moscow.

The great Bobby Orr, the best player in the NHL at the time, couldn't play in the series because of an injured left knee. But he convinced Boston Bruins teammate Phil Esposito (top, right), who was reluctant at first, to play. Esposito quickly became the team's leader and best player. In 1972 the Soviet Union was mostly an unfriendly image on network news, and the trip was an eye-opening experience. Red Berenson (centre) films the sights outside the Luzhniki Ice Palace. Ken Dryden and wife Lynda (bottom) embraced the adventure.

Posters advertising the series, featuring an odd Canadian flag, were hung around the city. Game 5 began awkwardly for Team Canada, when Phil Esposito stepped on a flower petal from a welcoming gift during pre-game introductions and fell. But he still managed to give the royal wave to Soviet leader Leonid Brezhnev, watching from a private box. Little did they know it would foreshadow a major pratfall by the team.

It is international hockey tradition for the teams to exchange gifts before games. Prior to game 8, the Canadians gave the Soviets Stetsons (above), and before game 5 the Soviets gave a welcoming gesture of a loaf of bread and bouquets of flowers. Game 5 would end with a blown 4–1 lead and another Team Canada loss. It could have been much worse after Paul Henderson crashed into the boards and suffered a concussion (centre), but he convinced the doctors and coaches to let him return. If they hadn't blown the lead, which goaltender Tony Esposito (bottom) blamed on himself, Henderson would have had yet another game-winning goal.

One of the lead architects of the series, Alan Eagleson, also head of the National Hockey League Players' Association, met with the media and hockey legend Jean Beliveau at practice after the game 5 loss, knowing every game was now must-win (top). The game 6 start in goal was given to Ken Dryden (centre), despite the shaky first few outings. Like the team, Dryden stood tall and produced a victory.

With just three years of NHL experience with the Philadelphia Flyers, twenty-three-year-old Bobby Clarke (top) was a rising star and a force with Team Canada. Playing on a line with Paul Henderson and Ron Ellis, they were the only unit that stayed together the whole series and their main assignment was to shut down one of the Soviets' top lines, featuring Valeri Kharlamov. In game 6, Clarke slashed Kharlamov on an already sore ankle, forcing Kharlamov, who had scored or assisted on all three Soviet game-winning goals and had six points in the series, to miss the seventh game. Physical play was always a big part of the Canadian game (bottom).

Tony Esposito (top), who was in goal for a crucial win in game 2, a tie in game 3, and who blamed himself for the game 5 collapse, was great in the seventh game victory. It was highlighted by Paul Henderson's game-winning goal, which he later called the greatest he had ever scored.

While they felt abandoned by the country when they left Canada after the fourth game, three thousand Canadian fans in Moscow restored the faith, and they were charged for the eighth and final game. Sticking to his original plan, coach Harry Sinden put a stoic Ken Dryden in goal, a move not endorsed by all of his teammates, but one that proved wise.

International officiating had been an issue from the start of the series, but it reached a controversial head during the games in Moscow, and especially in game 8. J. P. Parise, a physical winger—pictured here after a hard collision with Valeri Vasiliev (top)—was ejected after a feigned attack on referee Josef Kompalla, while Peter Mahovlich pleaded the Canadian's case (bottom).

The officiating and the ejection of J. P. Parise in game 8 prompted the frustrated Canadians to litter the ice with chairs and benches in protest, while the Soviet fans looked on in disbelief. They were shocked again when the soldiers, who circled the rink, grabbed Alan Eagleson after he charged the scorekeeper's box in an attempt to ensure Yvan Cournoyer's goal counted after the goal light wasn't turned on. Eagleson was rescued by the players and taken across the ice to the safety of the Canadian bench. The great Alexander Yakushev (bottom) continued to shine in game 8, opening the scoring and helping the Soviets to a 5–3 lead after two periods.

The goal. Henderson has scored for Canada. And the celebration. "Boy oh boy," recalls Phil Esposito, "I know there's a famous picture of Henderson jumping into Cournoyer's arms, and I was like two seconds late to be in that picture. But it's always in the memory. I remember jumping on him two or three seconds after. I told Paul, 'This is as close as I'm going to get to kissing another man.' I was in love with the man, right there."

Phil Esposito flashes a V for victory! And seconds later a handshake to end a series that changed the players and the hockey world forever.

From bums to heroes, Team Canada returns home victorious. Phil Esposito mobbed by fans (top), and Paul Henderson given a hero's ride by Tony Esposito and Alan Eagleson in the Toronto airport (bottom).

A Henderson game-worn sweater (top) was an attraction for fans and collectors alike. In 2010, that "piece of Canadian history" was bought for US$1,067,538 by a Toronto businessman, who wanted the sweater to go on a national tour to smaller communities and museums to be shared with fans. The previous owner donated some of the money to charity. Over time, the hockey cold war thawed. Several times, Russian president Vladimir Putin, seen here talking with Pat Stapleton (centre), invited the Canadians to anniversary reunions. Even Phil Esposito, who declared the series "war on ice," became friends with the Soviets, especially star winger Alexander Yakushev (bottom).

Team Canada. From a necessary but unwieldy roster of thirty-five players in the beginning, to the champions they were expected to be, just not in the way it was expected to happen. But great, nonetheless. The team of the century.

that's what I said, thank God it's over and I can go home, I can get back to Boston and play. And when we got back, I was on the ice the next day in training camp with the Bruins.

"But the celebration, it was wild in the beginning—the screaming and hugging and throwing beer at each other—but it seemed like twenty minutes after that we were just sitting there. It took me forever to get my equipment off. It always did. But I remember just saying to myself, 'Wow.' Wow. And I remember Paul Henderson's face. He had his mouth wide open and a big smile. His hair was matted because he wore a helmet. The sweat was pouring down. He was just sitting there and I went over to him and said, 'Great job, Pauly.'"

"Initially, we were ecstatic," said Ellis. "But then the emotion starts to hit you. We just sat there in our chairs and looked across and shook our heads. There's a great shot of Paul leaning back, exhausted. More emotionally exhausted than physically."

Early on, they started singing the anthem, everyone in the room.

"I'm not particularly patriotic or nationalistic and I'm not a flag-waver," Ken Dryden wrote in his book, a diary called *Face-off at the Summit*. "But singing the national anthem in that dressing room seemed like the only thing to do."

At some point after that, no one can remember just when, some can't remember at all, they broke into song again.

"I think at first they might have said, thank God it's over," said coach Harry Sinden, who was quick to mention at his post-game press conference that his players showed their integrity and character. "There was such great satisfaction in winning, a vindication, in many ways they redeemed themselves from what happened in the beginning. When we went in the room afterwards, some of them had tears in their eyes. And they began to sing the old Bob Hope tune, 'Thanks for the Memory' as they sat around, soaked with sweat. They were sentimental, that's the word I use to describe it, sentimental. We all were."

"I've never seen grown men cry like that," said backup goaltender Ed Johnston. "A lot of pride came into play—in yourself, your team, and your country."

"I think there was a loudness," said Dryden, "but then instead of the loudness carrying on, it grew quieter sooner than most."

"There was a numbness in the room, we had redeemed our honour," said Park. "We sat back, grabbed a beer, and said it's over, we won. It felt more like contentment than a celebration after a while. We got out with our dignity."

The twenty-seven-day war was over. And they all seemed to have a newfound belief in and feeling for what it meant to be a Canadian. Six weeks earlier most of them had been NHL enemies, guys who hardly knew each other, or not all, and those who did didn't particularly like each other. That's just the way it was. Now they were hugging and crying and drinking together, a true team brought together by adversity, a common purpose, and an amazing victory, celebrating in a style not quite the way they had imagined in the beginning.

"We felt tremendous joy," wrote defenceman Serge Savard in his book, *Forever Canadien*. "That victory was the greatest satisfaction of my sports career. I don't want to minimalize the impact of my first Stanley Cup in 1968, when I fulfilled my childhood dreams. But in 1972, I participated in a historic event."

"Until I scored that goal, I didn't know the difference between democracy and communism," said Henderson afterwards in the dressing room. "I knew what it meant to be Canadian."

In some ways, with all commotion, with all the bodies crowding in, it was difficult to entirely savour the moment and the overall achievement. But there was still time for that.

Soviet winger Vyacheslav Anisin made his way into the Canadian dressing room with a wrapped gift for Esposito, honouring him as the best player. It was a samovar, an attractive silver antique often used to boil water, typically to heat a teapot. Taken by surprise, Esposito grabbed one of his sticks to give back to the young Soviet.

"I was more emotional in this series than I ever was in the Stanley Cup," Esposito said in the dressing room. "What got me so motivated? Mostly it was the humiliation in that first game in Montreal . . . the fans booed in Vancouver and some of the crap we had to read in the papers."

"It definitely was more relief than excitement," said Cournoyer. "Everybody was exhausted, not just from playing hockey, but mentally. We were sitting there, and I don't think we knew what to say, or what to do, but you could see the satisfaction on everyone's face, it was so incredible. And our pride, too, don't forget that. It's funny because Dennis Hull was dressing beside me. He looked at me and he said, 'Yvan, is this like it is when you win a Stanley Cup?'"

"It was unbelievable," said Hull. "It was like a Hollywood story with the good guys beating the bad guys. I was sitting next to Yvan, and I asked him if this was what it was like to win a Stanley Cup. He said, rubbing it in, 'You don't know?' But then he admitted, 'This is ten times better.' I said, 'Good, then I've won the Stanley Cup ten times.' Yvan said, 'Show me your rings!'"

Once they had showered and changed, most retreated to the hotel, where champagne and a lot of noisy Canadians were waiting. The players and the staff soon made their way to the Metropole Hotel, not too far away, where a banquet had been scheduled to celebrate the two teams and no doubt a Soviet victory. Only a couple of the Soviet players turned up, including Alexander Yakushev and Vladislav Tretiak. The Canadians didn't stay long, making their way back to the hotel where the champagne and beer was poured until the sun rose on a new day.

In the *Globe and Mail* that morning, the final paragraphs of Dan Proudfoot's game story read:

"And while Eagleson raved about the Soviet Union being a two-bit country not worth a nickel, Esposito said the Russians had been a hell of a team. Nancy Eagleson, the Godfather's wife, said: 'Freedom always wins, freedom always wins.'

"Where was Bobby Orr?

"Cashman: He got too emotional watching the earlier games and I think he stayed at the hotel to watch this one on television."

Make it 16 million Canadians—plus one—who watched.

"What that team did, I don't think there has been a greater feat in sports," said Orr. "It was an unbelievable comeback against a great Russian team. I'd never seen anything like it."

"As we left our dressing room at the rink," wrote Sinden in his book *Hockey Showdown*, "I walked down the runway to take one final look. The lights were out over the playing surface. The score had been taken down. And in the stands, cleaning women were already going about their duties. And when I turned to walk away for the last time, I had the same feeling that I had when I was here in July. The best day in your life is the day you leave this place."

Next stop, Prague.

The game against the Czechoslovakian national team was further proof of how many expected the Summit Series to unfold, that Team Canada would cruise along and the four games in Moscow would not be the sweatshop they became. An extra game against the 1972 World Championship Czechs would be a nice stop on the way home, much like the week in Sweden was supposed to be a mini vacation, not a mini training camp.

Most of the Canadian players and staff, naturally, didn't have much sleep after their series-ending win. For most, the party extended through the night into the early morning hours when the team departed in a snowfall for the airport and the flight to Prague.

Now Sinden had a new problem: he would have to figure out who the soberest players were to make his lineup.

"Around five a.m., I opened a window to get some air and heard some happy Canadians—obviously inebriated—singing 'O Canada' and then I looked out and saw them parading in the direction of Red Square," said Dryden in his book.

When they arrived at the Moscow airport, without wives, who were returning directly home, they were greeted by the Canadian ambassador, Robert Ford, who read a congratulatory telegram from Prime Minister Pierre Trudeau. Also on that Aeroflot flight was Soviet coach Vsevolod Bobrov. "I'm going down to scout the Canadians," Dryden reported him saying.

"One of the funniest moments," said Seiling, "was when we were at the Moscow airport, waiting to leave. We were just sitting there, we don't know why we're delayed, but there had been a cleaner out working. He left for whatever reason, and he left behind a mop and bucket. Cash [Wayne Cashman] goes over and grabs the mop and turns it around and pretends it's a machine gun. He's firing at all the Russian guards and they don't know what to do. We're all laughing."

"When we flew to Prague," said Esposito, "I remember the referee [Franz Baader] was on the plane sitting in first class. J. P. Parise and me—you know those meals they have on the airplane and there's those little cherry tomatoes, fuck, we were throwing them at him. When I think about it that's terrible. How bad were we? But we won. I don't think we could ever get away with it today."

The other referee the Canadians despised, Josef Kompalla, was also on the flight, and in an interview with a German newspaper he said, "When I recall these matches, my flesh creeps. I am very glad I got home uninjured."

The game against the Czechs was especially nice for centre Stan Mikita, who was born in Sokolce but was sent by his parents, just a few years after World War II, at the age of eight, to St. Catharines, Ontario, to live with an aunt and uncle, who ultimately adopted him. It wasn't an entirely easy transition for Mikita, who was ridiculed by the other kids in school for being a "foreigner," but hockey became his escape and he became really good at it, eventually starring with the junior Teepees, joining the parent Chicago Blackhawks for the 1959–60 season. Mikita became a star in the NHL. At one time, he was one of the dirtiest players, but he transformed himself at the urging of his young daughter into a gentlemanly player. He was twice named most valuable player in the NHL, and he also won a scoring title. In the Summit Series, Mikita played the second and third games, earning an assist, and because he wasn't going to play in the final game in Moscow, Sinden let him leave a day early for Prague to spend time with his family. He watched the final game on TV.

But the big game for him was that game in Prague and his home-coming, with his mother, sister, and brother in attendance. Mikita, who was named captain for that one final game, played on a line with Frank Mahovlich and Cournoyer. He was given a three-minute standing ovation at the start.

"All the players knew how important this game was for Stan," said Savard. "He was the captain of our team that day. It was very moving to see him play in the country where he was born. Afterwards, he held his mother in his arms. She was crying and I also had a tear in my eye as I looked on."

Several players had tears in their eyes.

"At first, none of us after winning were very happy having to stop off in Prague to play," said Rod Seiling. "But once we got there, you never saw a person prouder to be a Canadian, happier to be in Czechoslovakia than Stan Mikita. When you think about his early life, a refugee coming to Canada, for him to go back to Prague having beaten the hated Soviets, you never saw a person happier to be a Canadian. It was so gratifying."

This was another scenario in which the Canadians really didn't have much to gain from winning, though a loss wouldn't exactly be a good way to finish up, either. Besides, they wanted to win for Mikita. And as much as the Czechs, whose country was under Soviet domination, were happy the Canadians had won the Summit Series, they had something to prove themselves.

Eight Canadians who played game 8 didn't dress in Prague: Henderson, Ellis, Bill White, Pat Stapleton, Guy Lapointe, Bergman, Jean Ratelle, and Rod Gilbert. Those who hadn't played much, if at all, were given a chance: Mikita, Mickey Redmond, Cashman, Goldsworthy, Marcel Dionne, Don Awrey, Seiling, Dale Tallon, and Brian Glennie. Dryden played the entire game and played well again in front of a singing, cheering crowd of 14,200, which was quite the contrast from the Moscow faithful. Sinden coached despite having a fever of 102 degrees Fahrenheit.

Canada led 2–0 after the first period on goals by Savard on a power play and Peter Mahovlich, but were tied headed into the third period. Penalties—surprise!—were an issue in the middle period, in which the Czechs outshot them, 12–3. Bohuslav Stastny was credited with both goals, one on the power play. At the end of the period, Clarke was given a five-minute major for high-sticking defenceman Frantisek Pospisil, the Czech captain.

Winger Jiri Kochta put the Czechs ahead on that power play early in the third period, but Savard, with Dryden pulled for an extra attacker, saved the day, tying the game with four seconds remaining. Another dramatic ending—just like in Sweden and Moscow.

"It was a special night for Mikita," said Clarke. "It was a subdued game after all the harsh emotions in Moscow. I was happy for Stan. I was happy we tied the game because, man, they had some talent on that team, too."

"I remember so vividly thinking, if we didn't win [in Moscow] they would never have sent a charter airplane for us to fly home," said Esposito. "I'm convinced of that. They would have thrown us to the fucking wolves. The government. Our government. That was my feeling, anyway. But they sent a nice Air Canada plane over for us. They picked us up in Prague and it was great."

Next stop, home—Montreal, then Toronto, and a hero's welcome.

CHAPTER 18

Calling the Shots

Legendary broadcaster Foster Hewitt, who brought the hockey world the famous, if slightly obvious, call "He shoots, he scores!" and opened his broadcasts with "Hello, Canada, and hockey fans in the United States and Newfoundland"—expanded his horizons in 1972. Hewitt was coaxed out of retirement at the age of sixty-nine to do the play-by-play of the historic Summit Series on CTV and CBC television from the four sites in Canada and the four games in Moscow, with former Canadian national team player and Toronto Maple Leaf winger Brian Conacher.

"Cournoyer has it on that wing. Here's a shot. Henderson made a wild stab for it and fell. Here's another shot. Right in front. They score! Henderson has scored for Canada . . ."

That was Hewitt's call of Paul Henderson's famous goal with thirty-four seconds remaining in the eighth and final game—the eventual series winner—one of the greatest Canadian sports moments ever.

On radio, another legendary broadcaster, this one in the making, called the action.

"Cournoyer steals it. A pass in front. Henderson was upended as he tried to shoot it. Here's another shot. Henderson right in. He scores. Henderson!"

Bob Cole grew up listening to Hewitt's broadcasts of Maple Leafs games on the radio. In 1956, the native of St. John's, Newfoundland, visited Toronto to give Hewitt an audition tape, not really expecting anything to happen. Instead, Cole was invited into Hewitt's office, where they listened to the tape and talked. Eventually, Cole was hired by VOCM radio in his hometown, and in 1969 he started calling Sunday night hockey games on CBC Radio. In 1973, he joined *Hockey Night in Canada*.

And in September of 1972, Cole was behind the radio microphone calling the play-by-play of the Summit Series.

Cole's colour commentator for the series was Fred Sgambati of the CBC, who originally wanted to do play-by-play himself, for at least some of the games. Allan Gilroy, the head of CBC Radio Sports, suggested that Cole call the games in Canada, while Sgambati call the games in Moscow. Cole threatened to walk from the assignment and eventually was allowed to call all the games, which Cole still ranks as the top assignment in his storied career.

"It has to be number one," he said. "Calling the 2002 Olympics in Salt Lake City was right up there, too. It had been fifty years since Canada had won Olympic gold in men's hockey. But 1972 was the biggest and most important sporting event in Canadian history. I didn't realize it at the time. But then you go home, talk to people across the country, and you realize how much Henderson's goal meant to everybody. I got letters from Canadians not only across Canada, but from around the world. People like a ship captain, who was so far from home, but listened to the games on the radio."

Cole, from start to finish in his career, was always meticulous about getting the pronunciation of players' names correct. Learning the names of the twenty-six Soviets was an extra challenge.

"The first game was on a Saturday night in Montreal," said Cole, who was thirty-nine years old at the time. "I found out the Russians were going to arrive on Wednesday. So I asked Allan Gilroy if I could go in [to Montreal] early. He eventually agreed it was a good idea. I walked up to the Queen Elizabeth Hotel and I was the only media person there as the Russians got off the bus. I met the team's interpreter. His name was Viktor, and it turned out he had studied English at Oxford University in England. We became friends right away.

"That afternoon, we went over the Russian roster. He pronounced the names for me and I spelled them out phonetically. I went back to my hotel and studied the names. The next day, I met Viktor for breakfast, and he asked me to say each name. After we got through the Russian lineup, he looked at me and said: 'Perfect.'

"Before the first game, I'm in the broadcast booth at the Forum, practising the names out loud. I come to defenceman [Gennady] Tsygankov. He was number seven. I say 'Se-gone-kov,' just like Viktor said. Well, Sgambati disagrees. He said he remembers that name from some junior event he covered in Salt Lake City. I felt strongly that I was right. Our producer, George Duffield, overheard our argument. He told me to go with Freddie's pronunciation. I was upset. I disagreed. It wasn't too much later that [PA announcer] Claude Mouton started to read the Russian roster to the crowd at the Forum. When he got to Tsygankov, he said, 'Gennady Se-gone-kov.' I looked at Freddie and George and said, 'Did you hear that?'"

Cole also developed a friendship with Russian coach Vsevolod Bobrov.

"Viktor introduced us one of those days before the series, at the Queen Elizabeth," recalled Cole. "I guess he thought I was somebody important. He took a liking to me. I'd often meet him before games in the dressing room. Their army officers would let me through and we'd go over his line combinations. I was the only Canadian media person allowed in their dressing room."

For years, while he was working for *Hockey Night in Canada*, Cole was one of the only media people, and often the only media person, whom NHL coaches would share their lineups and line combinations with the morning of a game. With Cole, they knew the information would remain private until he was on the air and the game was underway.

"You know my hero was Foster Hewitt," continued Cole. "I'd share the line combinations with him before games [in the Series] and he was so appreciative. This was such a big deal for me to help him out."

While he was in Moscow, working out of the Luzhniki Ice Palace, Cole scouted out his vantage point the day before the first game. The booth was glassed-in, which Cole didn't like. He preferred to hear the sounds from the arena, the players and the fans. Cole and *Globe and Mail* columnist Dick Beddoes attempted to remove the glass, but the army descended and made them stop. Eventually, though, Cole got his way.

Cole also accompanied the team to Prague for the exhibition game after the series wrapped up in Moscow.

"When we were in Prague for the final game against the Czechs, after the game, we were back at the hotel having a drink," said Cole. "The waiter came over to me and said, 'Somebody over there wants to say hi.' It was Bobrov [who had watched the game]. He raised his glass and I raised mine back to him."

Cole was on the same flight home from Prague with the victorious Team Canada.

"I sat with Harold [Ballard] for part of the flight," he said. "Alan Eagleson and Bobby Orr made their way up the aisle to talk to everyone. When they got to us, Harold's son, Bill, told Eagleson that he embarrassed the team and Canada in the final game in Moscow when he got upset when the goal light didn't go on. Orr got upset and said he'd punch Bill in the face if his dad weren't sitting beside him. After they left, Harold turned to Bill and told him that he didn't know when to keep his mouth shut.

"It was quite the party. We left Prague, refuelled in London, and it was on to Montreal. I went up to talk to the pilots as we were flying over Greenland. They told me it wouldn't be long before we would be over St. John's. I got on the PA system to announce we were now over Canada. Everyone cheered. I asked if they could patch us through to the tower in St. John's. They patched us through to the tower and the tower patched us through to CBC Radio. I told them Team Canada was on its way."

Upon arriving in Montreal, where an estimated crowd of ten thousand had gathered, Cole was forced into action, introducing the players as they departed the plane. He was scheduled to make his way home to St. John's the next morning.

"I was wearing my red CBC blazer when I got off the plane in Montreal," said Cole. "I was one of the first off, and this guy comes over to me to introduce himself. His name was Vic Chapman, the prime minister's press secretary. He asked me if I knew the players. Of course I did. He wanted me to introduce them as they came off the plane. So I did.

"I met the prime minister. [Trudeau] told me how much he enjoyed my work. When he found out I was staying the night in Montreal before flying back home to Newfoundland in the morning, he told me, 'No, you're not.' It turned out he was flying to St. John's on his Viscount for a campaign stop. It was quite the crowd waiting for me when I touched down at home in St. John's a few hours later. Of course, they weren't there to see me!"

Cole's call of that final minute was iconic.

"He scores. Henderson . . . And Kenny Dryden, I've never seen a goaltender skate that far from one end of the rink to the other . . . And the team officials are over the boards. Henderson has got to be the hero of the entire nation now. Thirty-four seconds left. They've got a 6–5 lead. Can they hang on?

"They drop the puck at centre ice now. Team Canada leading six to five. It goes back to the Russian blue line. Kuzkin goes back for it. Gives it to Gusev. Gusev a pass to the right side for Mikhailov. He shoots it in. Twenty seconds left. They're trying to clear it. [White] gets it through the middle down the ice. It's wide of the net and it's not called icing. Somebody could have played it. Twelve seconds left to go. Russia on the move. Here they come. Petrov coming out. And it's Gusev trying to get around. Off the boards. Dryden takes it. Three seconds left . . . The series is over!"

Cole retired in the spring of 2019—after fifty seasons of hockey play-by-play. A true legend in the business, he was given the Foster Hewitt Award by the Hockey Hall of Fame in 1996.

On French television, the games were broadcast on SRC (Radio Canada) with the legendary René Lecavalier doing the play-by-play alongside goaltender Jacques Plante for the games in Canada, with Richard Garneau taking over the play-by-play for the games in Moscow.

There were two other legends in the Luzhniki Ice Palace on the night of September 28, 1972—photographers Frank Lennon and Denis Brodeur, who both captured the famous image of Henderson, arms raised high in the air, celebrating his goal, Yvan Cournoyer applying a hug. The shot includes Soviet goaltender Vladislav Tretiak prone on his back, just the way he was when Henderson scored, looking at the two Canadians. Defenceman Yuri Liapkin is in the foreground, skating away in disbelief, while in behind are defenceman Valeri Vasiliev and centre Vladimir Shadrin, standing over Tretiak.

It is alternately a picture of unbelievable joy and crushing dejection.

Lennon was working for the *Toronto Star*. His photo of the Henderson celebration, which appeared on the front page of his newspaper the next day and across the Canadian Press syndicate, won him a National Newspaper Award for spot news photography and was named the Canadian Press Picture of the Year. It was also used for the design of the coin produced by the Royal Canadian mint in 1997 for the twenty-fifth anniversary of the series and a stamp created by Canada Post in 2017 as part of the Canada 150th anniversary.

Denis Brodeur, whose son is Martin, one of the best NHL goaltenders ever, had virtually the identical image as Lennon. Brodeur was for many years the official photographer of the Montreal Canadiens, as well as an Olympic bronze medalist goaltender with Canada in 1956.

He was at the series freelancing for the *Montreal-Matin* newspaper and gathering photos for a commemorative book. Three other notable photographers were also at the games in Moscow: George Cree of the *Montreal Gazette*, Melchior DiGiacomo with *Sports Illustrated*, and Brian Pickell of Hockey Canada.

Not unlike Bob Cole, who called countless Stanley Cup championships and the 2002 Olympic gold-medal game, Lennon and Brodeur both had illustrious careers. But they always insisted the Henderson picture was their best.

CHAPTER 19

O Canada

Once upon a time, the Montreal Canadiens were winning the Stanley Cup with such frequency that the mayor, Jean Drapeau, one day boastfully announced in a press release that this year's parade "will follow the usual route."

By 1972, Yvan Cournoyer had travelled that parade route—along Rue Sainte-Catherine and a seven-mile route in downtown Montreal—an incredible five times in his first seven years in the NHL. He would travel it five more times before injuries forced him to retire.

That quote was actually made sometime during the late 1970s, when the Canadiens were on a run of four consecutive Stanley Cup wins. But you get the idea, it happened a lot—five in a row to end the 1950s, the four in five years Cournoyer experienced during the 1960s, and six more in the 1970s.

It was pretty much a rite of spring in Montreal.

But in the fall of 1972, on October 1 to be precise, there was an entirely different kind of parade in a much different place.

Dorval Airport was the first stop, a little after 6 p.m., to drop off the first wave of villains-turned-heroes (remember, Montreal is where Team Canada lost the series opener, 7–3, and matters got much worse before they got any better) on the Air Canada flight from Prague. The likes of assistant coach John Ferguson, defencemen Serge Savard and Guy Lapointe, Cournoyer, and a few others stayed in Montreal, the team welcomed by Prime Minister Pierre Elliott Trudeau, Mayor Jean Drapeau and roughly ten thousand excited fans, some lining the windows in the terminal, some in a designated area on the tarmac.

"It was unbelievable," said Cournoyer. "I had won the Stanley Cup and I didn't see that many people in one place. When you win, the people are there. If we had lost, we wouldn't be talking about it now. We had to win. It's so great the feeling that you're the best."

Typical, and perhaps fitting for the series, was that there were politics involved upon arrival in Montreal. Essentially, Team Canada organizer Alan Eagleson was a prominent member of the Progressive Conservative Party, while the prime minister was a Liberal. And the country was in the midst of an election campaign.

"It was political from that very first game," said Phil Esposito. "When we came back, Trudeau was waiting at the back of the plane. It was one of those 727s that opened at the back. Eagleson says, 'We're not going out the back, we're going out the front,' and they went on and on for about ten or fifteen minutes."

There is a conflicting version that Eagleson wanted the players to exit from the back, while Trudeau waited outside the front of the plane for a photo opportunity. But you get the idea.

"Finally, I just sat down," said Esposito. "I was sitting with my brother, Tony, and Wayne Cashman. Both were—well, Cash for sure, I don't think he could have gotten off the airplane, let's just say that. Wayne had the worst injury I had seen in a long time when his tongue got split by a guy's stick when we were in Sweden. That was one of the most gruesome and gross injuries I had ever seen. Cash couldn't really talk, so he kept himself drunk, I guess."

According to some witnesses, not only was Cashman either sleeping, or passed out, but his pant legs had been cut off by a prankster. Dennis Hull was suspected by several and apparently had multiple victims.

"I sat there and Trudeau came up the airplane," said Esposito. "He came to me and my brother and Cash. Tony was sitting in the middle. He shook my hand, he shook Tony's hand, Wayne was sleeping. He said, 'Thank you.' I said, 'I'm sorry about all this bullshit.' He said, 'Politics.' That's all he said, 'Politics.' And I have never forgotten that."

Eagleson later insisted he never stopped the players from meeting Trudeau. Whatever really happened, eventually there was a gathering on the tarmac, the players and coaches loaded onto a handful of fire trucks for a parade past the terminal, where the fans had gathered. It was Peter Mahovlich who invited Trudeau onto one of the fire trucks amidst a stirring rendition of "O Canada."

"We had a good time in Montreal," said Mahovlich. "One of my cousins was one of Trudeau's security guards. We were on a fire truck, so I reached down and grabbed Trudeau and pulled him up. He was great and had a good time."

Savard, especially, had a good time. Ferguson had been clutching a hockey stick that he got autographed by all the players and management and carefully brought back from Moscow. Savard turned to Trudeau and told him Ferguson had gotten the players to sign the stick especially for him. It was a gift.

"Fergie never said a word," said Savard. "Trudeau shook hands and thanked John."

Ferguson later told reporters about losing his autographed stick, and the story made its way into the newspapers the next day. One of Trudeau's staff read the story and the stick was returned to Ferguson with a note, acknowledging the practical joke and congratulating him on the series win and his role as assistant coach.

Pat Stapleton, who had formed a terrific defence pairing with Chicago teammate Bill White, had a special souvenir himself, but it never found its way into anyone else's hands. At the end of the eighth game, while the celebration began in front of the Team Canada goal, Stapleton darted away and grabbed the game puck, the same one with which Paul Henderson had scored the game-winning goal. To get it out of the Soviet Union, and to make sure it wasn't taken away by the authorities, Stapleton had his wife, Jackie, stuff it down her brassiere. Stapleton insisted he kept that puck on his farm near Sarnia, Ontario—despite some teammates wanting him to donate it to the Hockey Hall of Fame—until the day he died in April 2020.

A prankster himself, Stapleton used to travel to alumni games and social events with the puck tucked in his pocket, although the original didn't have any markings, so it could have been any old puck.

"I got the goal, Patty got the puck," said Henderson. "They were just plain black pucks, you could pick up any one and say this is the one, but you see him go after it."

Meantime, another prankster was at it on the ground in Montreal.

"I remember we all had the same Team Canada luggage," said Hull. "To tell the bags apart, we had number stickers on our luggage. But instead of giving us a couple of sets, they gave us a dozen or so stickers. In Montreal, Bobby Clarke and I are talking to Trudeau. We asked him how he liked the series. I patted him on the back and stuck my number 10 sticker on his coat. Clarke then stuck on his number 28. Somewhere there is a photo of Prime Minister Trudeau with three number 10s and three number 28s on his back."

Next stop—the final stop—Toronto.

Upon arrival, Esposito walked down the stairs from the plane and proceeded to kiss the tarmac.

"I was so happy to be home," he said, declaring he would never go back to Russia. Little did he know. Esposito and seventeen other players and their families later returned to Russia and were glad they did. They were invited to celebrate the fortieth anniversary of the series and experience Moscow and a few other cities. Several were also invited to lunch at the home of Russian president Vladimir Putin with a handful of the Soviet players, including Vladislav Tretiak, Alexander Yakushev, and Boris Mikhailov.

Esposito's daughter, Carrie, who passed away in 2012, married a Russian, former Tampa Bay Lightning player Alex Selivanov.

Of the many memories and souvenirs the players and coaches brought home, there was also a lingering bitterness, or disappointment, about the reaction of some Canadians to how they had played, from the rough start in the first four games in Canada, to the rough-house games in Stockholm, to the Clarke slash and funny business in Moscow—to the amazing comeback and victory. Most Canadians had been converted to proud admirers of the team, but others, including some players, wouldn't let go.

Savard, for instance, had harsh words for some of the Montreal media as he was departing the airport, saying "Maybe some people would have been happier if we had lost the series . . ." He was roasted in the media, but his point was made.

Even Sinden acknowledged a few weeks later that the players and coaches were upset that some had painted them to be the bad guys, that part of the amazing victory had been clouded by criticism. But the reaction of the fans in Montreal and again in Toronto on the team's return helped to temper that disappointment and anger, at least for a while.

"It was an emotional roller coaster, the likes of which I had never been on my whole life," said Brad Park. "I was kind of sad when it ended. I never really enjoyed the benefits because we had to play the Czechs two days later and, when we came home, stop in Montreal, stop in Toronto, and then we had to disperse to our teams for the rest of training camp. We never really got to enjoy the fruits of our labour as a team. But we did drink the plane dry. When we stopped at Heathrow to get fuel, the bar was empty. By the time we got home, we had pretty much emptied it again. But it was well deserved. When we heard the stories about what it was like across Canada, how the entire country had shut down, it magnified it even more for us. Canada was a winner in this series, not just the team, because it unified the country. It made the country feel good again."

The team was taken to city hall in downtown Toronto via a thirty-six-car caravan, where an estimated eighty thousand fans were waiting, despite that it was dark and raining. Along the highway and downtown streets on the ride in from the airport, cars were stopped, fans waving and honking their horns.

"I don't think any of us really had a true sense of what was happening back home," said winger Ron Ellis. "We didn't know. You couldn't text back then. In Moscow, we saw the telegrams and the notes, but we had no idea people were taking time off work, kids were out of school, or so many were watching on TV. We thought everybody would be happy, but we didn't really know until we got on the Air Canada flight and the captain said, 'You guys will just not believe what's going on at home.' That's when it hit us."

One of the first indications for Paul Henderson was when he was handed a copy of the *Toronto Sun* newspaper.

"We were so intent on winning, nobody gave a rat's ass who scored, we just needed to win," said Henderson. "I never, ever once thought that I would be the 'hero' of the series, that never entered my mind. But then, on the way home, I saw the newspaper—'THE HENDER-SUN'—that was the front page of the *Toronto Sun*. That's when I started thinking, 'This may be a little more than I anticipated.'"

At Maple Leaf Gardens, the receptionists were answering the telephone with: "Maple Leaf Gardens—Home of Paul Henderson."

In the rain, with Ontario premier Bill Davis and mayor William Dennison in attendance, Sinden led the crowd in a rousing cheer of "Nyet, nyet, Soviet! Da, da, Canada," the rallying cry of the three thousand fans who made the trek to Moscow, followed by another singing of "O Canada"—a memory they will never forget.

Despite all the emotions—some bad, but most of them really good at that moment—Sinden was pleased with what his players were experiencing. It was the moment he had tried to share with them in the first days of training camp in mid-August in Toronto, when he spooled up the film projector and showed highlights of his Whitby Dunlops representing Canada and winning the 1958 World Championship in Oslo, Norway. The film got twisted, and there were a few moments of a young Sinden falling during the play, which brought laughter from the players. But Sinden's intent was to show them what a special and proud moment and experience it is to represent your country and win on the world stage.

That night in the rain at city hall in Toronto, in front of eighty thousand fans, the message was delivered.

"I wanted them to experience the indescribable thrill of winning for their country," Sinden later wrote. "That was my wish. It has been granted."

Epilogue

A Boston sportswriter covering an epic championship series between two basketball powerhouses once wrote that if one team was victorious it would be a "triumph of spirit, a mixture of cunning, planning, and hard work" and if the other team won it would be a "show of force, talent, brute power."

Leigh Montville summed it up by saying the "theatrics, either way, were wonderful." The same could easily be said of the meeting between the Soviet Union and Team Canada in 1972.

That the Soviets were so close to winning the Summit Series was a tribute to their skill, training, and determination to prove just how good they were. Spirit, cunning, planning, and hard work. Meanwhile, the Canadians were powered by equal parts grit and guile, heart and skill, and, as the players put it, driven alternately by almost a fear and an obligation to win, a stubborn refusal to lose. And pride. In other words, force, talent, and brute power.

And the theatrics were wonderful.

"We felt like we couldn't lose and we weren't going to lose," said Phil Esposito. "In many ways, we out-willed them."

"I think our players out-gutted them," said coach Harry Sinden.

269

And while Team Canada won the series, there really wasn't a loser (think bigger picture), and the game has forever been better for it—the unexpected charm being the changes that would follow, the influx of Europeans playing in North America and the tremendous international tournaments. Out of it all, of course, emerged many good things, including a mutual respect for how the other team prepared and played. That respect was undoubtedly born mere minutes into the series, but it was certainly cemented by the time the two teams lined up for the post-series handshake—28,800 seconds after the first puck drop.

"The series proved that we were as good as they were," said Soviet defenceman Vladimir Lutchenko.

"We definitely looked at the Soviets differently by the time the series was over," said Brad Park.

As for an actual thaw in the Cold War, that may not have truly arrived until fifteen years or so later.

When the series was finally over on September 28, 1972, long after the celebration in one dressing room had changed locations and they were already working on a second hangover, the two teams were invited to meet in a Moscow hotel for more formalities and a farewell toast. A celebration for all. Once again, these were the original plans made long before the series had started, when the expectations were that it would be nothing more than a friendly exhibition series and the two sides would be in the mood for a post-series social.

"We celebrated at the hotel," said winger Rod Gilbert, "but it was disappointing in one way. The Russians also were there with their wives, at least a few of them, but we couldn't talk to them. There were some speeches and then they disappeared. They weren't allowed to talk to us."

Others recalled only a couple Soviets turning up, but there was no mingling, no sharing of thoughts and feelings. The emotions were still quite raw on many levels.

The dictionary tells us détente is the "easing of hostility or strained relations, especially between countries." Well, détente wasn't truly achieved between the two teams until they met again years later.

"The best time [together] was in 1987," said Park. "We had the Relive the Dream reunion. The Soviets came over for three games—in Hamilton, Montreal, and Ottawa. We ended up winning all three. After the Montreal game, we went upstairs to a bar/restaurant in the Forum. I had a beer with [Valeri] Vasiliev. He was a defenceman, and during the series he was young, like me. We're trying to talk through an interpreter and getting along pretty well. But as we're leaving to walk back to our buses, he's walking ahead of me—[coach Viktor] Tikhonov is the head of their delegation—and because Vasiliev was having a couple of beers with me, Tikhonov went up and cuffed him on the back of the head, about ten feet in front of me. I ran up and grabbed Tikhonov by the arm and I looked him in the eyes and I said, 'No. Not here.'

"After the Ottawa game, through the interpreters, we told the Soviet players that when we got back to the hotel, to stay on the bus. So, when we got back, their delegation got off, but the players stayed on the bus. Myself and Cash [Wayne Cashman], we jumped on their bus and told the driver to follow our [Team Canada] bus. We rode with the Soviets. We took them to Hull, across the river in Quebec, and we took them to a strip club. We picked up the tab. Well, they had the best time. We both had the best time. That night, we put the 1972 series in the rear-view mirror as far as the animosity was concerned.

"Most guys I disliked when I played them—but I don't do that anymore. I'm not paid to do that now—I'm happy to see them because to a certain degree, guys I disliked to play against, they went through the same things I did as a player and the Soviets were no different. At the time, you hated them. But we put that behind us."

Not at a hockey rink in Canada or Moscow, but over post-game beers and no doubt vodka (and in a strip bar). It somehow feels like the hockey way to settle things and move on.

"[Back then] everything in Ottawa closed at eleven, so we went across the river to Hull," said Gilbert. "And the Russians were drinking vodka on the bus. We get to town and there's a big sign that says: 'Entering Hull.' Dennis was telling the Russians they named a town after him because we kicked their ass!"

"I don't know what happened in Hull, I wasn't there," insisted Yvan Cournoyer. "I heard about it. We became good friends. Back in '72, we didn't like them. It's our fault, they were better hockey players than we thought. After that, we became very good friends. Tretiak and I became good friends. One time, we were going to sign autographs in Toronto, and he was coming from Russia, with a stop in Montreal. We had about five or six hours to kill before we left, so I said come to my home, it's a beautiful day, you can swim at my house. I said, I never thought I would have a Russian in my pool.

"I was invited to Russia for the twenty-fifth anniversary. I don't know why, but I was the only one invited, with my wife. For five days, I had a private chauffeur. They had a banquet celebrating like they had won the series. I had pictures taken with all the players on the stage. I was giving a speech with a Canada sweater on, and the mayor of Moscow came up behind me with a Russian sweater with my name on the back. It was a complete surprise. They acted like they had won, but for them it was different and both teams came out as winners. If we had lost and they had won, I don't want to think about it! We wouldn't be talking about the series today, they wouldn't have let us come home."

"Sometimes I felt it was a real war on ice," said Boris Mikhailov. "We shook hands before and after the games, but I'm not sure it was the handshake of sportsmanship. We were hockey rivals and each of us wanted to show the world our superiority."

"I have seen an interview with Phil Esposito where he was remembering his attitude at the time, to the series and to the Russian players," said Yakushev. "And there was one unique phrase that really stuck out to me: 'If the coach had told me to go out and kill a Soviet player, I would have done it, because I had so much anger in me. It's not that I specifically hated the Soviet players, it was more the Soviet people. In that sense, I was prepared to go on the ice and do something that would take a player out of the game.' And so, the years have passed and Phil Esposito has turned one hundred and eighty degrees. He is on great terms with all the players, with our country, and in general with our people. This series didn't just improve the sports relations between the countries, but also on the human level. That also changed one hundred and eighty degrees and the people are now much more kind and friendlier. That's also great."

"If we had won eight games, no one would have thought about it again," said Paul Henderson. "Had we lost, it still would have been a game changer."

In the end, how did Team Canada ultimately battle back to win the series? The heroics of Henderson and Esposito and so many others aside, did they simply out-will the Soviets, out-gut them? Ken Dryden, in his tremendous book *The Game*, wrote that Canada winning the way it did "was like being shot at and missed." The legendary Soviet coach Anatoli Tarasov, who was replaced as coach of the national team the year before the series, said, "The Canadians battled with the ferocity and intensity of a cornered animal." Henderson once quoted Tarasov as saying, "We can skate with the Canadians, our skill level is there . . . the one advantage they have is their spirit."

"When you go through the Canadian junior programs, you learn what it takes," said centre Bobby Clarke, who is still remembered and, in some circles, criticized for his slash on Soviet star Valeri Kharlamov in the sixth game. It was another act that prompted many covering the series and many more watching from home to suggest the Canadians had disgraced themselves with their aggressive play. The Canadians defended it all by reminding that this was a war on ice, losing wasn't an option. And the world had a very different mindset at the time.

As journalist Dick Beddoes put it, "We did misbehave. I've always said hockey is war under wraps. The series reflected our hockey culture. We were what we are, and we won because of something Canadian—to do what you have to do to win. We're not gentlemanly in our national sport."

"You learn," Clarke continued, "whether you have the commitment or not. Some players have great talent, but they're not willing to commit to what it takes to be a good player. It's on a daily basis, every practice, every game, and in '72 there were stars in the league who came to work every day, that helped—even though Paul's goals were so important, it was only because someone else had scored before. Those goals were important because we won, but as important as those goals were, it still comes down to the team. It's always the team, never the individual."

A big part of the Canadians' success was that will to win at any cost, to do whatever it took, but it was also finding a respect for their opponent that essentially scared them straight. And to couple it with their own skill.

"It was that coming to learn to respect an opponent, that was significant," said Dryden. "You know the rule of always having to respect your opponent . . . every so often a team that isn't nearly as good as you are beats you, and why does that team beat you? It's not that they are suddenly a whole lot better than they were before, it's that you don't take them in a certain way. It means you aren't as good as you have to be and you end up getting beaten. We weren't as respectful as we needed to be, that's clearly the case. How would we have known that Soviet team beforehand? Okay, so you study the films, but what films existed at that time?"

It was a lesson learned the hard way. While, over time, Canadians learned from the Soviets in terms of preparation and skill development on and off the ice, the Soviets eventually learned from them about playing with an edge.

"In hockey, Canadians have always been good competitors," continued Dryden. "It's sort of an easy thing to say, but part of it's that we play games, we don't mess around with practice. Our history is playing games. It's not practising. One of our weaknesses over time was we weren't very good at developing ourselves away from games. But one of our strengths is we're really good at games. We develop the skill of games, which aren't necessarily the skills of practice that you then apply to a game.

"We know what to do, the different situations in a game. It's been part of our life's experience. We've been in countless games in our lives and in all kinds of different situations in which there was no way we were going to win. And we won. And in games when there was no way we were going to lose, and we lose. Even as exaggerated a set of circumstances as this series was, we had been in variations of it at different times in our lives before and we knew it was all about finding a way. And we hung in there until we did. That's what we knew."

As the late journalist Jim Proudfoot, brother of Dan, who also covered the series for the *Toronto Star*, wrote years later, after Canada had bounced back to defeat the Soviets in the 1987 Canada Cup, a series that was to that generation what 1972 was to the prior generation: "They [the Soviets] come over here with their fancy passing, artful patterns, and elaborate strategies and the Canadians admit it's gorgeous to behold, but what about some old-fashioned bodychecking, some energetic forechecking, an indomitable will to win—you can't beat it."

In some ways, in what was a clash of distinctly different styles, the Soviets refused to adjust in the series, to change their style of play.

"Our coaches didn't allow us to shoot the puck into their zone, we were instructed to cross the blue line only by passing," said defenceman Gennady Tsygankov. "Canada would dump the puck into our zone and chase after it. I don't know why our coaches thought this was a bad play. They scored a lot of goals this way."

But it was years later that hockey executive John Ferguson Jr., after watching a Canadian world junior team, said words to the effect that when it comes to hockey "you can't teach Canadian." As much as Team Canada knew it had to be physical to win, it shouldn't be overlooked that with all that grit and guts, there was also a ton of skill. And determination.

"In '72, we didn't want to let Canada down," said winger Dennis Hull, "or Canadian hockey down."

The videotape has sat on a shelf in Alexander Yakushev's home for longer than he can remember. Unwatched. And it will stay that way.

"The recordings of all eight games have been lying in my home for years," he said. "But frankly, I have never watched them, I have never even looked at them because of the pain. The pain of that last game is so great that I still can't digest it all. We think we made huge mistakes. The fact that we couldn't win the series is all on us. It's the end result that counts in any competition. Victory was within our grasp, but we lost and that's why we feel pain."

There are certainly enough highlight-reel moments for Yakushev to still have a look. He finished the series with a team-high seven goals and four assists. Five of those goals came in the final three games, all losses.

"We blew it," summed up goaltender Vladislav Tretiak.

"Unlike Alexander, I don't feel any lingering pain," said forward Boris Mikhailov. "The results of the game have had no effect on me. Why bother re-watching these games? They're all in my head."

Indeed, the Summit Series left an indelible mark with so many, from players to coaches to managers to fans alike. Incredible pain and unbridled joy. And it changed not only all the players involved, but ultimately the game itself. So, while Yakushev is right that it is the final result that ultimately matters, like so many have said there were no big losers in this series. That doesn't necessarily make losing any easier, but it's the truth. For the Soviets, proving they could play with the best professional Canadians was a victory in itself—for them and the game. It's the denouement that hurt and apparently continues to hurt them so much. Had the Canadians lost . . .

"It's hard to imagine what kind of welcome Team Canada would have received back home if they had lost," said Yakushev. "It's hard to imagine the reception and the evaluation of that team. The players probably would have heard a lot of criticism. The expectations before the series were that all games would end 8–0 or in double digits. Imagine that they had suddenly lost!"

"If they had lost, they would have been unemployed," deadpanned Mikhailov. "So, we thought, why win? Let them keep working and getting better contracts."

In many ways, of course, there was a winner and loser on the scoreboard, but while the Soviets lost, they still won—the paradox of sporting life.

"There are no losers here," continued Yakushev. "The series was fantastic, and it served not just Canadian or Soviet hockey, but hockey all around the world. So regardless of the pity I feel for myself, the series was a huge success and we should congratulate everyone— hockey fans on both sides and the players—and be grateful for the wonderful series."

"We opened a window inside the world of hockey," said Mikhailov. "Two different schools clashed—the Soviet and the Canadian. All the best part of the Canadian style, we took as ammunition, the importance of giving it all at the beginning and the end of periods of the game as a whole and the importance of one-on-one battles. Canadians have borrowed our passing and possession games, that's how they play now. After those games, Canadians became much more flexible instead of just playing a simple style, shoot from any angle and hope one goes in. So, from my point of view, those games gave a big push to the development of hockey."

And part of the reason why the Soviets still celebrate the series today, is they proved they belonged and could play.

"They proved to the hockey world they could play against the Canadian pros and on any given night they could win," said winger Ron Ellis. "We had nothing to win because it was expected of us. They had everything to win. That's why I feel they want to celebrate it so much with us. It meant so much to them and their hockey program."

"It doesn't happen very often, but I think we were both big winners," said Dryden. "Not just winners, but big winners. It changed them and it changed us."

A defining moment in the evolution of the game, an eye-opener for both teams.

You've probably heard the question asked before, or even wondered it yourself.

"The question you guys [the media] ask us," said Dryden. "'You've won a Stanley Cup, or you've won a few, which one matters the most?' You always get a lousy answer because it's a lousy question. Because the answer you want to give is they're like your children and you don't have a favourite. The fact is, you do remember certain ones. They do matter more, and others you don't remember, hardly at all. It's the same with any event in your life. Some come to matter more, some less.

"Anything you do, or have experienced, or any feeling that you have, you don't know how it's going to stack up. You don't know over time those things that you are going to feel more deeply or less deeply, that you're going to remember more or less. What moments survive and what don't. What really are historical and what weren't. It's a test of memory, and not only of what you remember, but how you remember.

"The fact is, for me and for just about everybody on Team Canada, that is the most memorable hockey experience that I have had. That's just the way it is. Some people might want to hear that it was this Stanley Cup win, or that Stanley Cup win, or coming in as a rookie, this and that . . . Maybe that could be, but it wasn't. It isn't. That's not how it feels. It's a fifty-year test of time and that's what the test has produced.

"This series happens to matter a lot more than most other series and more than any other series that I was a part of . . . the kind of change that it had, the effect it had on us, and the way we play and the way they play. That matters a lot. Ask those three thousand fans if it mattered. Ask them why it mattered and how it mattered. Ask those people who experienced it at home how they feel. I can't say all the ways in which it mattered, but it mattered a lot and to a lot of people, who were fifteen years old, or thirty-five years old, and they were living wherever they were living and they've had thousands of things happen to them in their lives, but it matters in a way that is surprising fifty years later. It's one of the things they remember and remember very deeply. Well, that says something. That's the real test of it."

"I played on four Stanley Cup–winning teams, nothing compared to that," said Peter Mahovlich, who won the Stanley Cup in 1971, '72, '76, and '77 with Montreal.

"If you lose the Stanley Cup one year, you can always win it the next year," said Cournoyer. "But if you lose the '72 series, that's it, you're not coming back, there's no more 1972. We said we have to win that series because everybody's going to crucify us. That goal was very, very important, not just for Canada but for us, too. For all the guys who played in that series, who would have had to come back and say 'we lost' that series. That would have been awful. We felt our reputations were on the line big time."

Harry Sinden, who won a Stanley Cup as coach of the Boston Bruins and another forty-one years later as an executive, said there are similarities between winning a Stanley Cup and winning the Summit Series, but they are also so very different.

"The exhilaration of both is pretty comparable," he said. "One player who had won the Stanley Cup several times said this meant so much to the players to win that series, with the way that it evolved and the way the emotions evolved. The fear of losing is always in a player's mind, even the good players, that's why they win, they're so afraid of losing. I know at least one of the Montreal Canadiens players, who won multiple Stanley Cups, said that to him this was bigger. Winning the Stanley Cup is great, but others have done that. No one else has done what we did then. Or since."

To a man—players, coaches, and team personnel alike—they all are grateful to the three thousand or so fans who travelled to Moscow for the final four games of the series and the thousands of others back home who sent telegrams and postcards and words of encouragement. It mattered.

One of those three thousand fans who made the trek, Pierre Plouffe, had his own Moscow adventure.

"After game six, I went with a friend over to the Intourist [Hotel] to have a drink with the Canadian players," said Plouffe. "I was friends from Montreal with Peter Mahovlich, John Ferguson, and Yvan Cournoyer. I was in a room drinking with Peter, Phil Esposito, Don Awrey, and John Ferguson. They told me I better go back to my hotel because I was getting drunk.

"Peter and Fergie and I went to the bar for one final drink. It was about one a.m. or two a.m. I ordered three drinks and the bartender, a woman, told me the bar was closed. I protested, saying that I had been in the bar other nights drinking until four a.m. I slapped down my hand and hit the top of a champagne bottle that was lying on its side. It spun down the bar and knocked some empty glasses, breaking them on the floor.

"She was mad. She started to blow a whistle and yelled at me in a very loud voice. I was scared and slowly walked backwards. I banged into and knocked over a table. A guy dressed in a black turtleneck sweater and black pants then approached me. He was the bouncer, I think. He was built, and he tossed me around like I was a piece of paper. I punched him, and it hurt my hand more than it hurt him.

"The police came. There was a lengthy discussion. There was a guy there from Toronto who understood Russian. He told me I was in trouble. They kept me there until the morning. I saw Pete [Mahovlich] before I left with the police, and he asked, 'You all right, kid?' I paid for the broken glasses and was driven back to my hotel. When I got back, the others from my group were having breakfast. I told them my story.

"We were supposed to go see the [Bolshoi] ballet that night. As I was getting ready for dinner before the ballet, the police knocked on my door. They told me I had to go with them to sign some papers at the police station. I signed the papers, but then they said we had to wait for a translator. Eventually, they put me in a cell by myself for the night. They took stuff from me, like my watch, and turned out the lights. I went to sleep, but I didn't know how long I slept because I had no watch.

"The next morning, my mother was asking people, 'Has anybody seen my son?' The Canadian Embassy was called. They found me, but a woman from the embassy was told that I was going to Siberia for five years for hitting the security guy, or policeman, they said, and for the damage at the bar. I was scared. I would be lying to you if I said I didn't cry. My mother wasn't even allowed to speak French to me at the police station, only English. All I could think was I would be shovelling snow [in Siberia] for the next five years.

"I had no sense of time. They came into my cell at one point and blindfolded me. But they took me to a place to watch the third game [game seven] on television. Imagine travelling all that way to watch a game on TV. My mother phoned Yvan Cournoyer, and he rallied some of the players [and Canadian government officials]. But I didn't have much hope at this point. I asked for two pieces of paper. With one, I made a deck of cards to play solitaire. On the other, I wrote down the alphabet and the Russian equivalent. I figured I might as well learn Russian if I was going to be there for five years.

"I figured I was going to watch the [eighth] game on television with the guards like we did the game before. But instead, they put me in a car and drove me to the arena. I watched the game sitting with the army guards behind the Russian bench. And they told me there would be no cheering. There wasn't a lot to cheer about anyway with Canada behind 5–3 [after two periods]. But then Cournoyer scores to tie the game, and I jump out of my seat. They pulled me back down to my seat."

Team Canada, of course, would mount an incredible comeback in the third period of a game that had every bit of drama and controversy you could imagine. Like the players, the fans very much had the feeling that it was team versus team, but it was also Canada versus Russia and it was more than a series, it was life.

And with thirty-four seconds remaining, Henderson scored for Canada.

"That game had everything happen," said Marie Garraway, another of the three thousand fans. "From high to low to high. When the goal was scored, we went crazy. We must have stood cheering for ten to fifteen minutes. They didn't like that. There were hugs and tears and smiles, you just couldn't believe that we pulled it off. It was one of the greatest comebacks ever, in the game and in the series. We were so elated.

"When they played 'O Canada' after the game, everybody sang their hearts out. It gave you goose bumps. I was so proud to be there. Of course, when we were going back to the hotel on the bus, everyone was singing. At the hotel everyone was partying, everyone mingled at that point. The lobby was packed, the music playing. It was so amazing to be a part of that—I'm a part of history. It wasn't supposed to be that, but we wound up being a part of history. That was pretty cool. When we got back, I went back to work, and everyone wanted to know what it was like. I just said, 'Hey, I invited you, you could have been part of history, too.'"

"To be there with three thousand Canadian fans, you had to cherish it," said Bill Watters, who was also there in Moscow. "You realized it was not just two hockey teams, it was two ways of living and we wanted ours to be the best. In the end, the Canadian inner spirit was hard to match."

Even some of the Canadian journalists who had been assigned to the series and had been, in the opinion of the players, overly critical for much of it, got caught up in the excitement.

"I was a mere kid of sixty-one," said nationally syndicated columnist Jim Coleman years later. "At the end of the game, I found myself, a nice old gentleman in my sincere three-piece blue suit, standing up on my seat and I was pointing up to Comrade Brezhnev, the head of the Soviet Union. I was giving him the exact same salute [the middle finger] as Alan Eagleson had given to the crowd fifteen minutes earlier.

"There was no neutrality there. They did everything to beat Canada by fair means or foul. This was 1972, and the Soviets were still the big bad bears, the Cold War was on, the Berlin Wall was up, these were the enemy."

Not unlike the players, the experience for the fans was a reminder of how good life was back in Canada. Winning a hockey series is one thing, remembering your roots and appreciating them was a nice by-product.

"It certainly was an eye-opener," said Garraway, "especially being a younger person. We grew up in Whitby, which wasn't Toronto, but we wanted for nothing. To go to a country like that and realize what you have makes you proud to be Canadian and realize how lucky you are."

"What a feeling to be there," said Plouffe. "We were the best in hockey. It was an experience of a lifetime. After the game, the police put me back into the car. I figured they were going to drive me back to the police station. Instead, they drove me to my hotel and told me to stay there for the rest of our trip. I didn't listen. I went back to the Intourist to celebrate with the players. When I got back to the hotel, a Russian official came up to me and asked me why I didn't stay at our hotel. They had followed me to the Intourist that night.

"After that, all I wanted to hear was the wheels going up on our plane. When we arrived back in Montreal, a few television crews and reporters were waiting for me to tell my story, but I just told them I had nothing to say."

A few weeks later, Plouffe had some visitors from the Russian Embassy. They apologized for the Moscow episode and presented him with some gifts, including one of those Russian fur hats. A few years later, Plouffe was asked to go back to Russia to coach some of their top water skiers. Plouffe's friends thought he was nuts for going, but he had a great time.

"I don't have anything bad to say about them," said Plouffe. "I made a mistake."

It seems détente was achieved on many levels.

"In Canadian history, we had the FLQ crisis in 1970, the taking of Vimy Ridge in 1917, and we had VE Day in 1945," said Beddoes. "VE

Day and the celebration in 1972 were the biggest this country has had. This is our national sport. You can't write about Canada without writing about that series. Napoleon didn't take Moscow, the Nazis got within twenty-one miles in 1943, but in a war of a different kind Team Canada conquered Moscow."

"I think that this series will be considered for a long time yet, as the most brilliant and memorable in the history of international hockey," said Yakushev.

"Both teams won in 1972," said Tretiak. "These games will be part of history as long as hockey lives. The winner was the game of hockey."

"They accomplished what they wanted to do," said Paul Henderson. "They wanted to prove they could play with the best in the world and they did that. We were the best and we had to win. To represent your country, a team voted 'team of the century' and that goal the 'sports moment of the century,' well, let's just say thank goodness for '72."

1972.

It says it all. The greatest. Ever.

Acknowledgments

Henderson has scored for Canada.

They are five words, one sentence, a legendary goal call that Canadians—make that hockey fans of a certain vintage—will never forget.

I know exactly where I was. Just about a week shy of my fourteenth birthday, a hockey-crazed kid, I convinced my parents to allow me to remain home from school. Not just for the historic eighth game but also for games 5 and 7. And after those final thirty-four seconds ticked off the clock and Team Canada had completed its amazing comeback, a group of us kids descended upon a nearby parking lot to play a game of road hockey: Canada versus the Soviet Union, a coin toss determining who was Canada. A quintessential Canadian day.

A very special thanks to all of Team Canada 1972 for the memories. And for giving their time, fifty years later, to reminisce about the days Canada stood still. The same thanks to the Soviets who shared their stories. Their memories were as vivid and accurate today as they were roughly thirty years ago when I first wrote a book looking back at the series. What has changed since then, and since the series was played, is their perspective. The mortal enemies have become friends

287

over time, understanding the other's way of life, remembering that 1972 was a wildly different time in the world on and off the ice, and appreciating just how good the other guys were.

There are many people to thank for helping with this project. Quotes and anecdotes came from various sources, including newspaper stories, books, and first-hand interviews I have conducted over the many years and for my previous book, *The Days Canada Stood Still*. The majority of quotes came from the most recent interviews, from the likes of coach Harry Sinden, and heroic players such as Phil Esposito, Paul Henderson, Brad Park, Ken Dryden, Yvan Cournoyer, Ron Ellis, Ed Johnston, Rod Seiling, Mickey Redmond, Guy Lapointe, Vic Hadfield, Wayne Cashman, Don Awrey, Dale Tallon, Red Berenson, Jean Ratelle, Pete Mahovlich, Bob Clarke, Bobby Orr, and trainer Joe Sgro. There were many others. I've tried to make a true representation of their thoughts and memories fifty years later.

And then there was the legendary Bob Cole, who called the series on CBC radio; reporter and friend Dan Proudfoot; David Honsberger, Chad Dawson, and John Yorke with the Team Canada 1972 group—all generously shared their time and recollections with me.

Among the books that were a great help was Ken Dryden's *Face-off at the Summit*; Serge Savard's *Forever Canadien*; Harry Sinden's *Hockey Showdown*; Andrew Podnieks's *Team Canada 1972*; Sean Mitton and Jim Prime's *The Goal That United Canada*; and Brian Conacher's *As The Puck Turns*.

A huge source of information was the book *1972: The Summit Series*, which was researched and written by Richard J. Bendell, Paul Patskou, and Robert MacAskill. Patskou, a hockey historian, along with Lora Evans, are the executive producers of the Hockey Time Machine zoom cast. Glenn Dreyfuss is the producer. They hosted Soviet players Vladislav Tretiak, Alexander Yakushev, and Boris

Mikhailov, and referee Steve Dowling, and it was the source of many quotes gathered for this book. Thanks also to Alex Braverman, who has had a hand in many of these ventures.

I also enjoyed watching again *Canada's Team of the Century*, more than twenty hours of complete game coverage and interviews.

A very special thank-you to long-time friend and colleague Tim Wharnsby, a top hockey reporter who assisted with some of the interviews and research for this book. His work was invaluable. Thanks as well to friend and colleague Wayne Parrish, former senior vice-president, editorial, at the *Toronto Star*, who helped arrange for copies of the front pages from throughout the series to appear in this book.

I want to extend a very special thanks to Justin Stoller, senior editor of nonfiction with Simon & Schuster Canada. This is the first book we have published together and Justin was a pleasure to work with, a steady and calming hand from start to finish. And thanks to President and Publisher Kevin Hanson, who made this happen, along with literary agent Brian Wood.

No doubt there are others who deserve to be thanked and acknowledged, so forgive me for slipping up, but consider yourself thanked, including my son, Mark, who knows how to navigate the waters at home when deadlines are approaching. He is truly an inspiration.

The reference to 28,800 seconds, in the conclusion, is a shout-out to the legacy venture Team Canada 1972. Under the guidance of the late Pat Stapleton, it launched the initiative 28,800 Seconds—The Power of Teamwork. Their stated goal is to give back and "to inspire every Canadian with the lessons learned from the Summit Series, particularly those highlighting what can be achieved through teamwork." It consists of three pillars: education, entertainment, and a charitable foundation. They know that hockey fans of different ages have different memories, understandings, and awareness of the series and as such they are speaking in a different way to the various demographics. Hopefully this book helps with that mission. The players certainly gave me their all and again are deserving of my deep thanks.

The series was as brilliant as it was game-changing, and its memory deserves to live on forever.

Henderson has scored for Canada.

It's funny, but Paul Henderson has often said the best goal he ever scored was the brilliant one to win game 7, but the most important was the winner in game 8. He called it a garbage goal! Even Vladislav Tretiak, who allowed the Henderson goal, says for Soviets that was a remember-where-you-were moment.

"I told Tretiak that he has become famous for letting in [Henderson's] goal," said Team Canada winger (and part-time comedian) Dennis Hull. "I said to him that 'if you had stopped it, you'd probably be a cab driver in Moscow today.'"

And here we are, fifty years later. 1972. The Greatest. Ever.

In Memoriam

– Team Canada –

GARY BERGMAN—Defence

Bergman was one of only seven Canadians to play in all eight games in the series against the Soviets. The others were Bobby Clarke, Yvan Cournoyer, Ron Ellis, Phil Esposito, Paul Henderson, and Brad Park. The native of Kenora, Ontario, who won a Memorial Cup with the 1958–59 Winnipeg Braves, was the most unheralded player to arrive at Team Canada's training camp. Signed by the Montreal Canadiens out of junior, he played a combined 267 AHL regular-season and playoff games with Buffalo, Cleveland, and Springfield before the Detroit Red Wings rescued him and gave him a shot.

Bergman made an immediate impact, helping the Red Wings advance to the 1965–66 Stanley Cup final against Montreal in his second NHL season. He would only play in four more playoff games the rest of his career. That's one of the reasons he was so appreciative of the opportunity Harry Sinden gave him with Team Canada. Bergman was well known to his Team Canada teammates. He had played with Red Berenson, Marcel Dionne, and Mickey Redmond in Detroit. Frank and Peter Mahovlich were former Red Wings. He also played with assistant coach John Ferguson in the AHL with Cleveland and later toiled with Bill Goldsworthy and J. P. Parise for a season with the Minnesota North Stars.

A defensive defenceman, Bergman returned to Detroit after the series against the Soviets and played some of his best hockey. He was named to the mid-season all-star game at Madison Square Garden in late January. He had a malignant melanoma removed from his back in 1994. He had no further problems until April 2000, when tests revealed his cancer had spread. He passed away at age sixty-two on December 8, 2000.

MIKE CANNON—Team Services

Cannon, who worked for Alan Eagleson as a manager with the NHL Players' Association, was an administrative coordinator for Team Canada and held a similar role for the 1976 Canada Cup. In 1972, he took care of all the visa problems, ticket arrangements, and any other wants and needs the players and management might have, as well as some of the logistics of team accommodations, etc. He became the Toronto Blue Jays' first director of travel in 1977 and held that role for three years.

His passion for baseball went beyond the Blue Jays. He coached the game at a minor level in Oakville. The Cannon Cup, the year-end midget all-star tournament in Oakville, Ontario, is named in Cannon's honour. Cannon passed away from throat cancer on May 31, 1995, at age forty-nine.

BOB DAVIDSON—Team Scout

Davidson was a fixture for forty-four years with his hometown Toronto Maple Leafs, first as a dependable player and later as the team's chief scout, who played an essential role in building the four Stanley Cup–winning teams in the 1960s. He spent his entire pro career as a rugged right wing with the Maple Leafs, winning Stanley Cups in 1941–42 and 1944–45. He played on Toronto's DAD line alongside Syl Apps and Gord Drillon. While not as offensively productive as his line mates, Davidson was counted on for his responsible defensive play, checking sniper Maurice "Rocket" Richard in his early days with the Montreal Canadiens. Davidson filled in as Maple Leafs captain in 1943–44 and 1944–45 when Apps joined the Canadian army for World War II.

After his playing days, Davidson remained with the Maple Leafs organization, first coaching their AHL affiliate in Pittsburgh and later becoming the club's chief scout from 1951 to 1978. His long-time association with the Maple Leafs ended before Christmas in 1978, when owner Harold Ballard pressured Davidson to resign. Ballard stooped to cutting Davidson's salary in half. The classy Davidson had had enough and retired.

He and Maple Leafs head coach John McLellan travelled to Russia to scout the Soviets before the 1972 series. Davidson passed on September 26, 1996, at the age of eighty-four.

KARL ELIEFF—Physiotherapist

Karl Elieff was known as "the Healer" to the Toronto Maple Leafs. He was one of the first physiotherapists in professional sports and kept the over-the-hill gang—as they were known—healthy enough to win four Stanley Cups in the 1960s. The final hurrah for this bunch arrived in the spring of 1967 when Toronto had the NHL's oldest team. Elieff also played a role in two Stanley Cups won by the Boston Bruins in the early 1970s because he helped Bobby Orr deal with his persistent knee problems, dating back to his first surgery on his left knee in 1968.

Many Maple Leafs and players from other NHL teams visited Elieff at his Parliament Street office, a few blocks away from Maple Leaf Gardens, in the off-season for maintenance and a piece of apple strudel, which he always kept on hand for his patients.

As Team Canada's physiotherapist, Elieff continued to work with Orr in the hopes he could play after another setback with his wonky knee. Elieff also was busy during the series with ailing players such as Frank Mahovlich (knee), Serge Savard (ankle), and others. Elieff passed away on March 24, 2015, at the age of ninety.

TONY ESPOSITO—Goaltender

Esposito played junior hockey for his hometown Sault Ste. Marie (Ontario) Greyhounds, then college hockey for Michigan Tech University, where he was a three-time, first-team all-American, winning the 1965 NCAA Championship with the Huskies. He began his NHL career with the Montreal Canadiens, called up from the central-league Houston Apollos, playing thirteen games during the 1968–69 season. His first NHL start was on December 5, 1968, against the Boston Bruins and brother Phil. Afterwards, their mother asked Phil if he had scored a goal on his brother, who was fourteen months younger. Phil replied: "No, Ma . . . I got two!" Tony made thirty-three saves in a 2–2 tie. He got his name on the Stanley Cup that season—the inscription reads A. Esposito—despite limited playing time, because he backed up Rogie Vachon after Gump Worsley was largely grounded by a fear of flying.

After that season, Tony was left unprotected in the intra-league draft by the Habs, who were deep in goal, including a prospect named Ken Dryden. Tony was claimed by the Blackhawks for $25,000, big money back in the day. In Chicago, he quickly became a star and was wildly popular for the next fifteen years. In his rookie season, he led the NHL with thirty-eight wins. He set a modern-day record that season with fifteen shutouts, winning the Calder Trophy as rookie of the year and the Vezina Trophy as top goaltender. Although not the first to use the "butterfly" goaltending style, Esposito certainly made it popular.

During his time with the Blackhawks, he led them to the 1971 and 1973 Stanley Cup final, both times losing to Montreal. Along the way, he was three times a first-team and two times a second-team all-star. He won the Vezina Trophy two more times, in 1972 and 1974, and was runner-up to Bobby Orr in the voting for the Hart Trophy, as the league's most valuable player, during his rookie season.

In the Summit Series, it was originally thought Esposito would back up Dryden, but he was quickly pressed into action, starting the second game, with Team Canada in desperate need of a win after their opening-night shocking loss to the Soviet Union. He wound up sharing the workload in the series, playing in the second, third, fifth, and seventh games—winning two, losing one, and tying the other. In the opinion of his brother, Team Canada would not have won the series without Tony Esposito.

"I believe in destiny," Tony said years later. "I believe it was destined that we were going to win because of the emotion and passion that we displayed. By no means were we the better team. They were the better team."

After retiring, he became general manager of the Pittsburgh Penguins for a few seasons and later was chief scout of the Tampa Bay Lightning, a franchise he helped build with his brother. The Blackhawks retired his number 35 in 1988, the same year he was inducted into the Hockey Hall of Fame. In 2017, he was named one of the "100 Greatest Players in NHL History."

Tony Esposito passed away on August 10, 2021, after a brief battle with pancreatic cancer. He was seventy-eight.

JOHN FERGUSON SR.—Assistant Coach

Ferguson was one of the most feared enforcers in hockey history, winning five Stanley Cups in eight years with the Montreal Canadiens. He led all rookies in 1963–64 with eighteen goals, but finished second in Calder Trophy voting to Montreal teammate Jacques Laperriere. Even though Ferguson retired as a player following the 1970–71 season, he was asked to play for Team Canada in 1972. He didn't feel right about suiting up because general manager Sam Pollock was after him to rejoin the Montreal Canadiens, too. So, instead, he accepted an invitation from Team Canada head coach Harry Sinden to be his assistant.

Ferguson, from Vancouver, was a valuable resource in player selections (Peter Mahovlich was one talent he pushed for) and kept up the spirits of the Team Canada players. Ferguson encouraged Bobby Clarke to take out Russian Valeri Kharlamov with a wicked slash to his ankle in game 6. Like it or not, Clarke's actions caused Kharlamov to miss the next game, and he was ineffective in the series finale.

The Team Canada stint was Ferguson's first foray behind the bench. He later coached and managed the New York Rangers, luring

Anders Hedberg and Ulf Nilsson away from Winnipeg in June 1978, only to be fired a few days later. The Rangers advanced to the Stanley Cup the following May. He then spent a decade as the Jets GM and later helped build into contenders the Ottawa Senators and the San Jose Sharks in their respective front offices. He passed away at sixty-eight on July 14, 2007, after a two-year battle with prostate cancer.

JOHN FORRISTALL—Trainer

John "Frosty" Forristall was a member of the Boston Bruins training staff for twenty years and part of their two Stanley Cup championships, in 1969–70 and 1971–72. Forristall and Bobby Orr were close friends. The two shared an apartment in Orr's first few seasons in Boston, until the Hall of Fame defenceman was married in 1973.

Forristall was nicknamed Frosty because he looked liked a snowman when he tended goal for North Quincy High School. When Bruins netminder Gerry Cheevers was hit with a puck on his mask in practice one day, it was Forristall who drew a stitch on the goalie's white face covering. A tradition was born. Cheevers added a stitch on his mask each time a shot struck him on his face in a game.

After his stint with the Bruins, Forristall worked for the Tampa Bay Lightning and later on the maintenance staff at the Toronto Blue Jays facility in Dunedin, Florida. Forristall was an assistant trainer for Team Canada. He passed away from brain cancer on May 30, 1995, at age fifty-one. Orr and wife, Peggy, took in Frosty when he was diagnosed with his condition in 1994.

ROD GILBERT—Right Wing

Known as "Mr. Ranger," for over eighteen professional seasons Rod Gilbert only played for two teams: the New York Rangers and Team Canada 1972.

But Gilbert's pro career was almost over before it began. During his final junior game with Guelph in 1960, he broke his back after stepping on debris and falling on the ice. He required spinal fusion surgery and almost lost his left leg to infection. But he made his NHL debut at the age of nineteen during the 1960–61 season, wearing a brace to support his back.

Gilbert hurt his back again in the late summer of 1965, while pulling a boat out of the water, and had a second spinal fusion surgery in February 1966. There were also severe complications from that operation, and Gilbert almost died when he choked on medication and lapsed into unconsciousness.

Born in Montreal on July 1, 1941 (Gilbert often joked, "It's nice of them to have a national holiday for me" in Canada), Gilbert signed with the Rangers in 1960 and told the team to also sign his boyhood friend, centre Jean Ratelle. Lucky for the Rangers and Gilbert, they did. Gilbert, Ratelle, and Vic Hadfield—all three played for Team Canada in 1972—became one of the best lines in the NHL during the 1971–72 season. Known as the GAG (Goal-A-Game) Line, they led the Rangers to the Stanley Cup final, only to lose to the Boston Bruins in six games. That season, Gilbert had forty-three goals and ninety-seven points, both career highs, and was named a first team all-star.

He retired at age thirty-six in November 1977. At the time, Gilbert had set or matched twenty team scoring records and was second only to Gordie Howe in NHL history for points by a right winger. He finished his career with 406 goals and 1,021 points in 1,065 games. He had 34 goals and 33 assists in 79 playoff games.

Gilbert is the leading scorer in Rangers history, first on their all-time goals and points lists, second in assists, and third in games played. He appeared in eight NHL all-star games. His number 7 was the first ever to be retired by the Rangers, on October 14, 1979. He was inducted into the Hockey Hall of Fame in 1982.

Like his NHL career, Gilbert's involvement in the Summit Series almost didn't happen. He was named to the Team Canada roster, but his contract with the Rangers had expired and he was being wooed by the rival WHA. It was determined that players had to be under contract to NHL teams to be eligible to play in the series. Both Ratelle and Hadfield re-signed with the Rangers, and Gilbert finally did, too, near the end of July that summer.

The GAG Line started the Summit Series together (the only complete line selected), but they were benched after the first-game loss in Montreal. The outcome was tough enough to deal with, but the post-game critique Gilbert received from his brother Jean really stung. He told Rod the Canadians were a "bunch of bums" and a "disgrace to your country." Gilbert and Ratelle were reunited in game 6 in Moscow, but with Chicago Blackhawks left winger Dennis Hull.

Gilbert had a goal and three assists in six games during the series and was regarded as being a terrific teammate. In Moscow, he and Paul Henderson were the only Canadians to earn points in all four games.

Said Rangers and Team Canada teammate Brad Park many years later about Gilbert: "He was the most wonderful man I ever met. Ever."

Gilbert passed away on August 22, 2021, after a lengthy illness. He was eighty.

BRIAN GLENNIE—Defence

Glennie did not dress for any of the eight games versus the Soviets. However, the physical, defensive defenceman did play in the first of two exhibition games in Sweden, a 4–1 win for Team Canada, and the final outing, a 3–3 tie with the Czech national team in Prague. Glennie was one of the few Team Canada members who had international experience before the series against the Soviets. He played for Canada at the 1968 Olympics in Grenoble, France, winning a bronze medal.

Before the Winter Games, he captained the Toronto Marlboroughs to the 1966–67 Memorial Cup. One of his teammates on that championship club was 1972 Team Canada defenceman Brad Park. After nine seasons in Toronto with his hometown Maple Leafs, Glennie finished his career with an eighteen-game stint for the Los Angeles Kings in 1978–79.

He was involved in an ugly incident at Maple Leaf Gardens on November 5, 1975. After Glennie delivered a clean check on Detroit Red Wings forward Bryan Hextall, Detroit tough guy Dan Maloney attacked and badly beat Glennie. He suffered a concussion. Maloney, a future Maple Leafs player and head coach, was charged with assault the next day but acquitted the following summer. Glennie's health declined late in his life. He passed away on February 7, 2020, at age seventy-three.

BILL GOLDSWORTHY—Winger

Goldsworthy had the temerity to don sweater number 9 for Team Canada after Rod Gilbert claimed his customary number 8, the same digit Goldsworthy wore for the Minnesota North Stars. Number 9 would have been Bobby Hull's number had the Golden Jet been allowed to play in the series. But Goldsworthy didn't mind the attention. He was a true character who kept his teammates laughing.

After helping the Niagara Falls Flyers win the 1964–65 Memorial Cup, he found himself in training camp for the Boston Bruins a few months later. In an exhibition game against the Montreal Canadiens, Goldsworthy munched on peanuts and licorice while sitting on the bench. The Habs were winning big, and the youngster wasn't playing. Bruins coach Milt Schmidt surprised Goldsworthy and sent him out for a late-game shift. There was a trail of peanut shells as he skated onto the ice. The next day, he was sent to Oklahoma City and plucked by the North Stars in the 1967 expansion draft.

In 1972, Goldsworthy played in games 2, 4, and 7. His early game crosschecking and elbowing penalties led to a pair of Soviet power-play goals in the first period in game 4. But he scored in the third period and assisted on Dennis Hull's late-game goal in the 5–3 loss.

Goldsworthy's number 8 was retired by the North Stars. He played his final NHL games early in the 1977–78 season with the New York Rangers, alongside his Team Canada teammates Phil Esposito, Rod Gilbert, and Don Awrey. Goldsworthy was the first Team Canada member to pass away, dying from complications of AIDS on March 29, 1996. Goldsworthy publicly admitted earlier that he had acquired the disease, saying "I can live a good life. I just can't live a long one."

Goldsworthy died at the age of fifty-one.

BOB HAGGERT—Executive Assistant to Harry Sinden

Haggert enjoyed an expansive ride in hockey. He began as a stick boy for the Toronto senior Marlboroughs in 1949 and decades later became a promoter and licensing guru for organizations such as the

NHL, NHLPA, MLBPA, and Labatt Breweries. He also was part of teams that won an Allan Cup, a Memorial Cup, and four Stanley Cups, celebrating with the 1949–50 Marlboroughs, 1953–54 junior Marlies, and the Toronto Maple Leafs in the 1960s, respectively.

In 1964, Haggert taped up the fractured leg of Maple Leafs defenceman Bobby Baun, who suffered the injury in the third period of game 6 of the Stanley Cup final. Baun returned to score in overtime, and Toronto defeated the Detroit Red Wings in game 7 for a third consecutive title.

Haggert was close with Maple Leafs coach/GM Punch Imlach. The pair had a ritual of being the last to leave the dressing room before the game. He departed the Maple Leafs in 1968 to become president of the Bobby Orr–Mike Walton Sports Camp. He later started his own business, Sports Representatives Ltd., a company that set up marketing deals for players.

He served as head coach Harry Sinden's executive assistant with Team Canada, handling the logistics of travelling the team to Montreal, Toronto, Winnipeg, Vancouver, Stockholm, Moscow, Prague, and back to Montreal and Toronto. He passed away on June 6, 2011, at the age of seventy-six.

AGGIE KUKULOWICZ—Interpreter

The Winnipeg-born Kukulowicz played four games for the New York Rangers in the early 1950s, scoring in his debut outing. He won a pair of IHL Turner Cups with the Saint Paul Saints in the early 1960s and the Allan Cup with the 1963–64 Winnipeg Maroons.

Kukulowicz was employed by Air Canada after his playing career concluded, working his way from baggage handler to being the airline's representative in Moscow. He later helped Canadian pro sports teams with their travel. Kukulowicz also spent time coaching hockey in Poland. He was fluent in Polish as well as Czech, French, German, Russian, and Ukrainian. His foreign language command landed him interpreter positions first for government officials and later for hockey executives, including super-agent Alan Eagleson.

He performed an interpreter role at many IIHF World Championships and alongside Eagleson for the 1972 series and all the Canada Cups. Kukulowicz passed away on September 26, 2008, at the age of seventy-five.

MICHEL "BUNNY" LAROCQUE—Goaltender

Larocque, at twenty, was one of three youngsters from the 1972 NHL draft invited to Team Canada's training camp to increase the total to thirty-eight players, enough to contest intra-squad games. Joining the future Montreal Canadiens goaltender were forward Billy Harris and defenceman John Van Boxmeer. The New York Islanders selected Harris first overall. The Habs chose Larocque sixth and Van Boxmeer fourteenth.

After Canadiens training camp that fall, Larocque and Van Boxmeer led the AHL Nova Scotia Voyageurs to the 1972–73 regular-season title and the Calder Cup final. The Voyageurs lost the final to Rick Dudley and the Cincinnati Swords. The following season Laroque found a spot on the Canadiens roster when Ken Dryden left to finish law school. Laroque won four consecutive Stanley Cups in the late 1970s as Dryden's backup. He also shared three Vezina Trophies with Dryden and a fourth in 1980–81 with Denis Herron and Richard Sevigny.

After his playing career, the native of Hull, Quebec, became a junior hockey executive. He was named the Quebec Major Junior

Hockey League's executive of the year, leading the Victoriaville Tigres as general manager to the 1989–90 President's Cup final. He was vice-president of the QMJHL when he passed away of brain cancer on July 29, 1992, at age forty.

RICHARD MARTIN—Winger

Before turning pro, Martin played a significant role with Team Canada teammates Gilbert Perreault and Jocelyn Guevremont in winning back-to-back Memorial Cup titles with the Montreal Junior Canadiens in 1968–69 and 1969–70. A native of Verdun, Quebec, Martin arrived in Toronto for Team Canada's training camp after a forty-four-goal rookie campaign with the Buffalo Sabres. He finished second in Calder Trophy voting to another Team Canada teammate, goalie Ken Dryden.

Before a knee injury cut his career short in 1980 at age thirty, Martin became one of the most prolific left-wing scorers, playing on the famed French Connection line in Buffalo with Gilbert Perreault and René Robert. Martin was named a first-team all-star in 1973–74 and 1974–75 and a second-teamer in 1975–76 and 1976–77.

Martin did not see action in any of the eight games in the series against the Soviets. Along with Perreault, Guevremont, and Vic Hadfield, the four left Moscow after the fifth game to report to their NHL teams for training camp, and incurred criticism for "deserting" Team Canada. Martin did play in the second of two exhibition games in Sweden before Team Canada arrived in Russia. He scored early in the third period to give Canada a 3–2 lead in the game that finished in a 4–4 tie. Martin also played for Canada in the 1976 Canada Cup, scoring three times in four games. On March 13, 2011, he passed away from a heart attack while driving near his Buffalo-area home. He was fifty-nine.

JOHN MCLELLAN—Team Scout

Championships followed McLellan early in his hockey career. As a junior, the centre from South Porcupine, Ontario, claimed his first title, a Memorial Cup, with the 1946–47 Toronto St. Michael's Majors and an Allan Cup three seasons later with the Toronto Marlboroughs. The legendary Joe Primeau coached both teams.

In his second year of pro, McLellan was promoted for a two-game stint with the Toronto Maple Leafs and was returned to the AHL Pittsburgh Hornets to win the Calder Cup in 1952. He won another Calder Cup with the Cleveland Barons five years later. He regained his amateur status to join the Belleville McFarlands in their march to a World Championship in 1959. One of his Belleville teammates that season was Team Canada forward Red Berenson.

McLellan then coached and won three consecutive championships with the Nashville Dixie Flyers of the Eastern Hockey League in 1965–66 and 1966–67, followed by another title with the Tulsa Oilers of the Central Professional Hockey League. He was promoted to coach the Maple Leafs in 1969 and coached the NHL club for four years. A few months before his final season as Toronto's coach, he and Bob Davidson went to Russia to scout the Soviet team in advance of the 1972 series.

In March 1979, Maple Leafs owner Harold Ballard asked McLellan, then the team's assistant general manager, to return as head coach after the bizarre firing of Roger Neilson. McLellan turned down Ballard, citing health reasons. A few months later, McLellan passed away, on October 24, 1979, at age fifty-one, suffering a heart attack while raking the leaves at his North Toronto home.

STAN MIKITA—Centre

Mikita was one of four co-captains on Team Canada with Phil Esposito, Frank Mahovlich, and Jean Ratelle. He played in game 2 in Toronto and game 3 in Winnipeg, setting up Mahovlich for the final goal in the 4–1 victory in the second game. At thirty-two, Mikita was the second oldest forward on Team Canada, twenty-nine months younger than Mahovlich. Mikita suffered a severe back injury in 1969 and was never the dominant player he had been earlier, even though he continued to produce.

In his second NHL season, he won a Stanley Cup with the 1960–61 Chicago Blackhawks and progressed to win the Art Ross Trophy scoring title four times, as well as the Hart Trophy in 1966–67 and 1967–68. He was born in the small village of Sokolce on the Slovak side of then Communist Czechoslovakia. His parents sent him to live with an aunt and uncle and settled in St. Catharines, Ontario, at a young age.

Canada played an exhibition game in Prague after the dramatic game 8 Summit Series victory in Moscow. It was an emotional evening as the Czechs and his family came out to honour the NHL star. Team Canada made Mikita captain for the game. Even though the Canadians were spent emotionally and physically from the series against the Soviets, they pulled out a 3–3 tie on a goal with four seconds remaining.

Mikita was diagnosed with Lewy body dementia in 2015 and passed away on August 7, 2018, at age seventy-eight.

DR. JIM MURRAY—Team Doctor

Murray was valedictorian for his University of Toronto medical school class in 1943. He also was a talented sportsman and recipient of the George Biggs Trophy, awarded to the graduate male student-athlete who contributed most to U of T athletics with the qualities of leadership, sportsmanship, and performance.

He was a captain in the Royal Canadian Army Medical Corps from 1944 to 1946. In 1953, Doc joined the Toronto East General and Orthopaedic Hospital, where he became head of plastic surgery and later surgeon-in-chief. He also was known as Dr. Hands because of his work as a hand specialist.

He was the Toronto Maple Leafs team doctor from 1948 to 1964, when the team won five Stanley Cups. In his last year, he attended to defenceman Bobby Baun's fractured leg in game 6 of the Stanley Cup final. Murray prescribed freezing in Baun's leg so he could return to action. Baun, of course, did reappear to score the overtime winner that night.

Dr. Murray made his own return to hockey in 1972 to keep a watchful medical eye on Team Canada. He passed away on April 4, 2003, at the age of eighty-three.

TOMMY NAYLOR—Equipment Manager

Naylor became part of the sporting goods industry at a young age. As a teenager, he began working for A.G. Spalding sporting goods as a messenger. But when the company's regular skate sharpener quit, Naylor pushed for the job and was hired.

He became a master skate sharpener and later took a job with the Toronto Maple Leafs to maintain all junior, senior, and NHL players' skates for decades. The cubbyhole underneath the northeast stairs at Maple Leaf Gardens where he performed his magic was a popular stop for players and others who made their way in the skating world. Canadian World and Olympic figure-skating champion Barbara Ann Scott would only allow Naylor to sharpen her skates.

He also was an equipment pioneer. He helped develop the portable skate sharpener. He made pads, blockers, and catching gloves safer for goalies, invented the skate guard, and created ankle protectors for defencemen. He was an easy choice to be added to the Team Canada training staff and travelled with the team to Moscow.

JEAN-PAUL (J.P.) PARISE—Winger

Parise was in the lineup for six of the eight games against the Soviet Union, checking in with two goals and two assists. He didn't dress for the series opener and game 4 in Vancouver. He played well at times on a line with Phil Esposito and established himself as a dependable penalty killer in the four games in Moscow.

Parise scored the opening goal in game 3, in Winnipeg, and combined with Wayne Cashman to set up Esposito to put Canada ahead 3–1 early in the second period. Parise also scored to put Canada in front 1–0 in game 5 and set up Esposito's late first-period short-handed goal to tie game 7 at 2–2. Parise led Team Canada with twenty-eight penalty minutes. But twenty-two of those came early in the series finale when West German referee Josef Kompalla called him for an interference minor and the subsequent ten-minute misconduct (and additional game misconduct) for his actions in protest.

Despite the incident, the native of Smooth Rock Falls, Ontario, returned home riding a high from the series. The left winger enjoyed his most productive NHL campaign with twenty-seven goals and seventy-five points in seventy-eight games, playing on a line with his Team Canada teammate Bill Goldsworthy and centre Jude Drouin. Parise was invited to play in the 1973 NHL all-star game.

He remained in the game as an assistant coach with the North Stars and later ran the prep school program at Shattuck-St. Mary's, where his sons Zach and Jordan played, as did Sidney Crosby and other NHL stars. Parise passed away on January 7, 2015, from lung cancer. He was seventy-five.

PAT STAPLETON—Defence

Stapleton won the 1959–60 Memorial Cup with the St. Catharines Teepees alongside his Team Canada teammate Vic Hadfield. After sitting out the series opener, Stapleton played in the remaining seven games and became an essential component with his Chicago Blackhawks defence partner, Bill White. Stapleton returned to the NHL after the series and scored a career-high ten goals in his final season with the Blackhawks. The following summer, he bolted for the cross-town Chicago Cougars in the WHA as their player-coach. He played for the WHA all-star squad that played the Soviets in 1974. Only Stapleton, Paul Henderson, and Frank Mahovlich played in both series.

Stapleton later was Wayne Gretzky's first coach in the professional ranks with the 1978–79 Indianapolis Racers, albeit for only eight games because the WHA franchise folded.

Stapleton was one of the pranksters on Team Canada. In November 2008, the Sarnia Legionnaires honoured former general manager Tom Norris Sr., who ran the junior B team when Stapleton played there in 1957–58. Stapleton presided over the ceremonial faceoff and claimed he used the puck from Paul Henderson's series clincher in 1972. A controversy was born. It does appear in the grainy video from September 28, 1972, that Stapleton bends over to collect the game puck, but every time one of his Team Canada teammates asked him where the puck was there was a different tale. Stapleton even jested he wasn't sure which of the hundreds of pucks he had in his possession was the keepsake from 1972. He served a vital role as board chair of the Team Canada 1972 group until he passed away on April 8, 2020. He was seventy-nine.

On May 31, 2021, it was announced that Sarnia Arena would be renamed after Stapleton.

BILL WHITE—Defence

After a brilliant three-year junior stint with his hometown Toronto Marlboroughs, White was stuck in the AHL for seven seasons (472 regular season and playoff games), until the expansion Los Angeles Kings signed him in 1967. Midway through his third season with the Kings, he was dealt to the Chicago Blackhawks, where he partnered with Pat Stapleton to make up one of the NHL's stingiest defensive duos. White was named to the NHL second all-star team for three consecutive seasons from 1971 to 1974.

Perhaps unsurprisingly, in both the campaign before the 1972 series and the season that followed, each member of the first and second all-star teams had been named to the original Team Canada roster. In 1971–72, the first team was comprised of Tony Esposito, Brad Park, Bobby Orr, Phil Esposito, Bobby Hull, and Rod Gilbert. The second team included Ken Dryden, Bill White, Pat Stapleton, Jean Ratelle, Yvan Cournoyer, and Vic Hadfield. The following season, the first team had Ken Dryden, Bobby Orr, Guy Lapointe, Phil Esposito, Frank Mahovlich, and Mickey Redmond. Tony Esposito, Bill White, Brad Park, Bobby Clarke, Dennis Hull, and Yvan Cournoyer made up the second team.

White was the second oldest defenceman on Team Canada at age thirty-three, ten months younger than Gary Bergman. He and Stapleton sat out the series opener but played the remaining seven games. The pair also led Team Canada and the Blackhawks in pranks, keeping the others loose. After his playing career, White was a mid-season replacement for head coach Billy Reay in 1976–77. His assistants were Team Canada teammates Stan Mikita and Bobby Orr. He also coached his Marlboroughs for a season in the late 1970s. White passed away on May 21, 2017, at age seventy-seven.

– Team USSR –

VSEVOLOD BOBROV – Head Coach

Before he took over as coach of the Russian national team, Bobrov was a household name in his country as an athlete, excelling in soccer, bandy, and hockey. He fought for Russia in World War II and competed in soccer at the 1952 Olympics. He helped his country win the IIHF World Championship in Stockholm two years later, at age thirty-two, and later gold at the 1956 Winter Olympics. In January 1950, a plane carrying eleven VVS MVO Moscow teammates crashed and killed everyone aboard. Bobrov had overslept and missed the Moscow-to-Chelyabinsk flight.

The legendary and long-time Russian hockey coach Anatoly Tarasov retired after the 1972 Olympics. Bobrov was named his replacement for the 1972 IIHF World Championship and continued his new role for the series against Team Canada. He was more of a players' coach, compared to Tarasov's iron-fisted ways. Bobrov was praised for his contributions to the Russian hockey scene, and one of the four divisions in the Kontinental Hockey League was named after him. The others are called Tarasov, Kharlamov, and Chernyshev.

Bobrov passed away on July 1, 1979, at age fifty-six.

ALEXANDER BODUNOV—Wing

Bodunov, a right wing, was part of the kid line for the Soviets in 1972 with left wing Yuri Lebedev and centre Vyacheslav Anisin. They were each twenty-one. Down 4–2 in game 3, Lebedev scored with five minutes and one second remaining in the third period, and Bodunov tied the game with ninety-two seconds left. Bodunov only played in games 3, 4, and 6. He was known for his shot. Again, with Anisin and Lebedev, he was part off the trio that helped engineer a massive upset for the Soviet Wings over the powerhouse CSKA Moscow in the 1973–74 Soviet League Championship. He helped Russia win the 1973 and 1974 IIHF World Championships. He passed away on May 11, 2017, at age sixty-five.

ALEXANDER GUSEV—Defence

Gusev was a top defencemen in Russia for more than a decade. He was good in both ends of the rink, made an excellent first pass, and had good vision. He played in six of the eight Summit games, sitting out games 4 and 6. He scored the game-tying 4–4 goal in game 5, which Russia won 5–4. Gusev also played in the 1974 series against the WHA all-stars.

He won the 1973 and 1974 IIHF World Championships and gold at the 1976 Olympics. He grew up in the CSKA Moscow organization with Valeri Kharmalov. The two became close friends. After a poor result in Vienna at the 1977 World Championship, national team head coach Viktor Tikhonov replaced Gusev with Slava Fetisov, a player Gusev mentored with CSKA Moscow.

Gusev passed away on July 22, 2020, at age seventy-three.

VALERI KHARLAMOV—Wing

Kharlamov was the first Soviet player to make an impact against Team Canada, scoring twice in the second period of the stunning series opener, including the game-winner. He wound up scoring three times and had four assists in seven games in the series. Two of his assists set up game-winners for the Soviets in Vancouver and game 5 in Moscow. He, of course, missed game 7 after Canadian centre Bobby Clarke whacked the smooth-skating left wing on the ankle in the sixth game.

Kharlamov was a decorated international star, having won eight IIHF World Championships and gold medals in the 1972 and 1976 Olympics. He was named four times to the World Championship tournament all-star team. He played on one of the most dominant lines in Russian hockey history with Vladimir Petrov and Boris Mikhailov on CSKA Moscow. In thirteen seasons, they won eleven league titles.

Kharlamov died on August 27, 1981, at age thirty-three, in a car accident. His wife, Irina, lost control of their car on the way home to Moscow from their cottage and hit a truck head-on. They both died, as did a relative in the back seat. There is a memorial plaque near the accident site. One of the four divisions in the Kontinental Hockey League is named after Kharmalov.

BORIS KULAGIN—Assistant Coach

Kulagin was Vsevolod Bobrov's assistant coach for the eight-game series. Kulagin was one of Russia's first-name hockey players in the

1940s and later became Anatoly Tarasov's right-hand man with CSKA Moscow in the mid-1950s. When Valeri Kharlamov fell out of favour with Tarasov in the late 1960s, Kulagin convinced his mentor to give Kharlamov a second chance.

Kulagin decided to leave Tarasov's shadow, moving to coach the Soviet Wings in 1971. Under Kulagin's leadership, the Wings emerged as a superior team and upended Tarasov's Red Army team in the 1974 league final. The outcome pushed Kulagin into the head coach position for the Soviet national team, replacing Bobrov. Kulagin coached the Soviets in the 1974 series against the WHA Team Canada and won the 1974 and 1975 IIHF World Championships and gold at the 1976 Olympic Games. However, Russia finished second at the 1976 World Championship and settled for bronze in 1977. The poor showings meant the end of Kulagin's reign as the country's national team coach. He passed away in 1988, at age sixty-four.

VIKTOR KUZKIN—Defence

At thirty-two, Kuzkin was the oldest defenceman on the Soviet roster. He was captain of the team in five of the seven games he dressed, sitting out the sixth game in Moscow. Before the series against Canada, he had already won seven consecutive IIHF World Championships in the 1960s and three Olympic gold medals in 1964, 1968, and 1972. With the Russians behind 3–0, Kuzkin assisted on Yuri Blinov's goal early in the third period that ignited a 5–4 come-from-behind victory in game 5.

Kuzkin later became an assistant coach at his beloved CSKA Russia with teammate Boris Mikhailov, working under Viktor

Tikhonov. At sixty-seven, on June 24, 2008, Kuzkin passed away from a heart attack related to a scuba diving accident near Sochi, a resort town off the Black Sea that played host to the 2014 Winter Olympics.

EVGENY MISHAKOV—Centre

At thirty-one, Mishakov was a veteran two-way forward for the Soviets against Team Canada, suiting up for six of the eight games. He sat out game 4, in Vancouver, and game 6 in Moscow. The Russian players were told not to fight, but Mishakov did not have a choice in the heated finale when he mixed it up with Canadian Rod Gilbert in a scrap early in the third period.

Mishakov performed for the dominant Big Red Machine team that won four consecutive IIHF World Championships from 1968 to 1971 and Olympic gold in 1968 and 1972. He passed away on May 30, 2007, at age sixty-six.

EVGENY PALADIEV—Defence

Paladiev only played in three games in the series. In game 2, Canadian forward Pete Mahovlich muscled his way around Paladiev for a massive short-hand goal to put Canada in front 3–1 in what finished as a 4–1 outcome. He played in game 4 but did not see any action in the four games in Moscow.

Paladiev, a dependable defenceman for Moscow Spartak, rebounded to play a significant role in Russia's World Championship seven months later. He passed away in 2010, at age sixty-one.

VLADIMIR PETROV—Centre

Petrov was the skilled centre on Russia's top line with Valeri Kharlamov and Boris Mikhailov. He played in all eight Summit games,
checking in with three goals and seven points. A two-way player,
Petrov was a reliable part of the Soviet special teams. He scored
short-hand goals in games 1 and 3 and a power-play goal to put
Russia up 2–1 in the first period of game 7. He remarked after the
series that he didn't contribute as much offence as he would have
liked because he was so concerned with his defensive responsibilities
going up against Canadian centres Phil Esposito and Bobby Clarke.

Petrov's final appearance for the Soviets internationally was at the
1980 Olympics when Russia was upset by the United States. But he
won eight IIHF World Championships between 1969 and 1979 and
Olympic gold in 1972 and 1976. He won five Russian League scoring
titles, four more at the World Championship, and was named to the
World Championship all-star team on four occasions.

He passed away on February 26, 2017, at age sixty-nine.

ALEXANDER RAGULIN—Defence

Ragulin played in six of the eight games against Team Canada, sitting
out game 3, in Winnipeg, and the series finale. He played alongside
his long-time CSKA Moscow teammate Alexander Gusev. Ragulin
set up Gusev to pull the Soviets even at 4–4 midway through the
third period of game 5 in an outing the Soviets won, 5–4. He was
named captain for the sixth game. At 220 pounds, Ragulin often
found himself out against Canada's Phil Esposito.

Ragulin was one of the most accomplished and decorated
defencemen in Russian hockey history, winning 10 IIHF World

Championships and Olympic gold in 1964, 1968, and 1972. He retired after his tenth World Championship, in 1973. He passed away on November 17, 2004, at age sixty-three.

VLADIMIR SHADRIN—Centre

Shadrin was somewhat overshadowed by a couple teammates, both of them stars—Alexander Yakushev and Valeri Kharlamov. But Shadrin was very good and, in fact, was a star in the Summit Series, finishing second in team scoring behind Yakushev, with three goals and five assists in eight games.

A two-time Olympic champion and five-time World Champion, scoring 45 goals in 71 games, Shadrin also played in the Soviet league from 1965 to 1979 with Spartak Moscow, along with Yakushev. He finished with 213 goals in 445 games. After that, he played four seasons in Japan with Oji Seishi. In 169 games with the Soviet national team over ten seasons, he scored 71 goals. He was inducted into the Russian and Soviet Hockey Hall of Fame in 1971.

"He was a true Spartak man to the tips of his fingers," said 1972 teammate Boris Mikhailov. "He wore the red-and-white jersey with pride. He was a wonderful player. In my view he was underrated. He was one of the best centres of his era, anywhere in the world."

According to reports out of Moscow, Shadrin was in hospital battling cancer when he died on August 26, 2021, after contracting the Covid-19 virus. He was seventy-three.

YURI SHATALOV—Defence

Shatalov did not receive an opportunity to play for the Soviet national team until he was twenty-seven, in 1972. A stay-at-home defenceman, he was a shot-blocker and physical blueliner. He only played in two outings in the series, game 3, in Winnipeg, and game 6 in Moscow. He was a significant defender when the Soviet Wings upset CSKA Moscow, his old team, in the 1973–74 Soviet League Championship. He passed away on March 20, 2018, at age seventy-two.

ALEXANDER SIDELNIKOV—Goaltender

Sidelnikov was goalie Vladislav Tretiak's sidekick on the international stage, including the 1972 series versus Team Canada. The national team teammates were the goalie tandem for victorious moments at the 1973 and 1974 IIHF World Championships and the 1976 Olympic Games in Innsbruck, Austria. Sidelnikov played for the Soviet Wings and upset Tretiak's CSKA Moscow in the 1973–74 Soviet League Championship final. He passed away on June 23, 2003, at age fifty-two.

SLAVA SOLODUKHIN—Centre

At twenty-one, Solodukhin was a young centre on the Russian roster in 1972. He only saw action in one outing in the series against Canada, game 3, in Winnipeg. He made his debut for the Soviet national team at the 1972 IIHF World Championship, scoring five goals in eight games in a tournament that saw Russia score ten or more goals in four of their games.

He played his entire career for SKA Leningrad. But he was added to CSKA Moscow for its tour against NHL teams in 1975–76. After eleven games into the 1979–80 season, he was found sitting in his car without a pulse due to carbon monoxide poisoning late in 1979.

GENNADY TSYGANKOV—Defence

Tsygankov was another legendary Soviet defenceman, playing in all eight games against Team Canada. He was a go-to blueliner for short-hand and power-play situations. His two assists in the series came on special teams, setting up Valeri Kharlamov for a short-hand goal in the second period of the 4–4 tie in Winnipeg and a power-play marker in the first period of game 7, a 4–3 loss. However, Paul Henderson beat Tsygankov for the game-winner in game 7.

Tsygankov won nine league titles with CSKA Moscow, six IIHF World Championships, and Olympic gold in 1972 and 1976. Late in his career, he was the first defence partner for Slava Fetisov. The two played a crucial role in Russia's victory at the 1979 Challenge Cup against the NHL all-stars. Tsygankov passed away from cancer on February 16, 2006, at age fifty-eight.

VALERI VASILIEV—Defence

Vasiliev was a physical and reliable defenceman for more than a decade on the Soviet national team, playing in six of the eight Summit games. He scored a power-play goal late in the second period of the series finale to put Russia ahead 5–3. However, his miscue helped to result in Paul Henderson's dramatic series clincher. After Henderson's "wild stab for it," the puck bounded off the boards to Vasiliev. But he failed to corral the puck, and it slipped to Phil Esposito. The Canadian centre knocked the puck to the front of the net, where Henderson finished the play.

It was about the only pockmark on the extraordinary career for the Dynamo Moscow defender. He won nine IIHF World

Championships, was named the top defenceman in 1973, 1977, and 1979, and was named to the tournament all-star team five times. He also won Olympic gold in 1972 and 1976 and captained Russia to its dominant 8–1 win against Canada in the 1981 Canada Cup.

Vasiliev recovered after a heart attack at the 1978 World Championship. He died of heart and kidney failure on April 19, 2012, at age sixty-two.

VLADIMIR VIKULOV—Wing

Vikulov was a skilled offensive player who was performing at his best when the series opened against Canada. He led the Russian League in goals scored in 1971–72 with thirty-four in thirty-one games and was the top goal scorer at the 1972 IIHF World Championship with twelve goals in ten games. Vikulov was named to the World Championship tournament all-star team in 1971 and 1972.

He played in six of the eight games against Canada and scored the game-winner in games 4 and 5. But he also had a team-worst plus-minus rating of minus-8. Vikulov finished his career with seven World Championships and Olympic gold in 1968 and 1972. He passed away on August 9, 2003, at age sixty-seven.

YEVGENI ZIMIN—Wing

At five-foot-eight and 163 pounds, Zimin was the smallest player on the Soviet roster. The quick and skilled right wing only played in two games but played an essential part in Russia's fantastic start. Down 2–0 in the series opener, he scored the Soviets' first goal midway through the first period and his team's sixth goal in the stunning 7–3 victory.

He scored the series clincher for Spartak Moscow in its championship run in 1969 for its second title in three years. He later coached the Russian under-eighteen team to a European championship, scouted for the Philadelphia Flyers, and became a television analyst. He passed away on December 28, 2018, at age seventy-one.

VIKTOR ZINGER—Goaltender

Zinger was the third goalie on the Soviet team, but he did back up Vladislav Tretiak for the four games in Canada. Zinger did not see any action in the series, and it was believed he suffered a broken finger before the series resumed in Moscow. He was a prominent goalie for the Russians in the 1960s, backing up Viktor Konovalenko when the Soviets won four consecutive IIHF World Championships between 1965 and 1968. They won a fifth straight with Zinger as the starter in 1969. He was also backup when Russia won Olympic gold in 1968.

He retired from Spartak Moscow in 1977 and later became coach of the organization's junior team. He passed away on September 24, 2013, at age seventy-one.

Team Stats

What follows are the "official" statistics as recorded during the playing of the 1972 Summit Series. In subsequent years, several hockey historians—including Richard J. Bendell, Paul Patskou, and Robert MacAskill in their fine book *1972: The Summit Series*—spent countless hours reviewing recordings of the games and found many discrepancies, especially with assists and in some cases with goals. On some plays, because the international television feed would occasionally break up in transmission from Moscow, accurately tracking all the points was impossible. And remember, back in the day, off-ice officials didn't review goals to ensure the scorer and those who earned the assists, along with other statistics, were always accurate.

POSITION (NO.)	PLAYER	NHL CLUB	HOMETOWN	AGE	GP	W-L-T	GAA	SV %	PIM
Goalie (1)	Eddie Johnston	Boston Bruins	Montreal, QC	36	0	0-0-0	0.00	0	0
Goalie (29)	Ken Dryden	Montreal Canadiens	Toronto, ON	25	4	2-2-0	4.75	0.839	0
Goalie (35)	Tony Esposito	Chicago Blackhawks	Sault Ste. Marie, ON	29	4	2-1-1	3.25	0.900	0

POSITION (NO.)	PLAYER	NHL CLUB	HOMETOWN	AGE	GP	G	A	PTS	PIM
Defence (2)	Gary Bergman	Detroit Red Wings	Kenora, ON	33	8	0	3	3	13
Defence (3)	Pat Stapleton	Chicago Blackhawks	Sarnia, ON	32	7	0	0	0	6
Defence (4)	Bobby Orr	Boston Bruins	Parry Sound, ON	24	0	0	0	0	0
Defence (5)	Brad Park	New York Rangers	Toronto, ON	24	8	1	4	5	2
Right Wing (6)	Ron Ellis	Toronto Maple Leafs	Lindsay, ON	27	8	0	3	3	8
Centre (7)	Phil Esposito	Boston Bruins	Sault Ste. Marie, ON	30	8	7	6	13	15
Right Wing (8)	Rod Gilbert	New York Rangers	Montreal, QC	31	6	1	3	4	9
Right Wing (9)	Bill Goldsworthy	Minnesota North Stars	Waterloo, ON	28	3	1	1	2	4
Left Wing (10)	Dennis Hull	Chicago Blackhawks	Point Anne, ON	27	4	2	2	4	4
Left Wing (11)	Vic Hadfield	New York Rangers	Oakville, ON	31	2	0	0	0	0
Right Wing (12)	Yvan Cournoyer	Montreal Canadiens	Drummondville, QC	28	8	3	2	5	2
Right Wing (14)	Wayne Cashman	Boston Bruins	Kingston, ON	27	2	0	2	2	14
Centre (15)	Red Berenson	Detroit Red Wings	Regina, SK	32	2	0	1	1	0

Position	Name	Team	Hometown						
Defence (16)	Rod Seiling	New York Rangers	Elmira, ON	27	3	0	0	0	0
Defence (17)	Bill White	Chicago Blackhawks	Toronto, ON	33	7	1	1	2	8
Centre (18)	Jean Ratelle	New York Rangers	Lac St. Jean, QC	31	6	1	3	4	0
Left Wing (19)	Paul Henderson	Toronto Maple Leafs	Kincardine, ON	29	8	7	3	10	4
Centre (20)	Peter Mahovlich	Montreal Canadiens	Timmins, ON	25	7	1	1	2	4
Centre (21)	Stan Mikita	Chicago Blackhawks	St. Catharines, ON	32	2	0	1	1	0
Left Wing (22)	J. P. Parise	Minnesota North Stars	Smooth Rock Falls, ON	30	6	2	2	4	28
Defence (23)	Serge Savard	Montreal Canadiens	Montreal, QC	26	5	0	2	2	0
Right Wing (24)	Mickey Redmond	Detroit Red Wings	Peterborough, ON	24	1	0	0	0	0
Defence (25)	Guy Lapointe	Montreal Canadiens	Montreal, QC	24	7	0	1	1	6
Defence (26)	Don Awrey	Boston Bruins	Waterloo, ON	29	2	0	0	0	0
Left Wing (27)	Frank Mahovlich	Montreal Canadiens	Timmins, ON	34	6	1	1	2	0
Centre (28)	Bobby Clarke	Philadelphia Flyers	Flin Flon, MB	23	8	2	4	6	18
Defence (32)	Dale Tallon	Vancouver Canucks	Noranda, QC	21	0	0	0	0	0
Centre (33)	Gilbert Perreault	Buffalo Sabres	Victoriaville, QC	21	2	1	1	2	0
Centre (34)	Marcel Dionne	Detroit Red Wings	Drummondville, QC	21	0	0	0	0	0
Left Wing (36)	Richard Martin	Buffalo Sabres	Verdun, QC	21	0	0	0	0	0
Defence (37)	Jocelyn Guevremont	Vancouver Canucks	Ste. Rose, QC	21	0	0	0	0	0
Defence (38)	Brian Glennie	Toronto Maple Leafs	Toronto, ON	25	0	0	0	0	0

POSITION (NO.)	PLAYER	HOCKEY CLUB	HOMETOWN	AGE	GP	W-L-T	GAA	SV %	PIM
Goalie (20)	Vladislav Tretiak	CSKA Moscow	Dmitrovsky District, Russia	20	8	3-4-1	3.88	.891	0

POSITION (NO.)	PLAYER	HOCKEY CLUB	HOMETOWN	AGE	GP	G	A	PTS	PIM
Forward (15)	Alexander Yakushev	Spartak Moscow	Moscow, Russia	25	8	7	4	11	4
Forward (19)	Vladimir Shadrin	Spartak Moscow	Moscow, Russia	24	8	3	5	8	0
Forward (13)	Boris Mikhailov	CSKA Moscow	Moscow, Russia	27	8	3	2	5	9
Forward (10)	Alexander Maltsev	Dynamo Moscow	Kirovo-Chepetsk, Russia	23	8	0	5	5	0
Forward (17)	Valeri Kharlamov	CSKA Moscow	Moscow, Russia	24	7	3	4	7	16
Forward (16)	Vladimir Petrov	CSKA Moscow	Krasnogorsk, Russia	25	8	3	4	7	10
Defence (3)	Vladimir Lutchenko	CSKA Moscow	Ramenskoye, Russia	23	8	1	3	4	0
Defence (25)	Yuri Liapkin	Khimik Voskresensk	Balashikha, Russia	27	6	1	5	6	0
Forward (22)	Vyacheslav Anisin	Krylya Sovetov Moscow	Moscow, Russia	21	7	1	3	4	2
Forward (11)	Yevgeni Zimin	Spartak Moscow	Moscow, Russia	25	2	2	1	3	0
Forward (9)	Yuri Blinov	CSKA Moscow	Moscow, Russia	23	5	2	1	3	2

Position	Name	Team	Birthplace						
Forward (18)	Vladimir Vikulov	CSKA Moscow	Moscow, Russia	26	6	2	1	3	0
Defence (6)	Valeri Vasiliev	Dynamo Moscow	Nizhny Novgorod, Russia	23	5	1	2	3	6
Forward (23)	Yuri Lebedev	Krylya Sovetov Moscow	Moscow, Russia	21	3	1	0	1	2
Forward (24)	Alexander Bodunov	Krylya Sovetov Moscow	Moscow, Russia	21	3	1	0	1	0
Defence (26)	Evgeny Paladiev	Spartak Moscow	Ust-Kamenogorsk, Kazakhstan	24	3	0	0	0	0
Defence (2)	Alexander Gusev	CSKA Moscow	Moscow, Russia	25	6	1	0	1	2
Defence (5)	Alexander Ragulin	CSKA Moscow	Moscow, Russia	31	6	0	1	1	4
Defence (7)	Gennady Tsygankov	CSKA Moscow	Vanino, Russia	25	8	0	2	2	6
Forward (8)	Vyacheslav Starshinov	Spartak Moscow	Moscow, Russia	32	1	0	0	0	0
Forward (29)	Alexander Martynyuk	Spartak Moscow	Moscow, Russia	26	1	0	0	0	0
Forward (21)	Vyacheslav Solodukhin	SKA Leningrad	Saint Petersburg, Russia	21	1	0	0	0	0
Defence (14)	Yuri Shatalov	Krylya Sovetov Moscow	Omsk, Russia	27	2	0	0	0	0
Forward (30)	Alexander Volchkov	CSKA Moscow	Moscow, Russia	20	3	0	0	0	0
Forward (12)	Evgeny Mishakov	CSKA Moscow	Moscow, Russia	31	6	0	0	0	11
Defence (4)	Viktor Kuzkin	CSKA Moscow	Moscow, Russia	32	7	0	1	1	8

Photo Credits

In order of appearance in the photo section.

Expo 67: John McNeill/The Globe and Mail/Canadian Press

War Measures Act: Peter Bregg/Canadian Press

Valeri Kharlamov drills with Boris Kulagin: Melchior DiGiacomo/Getty Images

Team Canada players do some stretches: Frank Lennon/Getty Images

Jacques Plante with Vladislav Tretiak: Denis Brodeur/Getty Images

Vladislav Tretiak: Melchior DiGiacomo/Getty Images

Brad Park shakes hands with Vyacheslav Solodukhin: Melchior DiGiacomo/Getty Images

Soviet players Yuri Blinov, Alexander Ragulin, and Valeri Kharlamov: Melchior DiGiacomo/Getty Images

Prime Minister Pierre Trudeau ceremonial faceoff: Melchior DiGiacomo/Getty Images

Frank Mahovlich skates with puck: Melchior DiGiacomo/Getty Images

Foggy ice in Montreal Forum: Melchior DiGiacomo/Getty Images

John Ferguson: Melchior DiGiacomo/Getty Images

Vsevolod Bobrov: Graphic Artists/Hockey Hall of Fame

Harry Sinden: Graphic Artists/Hockey Hall of Fame

Protesters outside Maple Leaf Gardens: The Canadian Press/Peter Bregg

Canadians for Fair Play Committee pamphlet: Courtesy of the author

Peter Mahovlich scoring: Graphic Artists/Hockey Hall of Fame

Phil Esposito, Peter Mahovlich, and Paul Henderson address media: The Canadian Press/Peter Bregg

Harry Sinden and John Ferguson address media: Barrie Davis/The Globe and Mail/Canadian Press

To Russia with Hull billboard: Don Dutton/The Toronto Star via Getty Images

Phil Esposito: John D. Hanlon/Getty Images

Bill White: Canadian Press

Frank Mahovlich pinning Tretiak: John D. Hanlon/Getty Images

Roadside on the way to Toronto airport: Barrie Davis/The Globe and Mail/Canadian Press

Wayne Cashman: Melchior DiGiacomo/Getty Images

Bobby Orr with Phil Esposito: Melchior DiGiacomo/Getty Images

Red Berenson with camera outside the Luzhniki Ice Palace: Melchior DiGiacomo/Getty Images

Ken Dryden and wife, Lynda: Melchior DiGiacomo/Getty Images

Soviet poster: Melchior DiGiacomo/Getty Images

Phil Esposito falls on ice: Melchior DiGiacomo/Getty Images

Phil Esposito takes a bow: Melchior DiGiacomo/Getty Images

Teams exchange gifts: Melchior DiGiacomo/Getty Images

Paul Henderson comes off ice: Melchior DiGiacomo/Getty Images

A frustrated Tony Esposito: Melchior DiGiacomo/Getty Images

Alan Eagleson et al. in arena: Melchior DiGiacomo/Getty Images

Ken Dryden: Melchior DiGiacomo/Getty Images

Team Canada bench celebrates a win: Melchior DiGiacomo/Getty Images

Bobby Clarke: Melchior DiGiacomo/Getty Images

Physical play in Moscow: Melchior DiGiacomo/Getty Images

Tony Esposito: Melchior DiGiacomo/Getty Images

Paul Henderson et al. celebrate game 7 win: Melchior DiGiacomo/Getty Images

Canadian fans in Moscow watch a game: Melchior DiGiacomo/Getty Images

Ken Dryden: Melchior DiGiacomo/Getty Images

J. P. Parise collides with Valeri Vasiliev: Melchior DiGiacomo/Getty Images

Referee Josef Kompalla with Peter Mahovlich: Melchior DiGiacomo/Getty Images

A chair thrown on the ice: Melchior DiGiacomo/Getty Images

Soviet crowd watching game: Melchior DiGiacomo/Getty Images

Alexander Yakushev shoots: Melchior DiGiacomo/Getty Images

Henderson's goal wins the series for Canada: Frank Lennon/Getty Images

Phil Esposito joins the celebration: Melchior DiGiacomo/Getty Images

Phil Esposito flashes a V for victory: Melchior DiGiacomo/Getty Images

The teams shake hands: Melchior DiGiacomo/Getty Images

Phil Esposito with fans in Canada: The Canadian Press/Peter Bregg

Paul Henderson on the shoulders of Tony Esposito and Alan Eagleson: Canadian Press

A Henderson game-worn sweater on display: AFP/Getty Images

Pat Stapleton with Vladimir Putin: Sergei Guneyev/Getty Images

Phil Esposito hugs Alexander Yakushev: KHL Photo Agency/Getty
   Images

Team Canada official photo: Graphic Artists/Hockey Hall of Fame

Index

Note: *Italic* page numbers indicate Team Stats for Summit Series hockey players.